GARDNER WEBB COLLEGE LIBRARY

GREAT LIVES OBSERVED

Gerald Emanuel Stearn, *General Editor*

EACH VOLUME IN THE SERIES VIEWS THE CHARACTER AND ACHIEVEMENT OF A GREAT WORLD FIGURE IN THREE PERSPECTIVES—THROUGH HIS OWN WORDS, THROUGH THE OPINIONS OF HIS CONTEMPORARIES, AND THROUGH RETROSPECTIVE JUDGMENTS—THUS COMBINING THE INTIMACY OF AUTOBIOGRAPHY, THE IMMEDIACY OF EYEWITNESS OBSERVATION, AND THE OBJECTIVITY OF MODERN SCHOLARSHIP.

GEORGE F. TYSON, JR. *teaches at the College of the Virgin Islands, St. Thomas, and is a Research Associate of the Island Resources Foundation, Inc. He is currently preparing a study on slave resistance and revolt in the British West Indies.*

GREAT LIVES OBSERVED

Toussaint L'Ouverture

Edited by
GEORGE F. TYSON, JR.

*Toussaint L'Ouverture is a negro and in the jargon of war
has been called a brigand. But according to all accounts
he is a negro born to vindicate the claims
of this species and to show that the character of men
is independent of exterior colour.*

—LONDON GAZETTE, DECEMBER 12, 1798

Toussaint, the first and greatest of West Indians. . . .

— C. L. R. JAMES

GARDNER WEBB COLLEGE LIBRARY

A SPECTRUM BOOK

PRENTICE-HALL, INC., ENGLEWOOD CLIFFS, N.J.

Library of Congress Cataloging in Publication Data

TYSON, GEORGE F, JR.   comp.
    Toussaint L'Ouverture.

    (Great lives observed) (A Spectrum Book)
    Bibliography: p.
    1. Toussaint Louverture, François Dominique, 1743–
1803.   2. Haiti—History—Revolution, 1791–1804.
I. Title.
F1923.T956   972.94′03′0924 [B]   72–13670
ISBN 0–13–925529–X
ISBN 0–13–925511–7 (pbk)

For T

© 1973 by PRENTICE-HALL, INC.,
Englewood Cliffs, New Jersey.

A SPECTRUM BOOK

All rights reserved.
No part of this book may be reproduced
in any form or by any means
without permission in writing from the publisher.

10 9 8 7 6 5 4 3 2 1

Printed in the United States of America

PRENTICE-HALL INTERNATIONAL, INC. (*London*)
PRENTICE-HALL OF AUSTRALIA PTY., LTD. (*Sydney*)
PRENTICE-HALL OF CANADA, LTD. (*Toronto*)
PRENTICE-HALL OF INDIA PRIVATE LIMITED (*New Delhi*)
PRENTICE-HALL OF JAPAN, INC. (*Tokyo*)

F
1923
.T956

Contents

Introduction

> The independence of St. Domingue is proclaimed, returned to our primitive dignity, we have claimed our rights, we swear never to yield them to any power on earth. The frightful veil of prejudice is torn to pieces. Be it so forever! Woe be to whomsoever would dare again to put together the bloody tatters!

With these proud words the black people of the former French colony of St. Domingue announced to the world on November 29, 1803, the foundation of the second independent nation in the Western hemisphere, and the first dedicated to the liberty and equality of black men. This truly revolutionary event culminated the most successful slave insurrection in history. After fifteen years of social, racial, and colonial conflict, former slaves and their free colored allies had flung off the bonds of servitude and discrimination to seize absolute control over their own destinies. In the process they fought and defeated French slaveowners, British and Spanish expeditionary forces, and the allegedly invincible armies of Napoleon Bonaparte. Nor were their historic achievements confined to a small island in the middle of the Caribbean Sea. The creation of a "Black Republic" generated shock waves of alarm throughout the plantation sphere, raising the possibility of other successful uprisings of the oppressed black masses and an end to white supremacy in the hemisphere. Henceforth, the institution of slavery could no longer be unquestionably accepted by even the most complacent slaveholders, for the very assumptions upon which their rule rested—negro inferiority, disunity, and docility—were permanently undermined.

A new nation had been forged on the anvil of war and revolution and along with it, new men, new leaders. Among them, the man most central to the Haitian revolution was Toussaint L'Ouverture. Through a combination of messianic ambition, military and political genius, and sincere dedication to the cause of his people, this remarkable man rose from slavery to become the ruler of the most prized colony in the world. It was he who molded the revolutionary army of slaves into an efficient, disciplined fighting unit; who defended the revolution by an astute mixture of statecraft and diplomacy; who restored economic stability to his ravaged country; who, through his personal achievements, inspired in his people, and in black people everywhere, a re-

1

newed sense of pride and purpose. Far more than the organizer and guardian of the revolution, Toussaint was the very personification of its ideals and contradictions.

Mystery and controversy have always surrounded Toussaint. Although works on the man and his age are legion, we know remarkably little about the man himself. In part this is due to his personality. He was essentially a man of action rather than words, a distrustful, taciturn individual who deliberately left little reliable information about his innermost thoughts, feelings, and motivations. But more particularly it has been the highly partisan emotions aroused by the Haitian revolution that have resulted in a lack of understanding.

In the course of the fierce debates on colonialism and slavery that raged in the last century, abolitionists and proslavery advocates, negrophiles and negrophobes, Haitian mulattoes and blacks, imperialists and anti-imperialists, historical popularizers and literary romantics were all attracted for their own didactic purposes to the story of Toussaint and the Haitian revolution. These polemics continued into the twentieth century, particularly after the American occupation of Haiti, which was justified on the assumption that blacks were incapable of self-government. In the 1930s the emergence of the *négritude* movement (in Haiti, a direct reaction to American occupation), coupled with a new wave of unrest by the colonized black masses, stimulated renewed interest in the formation of the first black nation and its most gifted revolutionary leader. Scholarly, but still didactic, reappraisals, epitomized by C. L. R. James' *The Black Jacobins,* were written by black men with an appreciation of the colonial context and the social legacies of slavery. Unfortunately, these impressive studies were obscured by a number of popular biographies, which not only were factually inaccurate but which distorted the historical setting. It is through these superficial works that most Americans know of Toussaint L'Ouverture.

Even within Haiti there remains a lack of consensus concerning Toussaint's role in the national heritage. There, evaluation has always been subject to strong racial and political biases. Generally speaking, when the mulattoes have held power Toussaint has been villified as antimulatto. But even black governments have sometimes disowned him because of his ambivalent attitude toward independence. Recently, the government of François Duvalier elevated Toussaint to the role of father of his country, but this image is only as secure as the Duvalier regime itself.

Up to the present, therefore, historical understanding of Toussaint has been obstructed by the fact that he has been all things to all men,

from bloodthirsty black savage to "the greatest black man in history."
Few writers have portrayed him as a complex individual, a former
slave, acting within the specific historical context of slavery and colonialism, confronted with unique and difficult choices and possessing
a limited range of responses. Yet, in a world still governed by social
injustice, racism, and neocolonialism the significant issues involved
in the Haitian revolution retain an obvious relevance. Until they are
resolved we should not expect dispassionate impartiality, but commitment that—as James's study illustrates—can be highly illuminating
when based on detailed archival research. Such at least is the basis
of this book. By presenting a multiplicity of viewpoints, together with
the words of Toussaint himself, it is hoped that the reader will not
only reach a fuller understanding of Toussaint, but will also perceive
how each generation has evaluated Toussaint on the basis of its own
concerns and commitments.

At the commencement of the French Revolution, the French colony
of St. Domingue was the most valuable in the world. Its economy—
based on the plantation system and slavery—was a source of wealth to
resident and absentee planters of over three thousand sugar, coffee,
cotton, indigo, tobacco, and cocoa estates, and to the French mercantile bourgeoisie, which supplied the slaves, advanced the capital, and
carried the cargoes. The colonial trade dominated by St. Domingue
was also crucial to the nascent French industrial sector, which proc-
essed the tropical products and supplied manufactured goods to African slave traders and resident colonists.

Yet, although immense fortunes were generated, the colonists had
long been discontented with the nature of their trade relations with
the mother country. By the terms of the "Exclusive," as instituted by
Colbert in the 17th century, the colony was required to ship all its
exports to, and purchase all its imports from, France. It was further
forbidden to establish local industries and was obliged to use only
French ships for the carrying trade. In return, France purchased tropical products solely from her colonies. This mercantilistic policy—the
basis of an obvious exploitation by the mother country—was bitterly
resented by the colonists, who were thereby forced to pay artificially
high prices for their imports, especially slaves, while receiving low
prices in France for their products. By 1789 the unfavorable nature of
the Exclusive had forced many colonists deeply into debt to the French
merchants.

Colonial society in St. Domingue was based on a three-caste system
in which class distinctions were complicated by cleavages of origin and
color. The ruling white society was highly diversified and divided, its

thirty-five thousand members united primarily by color. At the top stood the *grands blancs,* composed of the old creole plantocracy, local merchants, and a substantial group of French noblemen seeking to reestablish declining family fortunes through industry and/or marriage. This category also included a corrupt, slaveholding clergy and the somewhat aloof royal officials from France. Because of the lure of the metropolis—or, more correctly, because of the unpleasant features of colonial life—a high degree of absenteeism existed among the wealthier planters. Colonial society was thus deprived of a prime source of social and moral leadership. Nevertheless, a substantial group remained in the colony to set the standards of a creole society characterized by its ruthless pursuit of wealth, its independent spirit, and its pattern of conspicuous consumption, licentiousness, and brutality .

Below the *grands blancs* was a numerically larger group of plantation overseers, bookkeepers, artisans, small planters, shopkeepers, soldiers, and sailors known collectively as the *petits blancs.* Because of their color they enjoyed social and economic opportunities denied their counterparts in France. At the same time, their economic and social distance from the *grands blancs* made them highly receptive to republican ideas emanating from France, while their economic and physical proximity to the Negroes made them the principal carriers of militant racism.

Situated between the dominant whites and subordinate slaves was a distinct caste known as the *affranchis* (free people of color). This intermediate group comprised nearly 45 percent of the total free population in colonial society. Although they shared many of the rights enjoyed by the white people, they were denied full equality and were subject to periodic discriminatory regulations. Most were mixed bloods —progeny of extramarital liaisons between white men and black women—who received their freedom, and often their education and property, from paternalistc white fathers. Also included in this caste were a number of free blacks who had either purchased their freedom or been manumitted for meritorious service. Barred by law from professional occupations, the free coloreds resided principally in the countryside, either on their own plantations or employed on those owned by the whites. Quite a few were extremely wealthy: some sources have estimated that by 1789 free people of color possessed one-third of the landed wealth and one-fourth of the slaves of the colony. Still others constituted a virtual *lumpenproletariat,* scrounging a meager living on the outskirts of the towns and plantations. Such distinctions of origin, color, and wealth created tensions within the free colored community that were only slightly mitigated by a common desire to overcome legal limitations.

Dependent upon the whites for rights and privileges and sharing a common interest in the preservation of slavery, the free coloreds readily succumbed to the cultural hegemony of white creole society. They accepted without question the virtue of whiteness in both color and culture, growing to despise the slaves for their blackness, their servility, and their Africanisms. This antagonism between potential allies was deliberately encouraged by the French, who were well aware that a policy of divide and rule was their most effective method of social control in a society where they were overwhelmingly outnumbered by a hostile labor force. However, despite the willingness of the *affranchis* to serve as allies in preserving the precarious internal security of the colony, the whites stubbornly refused to incorporate them into the ruling class by granting them full citizenship because they were convinced that rigid racial distinctions formed an equally essential bulwark against slave unrest. As one official dispatch explained the discriminatory regulations:

> This law is hard, but it is both wise and necessary in a land of fifteen slaves to one white. Between the races we cannot dig too deep a gulf. Upon the Negro we cannot impress too much respect for those he serves. This distinction, rigorously upheld even after enfranchisement, is the surest way to maintain subordination; for the slave must thus see that his color is ordained to servitude, and that nothing can make him his master's equal.

After 1758 the whites, alarmed by the increasing wealth and numbers of the free people of color, subjected them to a series of discriminatory laws. Restrictions were imposed upon their dress, occupation, and right of assembly; they were assigned separate seating in public places; their freedom of movement was curtailed; they could be re-enslaved for certain crimes. Unsuccessful attempts were made to limit their property rights. Upper-class white society was generally closed to them, and they were exposed to ill-treatment and humiliation at the hands of even the lowliest white man. Initially, the free coloreds acquiesced in these persecutions, by channeling their energies into even greater economic and cultural competition with the whites. But when success in these areas brought them no closer to the equality they desired, and as the few remaining avenues of mobility were closed by new regulations, they grew increasingly embittered. Prior to 1789, however, they avoided a direct confrontation with the whites, fearful of provoking a wider social unheaval that would involve the slaves.

Thus, on the eve of the French revolution, the free people of color found themselves ensnared in a cruel dilemma. Craving equality with the whites, they had turned their backs on the blacks; for a variety of economic, social, and cultural reasons they had come to accept the slave system. These decisions implied at least a tacit acceptance of the very color line they hoped to overcome. Moreover, it meant that their status depended less upon their own exertions than upon the attitude of their white patrons toward the threat of the black masses. As long as this threat persisted the whites would resist their claims to equality, and as long as the free coloreds refused to make common cause with the slaves they had little alternative but to remain quiescent in the face of white discrimination. By 1789, although these contradictions had rendered many free people of color incapable of decisive action on their own behalf, they had convinced others that it would be impossible to extricate themselves from their ambiguous condition as long as the old regime survived.

At the bottom of the social hierarchy were the slaves, some four hundred fifty thousand of them. Negro slavery in St. Domingue, as in the rest of the hemisphere, was harsh and brutalizing, particularly after the sugar boom began in the 1750s. The vaunted *Code Noir* promulgated by the French government in 1685 in an effort to place the master-slave relationship on a humane basis was, almost from the outset, a dead letter. The Catholic Church, a slaveholding institution itself, was unwilling and unable to exert any effective moral influence. The master's power was absolute, and the treatment of the slave dependent only upon his whim and economic calculations. Two factors guaranteed that these were generally unfavorable to the slave. Slavery everywhere rested upon terror and dehumanization, but in St. Domingue, where the slaves outnumbered their masters fifteen to one, it was essential to convince the blacks constantly of their powerlessness. To this end vicious and arbitrary punishments became a matter of policy as well as of inclination. Furthermore, profit calculations operated to the slaves' disadvantage, for it was commonly believed to be cheaper to work a slave to death within a few years and purchase a new one than to maintain him through old age. As a consequence, slave mortality was fantastically high, and vast numbers of imports were required every year. The fact that after 1783 St. Domingue benefited from steadily rising sugar prices meant that in the last years of slavery the slaves were driven harder than ever.

In order to survive in this environment of calculated cruelty and debasement, the slaves learned to accommodate themselves through a unique amalgam of retained Africanisms and New World adaptations —such as the practice of voodoo—thereby creating a vibrant folk culture that would survive long after emancipation. There was also a vigorous tradition of resistance. Poisoning was particularly common and dreaded by the whites. Runaways were frequent; large, permanent Maroon communities were established in the unsettled mountains from the 17th century onward. The Maroons, who served as a rallying point for disaffected plantation slaves, kept up persistent guerilla warfare, while successfully defending their settlements against numerous expeditions. *Marronage* became so endemic that a special force, the *maréchaussée*, was formed to hunt down runaways. The fact that these horse patrols were manned by the free people of color only deepened the rancor between slaves and their free brethren. Although no major slave revolt preceded that of 1791, there had been several conspiracies: in 1679, 1691, 1703, 1704, 1758, 1775, and 1778. The abortive revolt of 1758 was the most ambitious of these. Organized by the legendary Mackandal, a Maroon voodooman with extensive influence among the blacks, its plan called for the plantation slaves systematically to poison their masters, after which the Maroons and slaves were to drive the surviving whites from the island. Some poisonings did occur, but the revolt failed to materialize when Mackendal was betrayed and executed.

The political framework for the governing of this volatile population was provided solely by France. Colonial affairs were directed in France by the Ministry of the Marine. Its chief agents in the colony were the Governor, who dealt with military affairs, and the Intendant, who supervised the administration. They were supported by myriads of royal officials sent from France to manage local affairs. The military force consisted of a permanent garrison of regular troops, supplemented by a large but undisciplined colonial militia. There existed no system of colonial self-government through representative assemblies as in the English colonies. The entire arrangement grew increasingly irritating to the colonists, who since their origins as buccaneers had prided themselves on a strong tradition of independence from French rule. The fact that the administration of justice rested in the hands of royal officials who were responsive to the pressures of the French merchants was another source of resentment to the indebted colonists.

In short, at the outset of the revolution in France the inhabitants of St. Domingue harbored many grievances that they hoped would be redressed by the revolution. The whites wanted modification, if not repeal, of the Exclusive, relief from the tightening controls of the mercantile bourgeoisie, some measure of self-government, the right to hold public office, and judicial reform. The free persons of color desired the removal of all forms of discrimination and full rights of citizenship. The slaves sought what they had always sought: freedom.

The history of the Haitian revolution divides logically into two stages. In both, events in St. Domingue intersected with the course of the revolution in France, but in the first (1788–1794) the initiative came from the whites, and events in the colony were propelled forward by rapidly changing developments in France. The fall of the French Jacobins in 1794 concluded this period. At that point, while the revolutionary impulse of the *sans culottes* in France was checked by the men of Thermidor, in St. Domingue it was continued by the black masses. With their upsurge Toussaint L'Ouverture emerged as the pivotal figure in the Haitian revolution, and increasingly the French were compelled to respond to his initiatives. The independence of Haiti in 1804 was the culmination of this second period.

In November 1787 the bankrupt Louis XVI of France announced his intention to convene the Estates-General to discuss raising new revenues and possible reforms in France and her Empire. To this invitation the planter aristocracy of St. Domingue, like its counterpart in France, was quick to respond.

Inherent in any colonial situation lurks the fundamental conflict between the metropolis seeking to centralize its control over its possessions and the colony equally determined to obtain some measure of autonomy. This issue impelled the *grands blancs* of St. Domingue to seize the opportunity offered by the convening of the Estates-General to press for greater economic and political independence. Acting without authorization from France, they selected delegates to sit in the Estates-General and drew up a cahier of grievances designed to render the planter class a privileged aristocracy, monopolizing power and place in a self-governing colony. Their activities were directed in France by a group of absentee planters known as the Colonial Committee. Initially, the efforts of this committee were directed toward the Court and royal administration, but when their attempts failed, they shrewdly shifted tactics by joining the Third Estate on the day of the Tennis Court Oath. The subsequent victory of the Third Estate guaranteed success for their claims. By decrees of September 1789 and March 1790 the National Assembly agreed to the principle of colonial self-government, granted a Colonial Assembly based on a restricted, all-white franchise, and permitted six deputies from St. Domingue to sit in the French Assembly.

However, this alliance with the revolution proved to be a double-edged sword. Whatever their origins, all colonial independence movements inevitably intensify preexisting class conflicts and release pent-up demands for social change. In the case of St. Domingue this was doubly true, since the revolutionary principles of liberty and equality were suddenly injected into a society based on the most naked form of social and racial injustice. It was this perpetual interplay between the movements for independence and social change that provided the internal dynamic of the Haitian revolution. It was the genius of Toussaint L'Ouverture that he alone was able to manipulate and unite these forces to serve the ends of the blacks.

Clear evidence that the bonds of colonial society were indeed loosening came when the *petits blancs*, activated by events in France, challenged the authority of the planters and gradually gained control of the Patriot party that dominated the new Colonial Assembly. Under Patriot direction the Assembly produced a constitution granting itself supreme authority over internal affairs and a check on all trade regulations decreed by France. This popular movement toward ever greater colonial independence alarmed the local royalist officials as well as many of the socially conservative *grands blancs*. The result was a virtual civil war, from which the Patriots emerged triumphant by mid-1791.

Coincident with the challenge of the *petits blancs*, the free people of color intensified their demands for full rights and privileges. News of the Declaration of the Rights of Man and the granting of a Colonial Assembly had excited their expectations and ambitions. Their representatives in France—such as Julien Raymond, ably assisted by the *Amis des Noirs*, a heterogeneous group of colonial reformers inspired by the British abolitionists—pressed their claims in the French Assembly. Following repeated rejection of their claims by both National and Colonial Assemblies, some of the more radical people of color rose in rebellion in October 1790. This revolt, led by a mulatto from France, Vincent Ogé, was ruthlessly put down by the colonists, and a wave of terror spearheaded by the *petits blancs* commenced. Indeed, their astute manipulation of the racial issue largely accounts for the emergence of the *petits blancs* as a major political force during this period.

In France, meanwhile, the National Assembly had become more sympathetic to the people of color. Swayed by the execution of Ogé, but more importantly by the independent mood of the white colonists, it seized upon the claims of the free coloreds as a means of reasserting French authority over its dissident colony. A decree of May 1791 granted full citizenship to all free people of color born of free parents. Although this order affected only four hundred persons, it effectively affirmed the principles of full citizenship for nonwhites and the right of France to legislate for the internal affairs of the colonies. The alarmed Patriots responded by calling for a new Colonial Assembly to resist this attack on local self-government and the racial structure of colonial society.

In this atmosphere of intensified colonial, class, and racial conflict the slaves conceived their revolt. The precipitants of the revolt were many. Exploitation of the slaves had increased as a result of mushrooming prices of colonial products in revolutionary France. The slave population had swollen by over one hundred thousand new Africans imported between 1788 and 1791, and these insufficiently acculturated slaves provided the mass base of the insurrection. Finally, slave expectations had been heightened by the circulation of revolutionary doctrines and by divisions among their masters.

In the crucial area of preparation and organization the revolt was far superior to any previously attempted in the hemisphere. Leadership came from both religious authorities and slaves with leadership roles on the plantations. For example, Boukman, the organizational genius, was both a high priest of voodoo and a plantation headman. The widespread practice of Voodoo provided an ideal organizational structure, as well as serving as a medium through which news and enthusiasm for the revolt were transmitted. From the outset the goal of the conspirators was that of most West Indian revolts: liberation and independence.

On the night of August 22, 1791, thousands of slaves in the vicinity of the city of Le Cap rose to avenge themselves on their oppressors. Within days one hundred thousand were in open rebellion and the entire northern plain was engulfed in a paroxysm of blood and fire. The terrified white population, their deepest fears suddenly realized, huddled in the towns awaiting aid from France.

This new element changed the calculations of all other parties. The need for the connection with France was obvious, and everywhere royal officials, people of color, great and lesser whites reconciled their differences to confront the threat from below. After some months, however, this united front collapsed; for when word arrived that the National Assembly had reversed itself and rescinded the May Decree, the *petits blancs* turned on the people of color in Port-au-Prince and massacred hundreds of them. The southern and western provinces were now plunged into new conflicts as the mulattoes, led by André Rigaud, formed an army, raised the slaves, and forged an alliance with the royalists.

With the colony in chaos, three Civil Commissioners arrived from France in December 1791 to stabilize the situation. However, their efforts to induce the slaves to surrender and to persuade the Colonial Assembly to grant rights to the free people of color were frustrated by the Patriots, who stubbornly resisted French interference in local affairs.

On April 4, 1792, the French Assembly, now dominated by the liberal representatives of the French mercantile bourgeoisie, reversed itself once more and issued a decree giving full citizenship to the people of color. The decision was motivated less by a commitment to the principles of the Rights of Man than by a desire to restore order and stability, so favorable to commerce. As was the case throughout the French revolution, the bourgeoisie had furthered their particular class interests by identifying them with the universal principles of liberty and equality. That their primary consideration was economic self-interest became manifest when they refused to extend these principles to the slaves. Three new Civil Commissioners, headed by Léger Sonthonax, and six thousand troops were sent to St. Domingue in September 1792 with instructions to reestablish the control of the French Assembly over local affairs and to restore order by relying upon the people of color to crush the slaves and counter-revolutionaries.

The Commissioners found it difficult to make headway. Colonial support for the royalist cause mounted, particularly after the execution of Louis XVI, while the rebel slaves, aided by the Spanish, kept up unrelenting guerilla warfare. In June 1793 the Commissioners were confronted by a new threat, when the *petits blancs* of the north, jealous of the growing influence of the people of color and resentful over the dissolution of the Colonial Assembly by the Commissioners, revolted in Le Cap. To quell this unexpected uprising Sonthonax sent both free coloreds and armed slaves into the city, which was destroyed in the fighting. For many of the colonists the destruction of Le Cap symbolized the end of white supremacy in St. Domingue, and a mass migration followed.

In a desperate effort to retain control of the situation, Sonthonax proclaimed full Negro emancipation on his own authority in August 1793. Initially this move backfired. The rebel slaves were slow to leave the Spanish, recruits from the plantations were few, and many of the slaveholding people of color deserted to the counterrevolution. In September, the Royalists of the south signed a convention with the British transferring their allegiance to England in exchange for British intervention. The first English troops landed to a mixed reception. Soon, however, many whites and people of color joined them, and with their assistance the coastal cities of the South and West were secured. These successes culminated with the surrender of Port-au-

Prince in May 1794. Simultaneously, the Spanish and their slave allies occupied nearly the whole of central Haiti. At this critical juncture Toussaint L'Ouverture, the most capable rebel slave leader, was induced to join the French Republic.

Toussaint had been no ordinary slave. Endeavoring to account for his remarkable abilities, most biographers have stressed, respectively, his African heritage, his familiarity with European culture, and his religious faith. To some it was his father, allegedly an Arada chief, who instilled in his son a profound respect for African traditions and who prepared him for his subsequent role as leader of his people. Others have emphasized that unlike most slaves Toussaint was taught to read and write, thereby acquiring motivation from European books such as Abbé Raynal's *History of the Indies* (in which it was predicted that a black Sparticist would someday appear to overthrow slavery), and military expertise from Caesar's *War Commentaries*. Finally, some writers, pointing out that Toussaint was a devout Roman Catholic, have argued that he was inspired chiefly by the moral precepts of Christianity and was often guided by the advice of priests.

Although each of these influences was undoubtedly important, the most decisive factor shaping Toussaint's perceptions, attitudes, and conduct—a factor commonly overlooked by most commentators—was his slave experience, particularly his creole birth and his background as a plantation headman.

The strength of his African heritage was considerably diminished by the fact that he was a creole, born on the large Bréda plantation sometime around 1744. As such, his assimiliation into slave society was far greater than that of the newly imported Africans, who retained direct awareness of a former condition. His knowledge of the French language and his Roman Catholicism facilitated this detachment from African culture. Furthermore, for the creole it was generally the white master who exercised a formative influence in his early development. All the more so for Toussaint, who lost his mother while a youth, and whose master was exceptionally humane and generous, especially to Toussaint, who was never punished or ill-treated.[1] Throughout his life Toussaint reciprocated this kindness. He was a model slave. Loyal and trustworthy, he rose rapidly within the plantation hierarchy from herdsman to coachman to steward. In the process he acquired self-confidence, wealth, and privileges, as well as substantial influence among his fellow slaves.

The social role of such slave headmen (a category including drivers,

---

[1] We refer here to the manager of the Bréda estate, Bayou de Libertas, and not to the owner, M. Noé, who was an absentee planter.

stewards, boilers, artisans, watchmen) was to serve as intermediaries between oppressor and oppressed. Specifically, they transmitted the directives of the white master, supervised their implementation, disciplined, absorbed slave discontent, and curbed unrest. To a far greater extent than has generally been appreciated it rested with the headmen —who unlike the house slaves were actively engaged in the productive process— to maintain order on the estate and regulate the operation of the plantation economy. In return this elite could expect to be rewarded with preferential treatment, could enjoy the confidence of the whites, and could share in their authority while holding high status among the slaves. It was not an easy role to maintain, however, involving as it did an ambiguous and ambivalent attitude toward both whites and blacks, a complex mixture of love and hate. Toward the slaves it engendered an attitude of aloofness and superiority. Yet their society alone provided a source of friendship, respect, and love. Toward the whites it necessitated a high degree of accommodation and compliance. The headman had to deal directly with the whites on a day-to-day basis and, even more than for the average slave, survival considerations required that he be deferential and passive yet crafty and resourceful. Above all it was incumbent upon him to understand the psychology of the master, while preventing the master from deciphering him. It meant living in a state of constant inner tension, for the headman grew to know his own worth and strength but was obliged to conform to the white man's stereotype of the self-effacing, ignorant, docile black. It is no wonder, therefore, that these headmen were most frequently the leaders of West Indian slave revolts.

Toussaint learned this role well. As we shall see, it provides the key to understanding his incredibly successful career as soldier, administrator, statesman, and diplomat. Unquestionably, slavery prepared Toussaint for leadership, provided him with tools to manipulate effectively both white and black, and shaped his notions of society and government. It is true that the revolutionary struggle was also highly formative. But to that struggle Toussaint brought a fully developed personality—a personality nurtured in slavery, which, for a time, allowed him to dominate the situation.

His slave background was also responsible for many of the paradoxes of his rule. For although it had familiarized Toussaint with the desperate longing of the slaves for freedom, dignity, and self-respect, it also taught him their potential for self-destructive rage, their ignorance, and their lack of self-discipline. In short, it convinced him of their need for firm direction from above. Despite all his efforts on their behalf, Toussaint always regarded the blacks with a certain disdain, never placing full confidence in them. Conversely, he could never bring himself to break completely with the whites, for whom he held a grudging respect. Throughout his life Toussaint relied upon a white authority figure to justify his actions. At various times this role was filled by his master, the King, Laveaux and Sonthonax, Catholic priests, even Napoleon Bonaparte. This psychological dependence was reinforced by his awareness that the prosperity of the blacks was dependent upon white capital and expertise, just as the security of St. Domingue required some connection with France. It is true that during the course of the revolution Toussaint successfully extricated himself from the hegemony of each of these white men and that, furthermore, his attachment to the whites was often no more than rank expediency. But it is no less true that in 1802 he finished the revolution as he had begun it—unable to emancipate himself decisively from the white man and embrace fully the cause of the blacks.

In the end this posture proved untenable. It involved Toussaint in a series of contradictory policies that ultimately cost him the loyalty of the blacks, who after years of exploitation and conflict had no further use for the whites no matter what the economic and social costs. It led to his betrayal by the whites, who had no further use for a powerful black leader. And because of it the unequivocal African field slave, Jean Jacques Dessalines, led the final struggle for independence.

Toussaint's activities in the early stages of the slave revolt are the least known of his career. It is unlikely that he played any role in the formation of the revolt of August 1791. When it erupted he remained loyal to his master, electing to stay on his plantation and protect it from the rebels. He maintained this stance for over a month, until he realized that the slave revolt stood a favorable chance of success. Then, after escorting his master to safety, he joined the rebels in the mountains, where he was given a position as physician. His intelligence and military skills were soon recognized and he steadily advanced to a position rivaling that of Jean François and Biassou, who had assumed leadership following the death of Boukman.

When in December 1791 Jean François and Biassou, in an extraordinary act of treachery, offered to surrender the rebel slaves to the Civil Commissioners in exchange for the freedom of the rebel leadership, Toussaint played a major role in the negotiations. The refusal of the Patriots to ward freedom to any of the rebels ended this sordid affair. Thereafter, Toussaint resolved to earn his freedom and that of his followers through his own efforts. He began organizing a disciplined band of rebels, skilled in the art of guerilla warfare and personally attached to him. During the next two years this force won an impressive series of victories over the French armies, while Toussaint's humane policy of "no reprisals" resulted in the surrender of a number of towns. By December 1793 his forces, allied with the Spanish and French royalists, occupied the whole of central Haiti, posing a major threat to the French in the north and west.

Toussaint's loyalties during this period were to the Spanish and French kings, who alone, he believed, were willing and able to offer freedom to the rebels. Sonthonax's decree abolishing slavery in St. Domingue failed to impress him. But when news arrived that the Jacobin-controlled French Assembly had officially emancipated the slaves on February 4, 1794, he decided to cast his lot with the French Republic. Undoubtedly this decision was partially motivated by the fact that Toussaint's personal ambitions were blocked in the royalist camp by Jean François, but the primary consideration was that the French Republic alone offered freedom to *all* the slaves. By a series of brilliant maneuvers Toussaint drove the Spanish forces out of the North, then joined with Rigaud to contain the British in the ports of the South and West. As a consequence of these victories the French became increasingly dependent upon the former slaves, and Toussaint acquired great personal influence over the French military commander General Laveaux. The people of color, especially in the North, came to resent this growing ascendancy. Led by the mulatto, Villate, they staged a coup in Le Cap in March 1796 and arrested Laveaux. But this attempt to regain control of the revolution from the blacks failed when Toussaint rushed to the capital and forced Villate to release Laveaux, thus placing the Frenchman permanently in his debt. On April 1, 1796, Laveaux rewarded Toussaint by proclaiming him Lieutenant Governor of the colony.

A month later a third group of Civil Commissioners arrived from France. Led once again by Sonthonax, they were instructed by the Directory to expel the English and reestablish full French authority over the colony. Convinced that the people of color now represented the greatest obstacle to French control, Sonthonax pursued a problack policy, naming Toussaint Commander-in-Chief of the French armies. In the South, where Rigaud had restored prosperity through forced labor and American trade, the Commissioners encouraged rivalries between blacks and browns, but with little success.

Toussaint, meanwhile, was forming his own conception of who should govern the colony. Since the fall of the Jacobins, he had watched colonial interest groups assuming a greater prominence within the French government and had grown anxious lest France should some day attempt to restore slavery. He was persuaded that in order to insure the social gains of the revolution, negro unity and the revival of prosperity were essential. These goals, he believed, could be realized only by a black government at the head of a genuine national movement. By 1797, therefore, he had resolved to make a bid for absolute political power and to identitfy the cause of the blacks with the movement for local self-government that had been successfully defused in 1794 when the French government freed the slaves.

In August 1797 he forced Sonthonax to return to France on the pretence that the Frenchman wanted him to murder all the whites and declare independence. Interpreting this action as a clear indication of Toussaint's personal ambition, the French dispatched a new agent, General Hédouville, to bring the black chief under control. Until Hédouville's arrival Toussaint had enjoyed great solidarity with Rigaud, their forces cooperating to inflict a series of crushing defeats upon the English. But as soon as Hédouville arrived, in April 1798, he began intriguing with Rigaud to undermine Toussaint's project of forging a truly nationalist movement. Toussaint, meanwhile, had forced the English to agree to withdraw their forces from the colony. In the resulting treaty he signed a secret clause stating that he would not invade Jamaica and promising the English extensive trading privileges. At the same time he rejected English offers to support him as king of an independent nation. This treaty not only enhanced Toussaint's prestige, but substantially improved his bargaining position with the French by raising the possibility of an alliance with England. Hédouville found himself outmaneuvered. He reacted by openly encouraging racial conflict between blacks and browns. Exasperated by this treachery, Toussaint expelled the Frenchman from the island in October 1798. However, before his departure Hédouville publicly urged Rigaud to resist Toussaint, pledging official French support for such an effort.

Toussaint held no racial biases. Convinced that a united front of blacks and browns was the surest guarantee of freedom, he was prepared to cooperate with Rigaud and govern jointly with him. Encouraged by the French, Rigaud refused to negotiate. In April 1799, following several unsuccessful efforts to reach agreement, Toussaint invaded Rigaud's southern stronghold.

From the outset this tragic conflict was greatly influenced by the diplomacy of the great powers. On his return to France, Hédouville had advised the Directory that Toussaint intended to declare independence and urged aid for Rigaud. This policy was adopted, but assistance to Rigaud was extended only to the extent that it would prolong the civil war and weaken both participants. The British, fearing that a stable black government in St. Domingue would directly or indirectly provoke slave rebellions in their vulnerable West Indian colonies, followed a similar policy. For the Americans, on the other hand, desire for profits outweighed fear of slave insurrection. The administration of John Adams was prepared to accept, even aid a black government as long as it was commercially dependent on the United States.

With the assistance of American arms and vessels, Toussaint finally broke the determined resistance of the mulattoes in July 1800, forcing Rigaud to flee the island. In the aftermath, despite Toussaint's promise of no reprisals, Jean-Jacques Dessalines, as Governor of the South, instituted a wave of terror against the people of color and thousands were slaughtered before Toussaint called a halt.

One further obstacle remained before Toussaint became master of the situation. His rebel background had taught him that the security of St. Domingue was dependent upon control of the Spanish part of the island. Accordingly, in May 1800 his forces invaded Spanish Santo Domingo and within six months had made a triumphant entry into the Spanish capital.

Between 1798 and 1802 Toussaint turned his attention to the crucial task of reconstruction, to the establishment of an administration that would unify the colony and would restore tranquility and prosperity. Dedicated above all to the freedom of the blacks, his overriding aim was to consolidate their liberty against internal and external foes. The policy he adopted was one of moderation and reconciliation. In its outlines it envisaged a multiracial society founded upon the plantation system, ruled by a benevolent despot in accordance with republican principles, and loosely linked to Republican France. The basic difference from the past was that government would be geared to the needs of the blacks as well as the whites. For that reason black rule was imperative. Toussaint resolutely set out to realize this vision and thereby convince France that only a black government could rule the colony profitably in accordance with the principles of the French revolution. Concurrently, he sought to demonstrate that, contrary to planter propaganda, the Old Colonial System was not dependent upon slavery. In so doing, either consciously or unconsciously, he threatened to undermine the central prop of the slave system within the European mother countries, where slavery was conceived of largely as the only (albeit distasteful) means of amassing the colonial wealth so essential to the national economy. Thus, although some might question Toussaint's refusal to spread revolution throughout the hemisphere, as many of his contemporaries feared he would, his policy of restoration within the framework of empire was just as revolutionary in its implications. For if free, self-governing black men could continue to produce colonial wealth for the mother country at a rate equivalent to that of a slave colony, then clearly slavery and white supremacy had become anachronistic.

Toussaint was aware that these projects were fraught with enormous difficulties, that his very success might render him more intolerable to friend and foe alike; so, simultaneously, he prepared his military defenses and placed his people in a state of seige.

Any discussion of Toussaint's domestic program must recognize that he lacked any model or ideology of development. To a great extent this accounts for his social conservatism and reluctance to sever the connection with France. But these tendencies also proceeded from Toussaint's own predispositions. His conception of society and government drew much from his slave background, reinforced by his military experience. His training as a headman had taught him the virtues of order, duty, discipline, and paternalistic authority, and they became the watchwords of his rule. In effect, he perceived society at large as a plantation and would govern it accordingly.

One of Toussaint's most frequently expressed dictums was: "The liberty of the blacks can only be consolidated through the prosperity of agriculture." The plantation system, which he considered the key to this prosperity, was therefore retained; however, it was to be organized on a new basis. Forced labor was imposed, but hours were regulated and safeguards established to insure that the blacks were given humane treatment and maintenance. Profits were divided: one-fourth going to the workers, one-fourth to the owner, and one-half to the state. A passport system was introduced, and strict controls were exercised over the activities of the workers.

Retention of the plantation system, fear of foreign invasion, and the need for unity necessitated a strong central government. This requirement coincided with Toussaint's preference for a system of paternalistic authority. Despite his espousal of republican theory and practice, the state he created can only be termed a military despotism. The locus of power was to be found not in the sham Colonial Assembly, but in the twenty-thousand-man army, which enforced internal order and secured the country against a hostile outside world. The chieftains of this army were responsible for local government, but they received their instructions directly from Toussaint, who, as Commander-in-Chief, retained their loyalty through a combination of charisma, coercion, and reward. The Constitution of 1801 officially concentrated all power in the hands of Toussaint and granted him the right to designate his successor.

Although his rule was designed to guarantee the interests of the black majority, Toussaint firmly believed that "the blacks, the people of color and the whites, when governed by laws, must be equally protected and equally punished." Convinced that the colony could not progress without white assistance in the form of capital, expertise, and advice, he pursued a policy of racial harmony. Accordingly, the plantations were restored to those former owners who would return, even though they may have formerly fought against the blacks. Many accepted this offer. Whites were favored with key government and military posts, and Toussaint relied heavily upon their counsel. Nor was there discrimination against the people of color, who likewise occupied important positions, especially in the expanding state bureaucracy.

Toussaint's diplomacy during these years has generally been condemned as one of hypocrisy and duplicity—as if that practiced by his adversaries was somehow different. The truth of the matter is that Toussaint simply beat his adversaries at their own game. Trained from birth to distrust white men, to understand, even to anticipate them, he was ideally equipped to match wits with the diplomats of the great powers. The object of his diplomacy was to maintain his freedom of action internally and free trade externally while retaining the connection with France for purposes of development and protection. Coincidently, he maneuvered to gain time to strengthen his forces against any attempt to restore slavery. His tactic was to keep his opponents off balance by disguising his real intentions, to manipulate them in such a way that they believed they were manipulating him.

Well aware that no slave power could long tolerate a black government in its midst, he endeavored to offset the threat he posed by offering substantial commercial advantages and disclaiming any intention of instigating slave unrest in the Caribbean or the United States. His task was facilitated by a favorable international situation. England and France were at war, and the United States was involved in a quasi war with France. Toussaint astutely took full advantage of this opportunity. He kept France at bay by professing a nominal allegiance but implied that in case of interference he would ally himself with England. To the English and Americans he granted extensive trading rights, stopped French privateers from using Hispaniola as a base for raiding their shipping, pledged not to attack their slave territories, and encouraged them to believe that he intended to declare independence from France if he received their support.

Initially, all these policies paid dividends. The plantations flourished, new lands were cultivated, roads were built, trade revived to two-thirds of its prerevolutionary height. Massive public works projects were undertaken, the cities were rebuilt, and a number of schools —open to all races—were constructed. A new black ruling class began to emerge, and the black population at large was acquiring some degree of self-confidence and pride. The colonial whites responded favorably. And why not? Their estates had not been broken up. Their labor was disciplined. And Toussaint's administration appeared to have brought them the very gains they had sought at the outset of the revolution: local self-government and free trade. They believed Toussaint to be their creature. Toussaint fostered this illusion but held the reins of power tightly in his own hands.

His diplomacy was equally successful—in part because the white diplomats, like the white colonists, responded to him as they would to any slave. They consistently underestimated him, flattered him, and misunderstood his intentions and determination. Their error was crucial, for Toussaint's diplomacy, although failing in its primary objective of convincing France that a black government was more capable than a white, did earn the time necessary to prepare the defenses of St. Domingue and to encourage the development of a national consciousness. Continuation of free trade meant that plantation products reached the most favorable markets, and with the profits Toussaint purchased essential military supplies. Indeed, it was in these years that the foundation of an independent nation was securely laid.

By the end of 1801, however, Toussaint was confronted with grave domestic and international crises. Many blacks had become disillusioned with his rule. They resented the policy of forced labor and the favors extended to the whites. Feeling that Toussaint had abandoned their interests, they could see little justification for his despotism and diplomatic intrigues. A few petty chieftains, including the Maroons, had resisted Toussaint's rule all along by establishing their own fiefdoms deep in the mountains. But it was Moise, Toussaint's adopted nephew and rumored successor, who took the lead in opposing Toussaint and championing the cause of the blacks. In September 1801 Moise led a major revolt against the whites of the North. Toussaint quickly quashed this threat and had Moise executed. But the die was cast. Toussaint's influence over the blacks was on the wane; his reluctance to confide his real intentions to them had cost him their trust.

More significantly, the international basis of his rule had collapsed. In October 1801 the British and French concluded their hostilities by the Treaty of Amiens. In the United States the new Jefferson administration, more responsive to Southern slaveowners than to northern merchants and desiring improved relations with France, had already cooled toward the idea of an independent black republic. Bonaparte, prodded by his backers among the mercantile bourgeoisie and by his own dreams of a vast empire in the Western Hemisphere, organized a fleet under the command of his brother-in-law, General Leclerc, to depose the "gilded African." Leclerc's secret instructions were: first, win over Toussaint's lieutenants; second, arrest and deport Toussaint; third, disarm the blacks; fourth, restore slavery. Napoleon's official explanation that Toussaint had to be overthrown to guarantee the security of the Western Hemisphere earned him British assistance and American neutrality.

In January 1802 the French force, sixteen thousand strong, arrived off Le Cap. Acting under Toussaint's orders, Henri Christophe refused to allow them to land, then burnt Le Cap to the ground. Nevertheless, the French came ashore at several points along the coast, and within days the entire northern plain was under their control. Toussaint's troops in the South and in Spanish Santo Domingo surrendered without a fight. The whites joined the French, as did the persons of color and Maroons. Toussaint conducted a vigorous but futile resistance. He was now reaping the harvest of discontent and distrust he had sown among the blacks. Many of his generals and their armies deserted to the French, while the black laborers, whom Toussaint had expected to rise *en masse,* remained apathetically on their estates. Discouraged, Toussaint surrendered to Leclerc in April 1802, then retired to his estate. But he was far too dangerous to be left free. A month later, on the pretence that the black leader was preparing a new rebellion, Leclerc tricked him and deported him to France. When he arrived, Toussaint pleaded for a hearing, but it was denied, and he was cast into the dungeon at Fort de Joux in the Jura Mountains. He became seriously ill during the freezing French winter and died on April 7, 1803.

When news of his death reached St. Domingue the colony was in the final throes of its struggle for independence. The treachery surrounding Toussaint's arrest had alarmed only a few of his most dedicated followers, who took to the hills to establish the resistance. As French rule became increasingly intolerable, the ranks of the rebels grew. However, the insurrection only became general when word leaked out that slavery had been restored in Guadeloupe. The blacks cherished their hard-earned freedom and, thanks to Toussaint, knew how to defend it. In October 1802 Dessalines and Alexander Pétion deserted the French to take command of the national liberation movement.

Already decimated by yellow fever, the French now encountered a genuine, popular insurrectionary movement. They responded as have all occupying powers when confronted with a similar phenomenon. Pouring in reinforcements, relying upon superior firepower, they initiated a war of extermination in which no distinction was made between civilian and military populations. The blacks responded in kind. Barbarous atrocities were committed by both sides. As it became obvious that the stubborn resistance of the freedom fighters could not be overcome, the French systematically devastated the countryside to render it uninhabitable and destroy the basis of the economy. After a year of bitter fighting, Napoleon reluctantly withdrew the remnants of his army, leaving the blacks of St. Domingue in absolute control of their own destiny.

Chronology

1744?	Toussaint born into slavery on the Bréda plantation in St. Domingue.
1787	
(November)	Louis XVI of France promises to summon Estates General.
1788	
(February)	*Amis des Noirs* founded in France.
(July)	Colonial Committee founded in France by absentee planters.
(September)	Colonial Committee demands right of colonial representation in Estates General.
(December)	Planters in St. Domingue draw up cahier of grievances seeking greater autonomy.
1789	
(January)	People of color petition for full rights in St. Domingue.
(June 20)	Colonial Committee joins Third Estate on day of Tennis Court Oath.
(July 14)	Storming of the Bastille in France.
(August 26)	Declaration of Rights of Man and Citizens drawn up in France.
(September)	French Assembly grants a Colonial Assembly to St. Domingue.
(October)	People of color address French Assembly, claiming Rights of Man.
(November)	Widespread persecutions of people of color begin in St. Domingue.
(December)	French Assembly rejects claims of people of color.
1790	
(March 8)	Decree of French Assembly leaves question of rights of people of color to Colonial Assembly in St. Domingue.
(March)	First major revolt of people of color.
(April 15)	First Colonial Assembly meets.
(May)	Colonial Assembly issues a constitution giving itself sweeping powers. This act prompts civil war between royal officials and colonists.
(August)	Colonial Assembly forcibly dissolved by government troops.
(October 12)	French government officially dissolves Colonial Assembly.
(October 28)	Ogé rebellion in St. Domingue.
1791	
(March)	Military reinforcements from France mutiny and join colonists.
(May 15)	French Assembly grants full equality to people of color born of free parents.
(August 9)	New Colonial Assembly meets to oppose May Decree.
(August 22)	Massive slave revolt in the North.

(September?)	Toussaint joins rebel slaves.
(September 24)	May Decree rescinded by French Assembly.
(November 21)	*Petits blancs* massacre people of color in Port-au-Prince.
(November 29)	Three Civil Commissioners arrive in St. Domingue.
(December)	Civil Commissioners fail to come to terms with rebel slaves.

1792

(April 14)	French Assembly decrees full rights and privileges to all people of color.
(May)	War commences between French St. Domingue and Spanish Santo Domingo.
(September 18)	Three new Commissioners arrive in St. Domingue to enforce April Decree.
(October 12)	Commissioners dissolve Colonial Assembly and assume full control over colony.

1793

(January 21)	Louis XVI executed.
(February)	France goes to war against England and Spain.
(June 19–20)	*Petits blancs* revolt against Commissioners fails.
(August 29)	Sonthonax, on his own authority, proclaims slave emancipation.
(September 3)	Royalists in St. Domingue request English intervention.
(September 19)	British expeditionary forces land in St. Domingue.
(December)	Toussaint's army occupies central Haiti after a series of victories.

1794

| (February 4) | French Assembly officially abolishes slavery. |
| (May 6) | Toussaint deserts the Spanish to join the French. |

1795   Toussaint's army drives the Spanish from St. Domingue.

1796

(March 20)	People of color, led by Villate, revolt against General Laveaux. Toussaint rescues Laveaux and crushes rebels.
(April 1)	Toussaint proclaimed Lieutenant Governor of St. Domingue.
(May 11)	New Commissioners arrive from France to pursue problack policy.

1797

(March)	Elections in France bring large number of reactionaries into French Assembly.
(May)	Toussaint made Commander-in-Chief of the French armies in St. Domingue.
(August 20)	Toussaint forces Sonthonax to return to France.

1798

(April 21)	General Hédouville arrives in St. Domingue.
(May)	English evacuate St. Domingue following agreement between Toussaint and General Maitland.
(October 20)	Toussaint expels Hédouville and assumes effective control.

1799

| (April) | Civil war begins between Toussaint and Rigaud. |

1800

(May)	Toussaint's armies invade Spanish Santo Domingo.
(July)	Rigaud defeated by Toussaint.
(October)	Toussaint proclaims policy of forced labor throughout Hispaniola.

1801

(January)	Santo Domingo surrenders to Toussaint.
(July)	Toussaint publishes Constitution granting him power for life.
(September)	Moise rebellion against Toussaint.
(October 1)	Peace of Amiens ends war between France and England.
(November 25)	Toussaint proclaims strict military dictatorship.

1802

(February 6)	Leclerc expedition invades St. Domingue as Toussaint retreats to mountains.
(April)	Christophe surrenders and joins the French.
(May 1)	Toussaint and Dessalines surrender.
(June)	Toussaint arrested and sent to France.
(July)	News arrives in St. Domingue that the French have restored slavery in Guadeloupe.
(October)	Dessalines and Pétion join rebellion against the French.

1803

(April 7)	Toussaint dies in Fort de Joux.
(November 29)	French forced to evacuate St. Domingue.
(December 31)	Haiti declared an independent republic by its black leaders.

PART ONE

TOUSSAINT LOOKS AT THE WORLD

1

Toussaint Calls the Slaves to Arms

The following two proclamations are among the first issued by Toussaint. Intended to offset Sonthonax's unofficial emancipation of the slaves on August 29, 1793, they reflect Toussaint's conviction that the blacks should gain their liberty by their own struggle rather than as a gift from the whites. In the first proclamation, the messianic element of Toussaint's leadership is obvious. Throughout his political career, Toussaint endeavored to capitalize on the religious ecstaticism that had characterized the slave rebellion from the outset. There can be no doubt that this was not merely political expediency but that he shared the general "delirium"—as he liked to call it—of his brothers. However, he did attempt, with varying degrees of success, to shift the locus of this prophetic movement from the beliefs and practices of African voodoo to Western Christianity. The second proclamation makes it clear that during the period he was fighting in the service of the Spanish his commitment was not to the cause of royalism but to the liberty and equality of the blacks.[1]

PROCLAMATION OF 25 AUGUST 1793

Having been the first to champion your cause, it is my duty to continue to labour for it. I cannot permit another to rob me of the initiative. Since I have begun, I will know how to conclude. Join me and you will enjoy the rights of freemen sooner than any other way. Neither whites nor mulattoes have formulated my plans; it is to the

[1] From Ralph Korngold, *Citizen Toussaint* (London, 1945), p. 85.

Supreme Being alone that I owe my inspiration. We have begun, we have carried on, we will know how to reach the goal.

PROCLAMATION OF 29 AUGUST 1793

Brothers and Friends:

I am Toussaint L'Ouverture. My name is perhaps known to you. I have undertaken to avenge you. I want liberty and equality to reign throughout St. Domingue. I am working towards that end. Come and join me, brothers, and combat by our side for the same cause.

2
Toussaint Joins the French Republic

In the next two selections, Toussaint presents his reasons for joining the French in May, 1794. In the first he stresses the ideological factor. The Spanish and French royalists were only using the slaves with the ultimate intention of returning them to slavery. Freedom could be achieved solely through a French victory. In the second excerpt—from an official report to the Ministry of the Marine in 1799, which Gerard Laurent refers to as Toussaint's "political testament"—Toussaint offers his interpretation of the early stages of the St. Domingue revolution and suggests that he deliberately chose to join the French at a critical moment when he could wring the maximum number of concessions from Laveaux. Notable in his analysis of events is Toussaint's opinion that the slaves joined the Spanish only after the whites had bought off the persons of color who had initially been their allies.

Some writers have suggested two other motives for Toussaint's decision to join the French: He had fallen out of favor with the Spanish and English, and his ambitions to further advancement were blocked by Jean François.

LETTER TO GENERAL LAVEAUX, 18 May 1794 [1]

It is true, General, that I had been deceived by the enemies of the Republic; but what man can pride himself on avoiding all the traps of wickedness? In truth, I fell into their snares, but not without knowing the reason. You must recall the advances I had made to you before the disasters at Le Cap, in which I stated that my only goal was to unite us in the struggle against the enemies of France.

Unhappily for everyone, the means of reconciliation that I proposed —*the recognition of the liberty of the blacks and a general amnesty*— were rejected. My heart bled, and I shed tears over the unfortunate fate of my country, perceiving the misfortunes that must follow. I wasn't mistaken: fatal experience proved the reality of my predictions. Meanwhile, the Spanish offered their protection to me and to all

---

[1] From Victor Schoelcher, *Vie de Toussaint-Louverture* (Paris, 1889), pp. 98–99; trans. George F. Tyson, Jr.

those who would fight for the cause of the kings, and having always fought in order to have liberty I accepted their offers, seeing myself abandoned by my brothers the French. But a later experience opened my eyes to these perfidious protectors, and having understood their villainous deceit, I saw clearly that they intended to make us slaughter one another in order to diminish our numbers so as to overwhelm the survivors and reenslave them. No, they will never attain their infamous objective, and we will avenge ourselves in our turn upon these contemptible beings. Therefore, let us unite forever and, forgetting the past, occupy ourselves hereafter only with exterminating our enemies and avenging ourselves, in particular, upon our perfidious neighbors.

LETTER TO THE MINISTER OF MARINE, 13 APRIL 1799 [2]

The first successes obtained in Europe by the partisans of liberty over the agents of despotism were not slow to ignite the sacred fire of patriotism in the souls of all Frenchmen in St. Domingue. At that time, men's hopes turned to France, whose first steps toward her regeneration promised them a happier future; . . . they wanted to escape from their arbitrary government, but they did not intend the revolution to destroy either the prejudice that debased the men of color or the slavery of the blacks, whom they held in dependency by the strongest law. In their opinion, the benefits of the French regeneration were only for them. They proved it by their obstinate refusal to allow the people of color to enjoy their political rights and the slaves to enjoy the liberty that they claimed. Thus, while the whites were erecting another form of government upon the rubble of despotism, the men of color and the blacks united themselves in order to claim their political existence; the resistance of the former having become stronger, it was necessary for the latter to rise up in order to obtain [political recognition] by force of arms. The whites, fearing that this legitimate resistance would bring general liberty to St. Domingue, sought to separate the men of color from the cause of the blacks in accordance with Machiavelli's principle of divide and rule. Renouncing their claims over the men of color, they accepted the April Decree [1792]. As they had anticipated, the men of color, many of whom were slaveholders, had only been using the blacks to gain their own political demands. Fearing the enfranchisement of the blacks, the men of color deserted their comrades in arms, their companions in misfortune, and aligned themselves with the whites to subdue them.

Treacherously abandoned, the blacks fought for some time against

[2] Trans. George F. Tyson, Jr.

the reunited whites and the men of color; but, pressed on all sides, losing hope, they accepted the offers of the Spanish king, who, having at that time declared war on France, offered freedom to those blacks of St. Domingue who would join his armies. Indeed, the silence of pre-Republican France on the long-standing claims for their natural rights made by the most interested, the noblest, the most useful portion of the population of St. Domingue . . . extinguished all glimmer of hope in the hearts of the black slaves and forced them, in spite of themselves, to throw themselves into the arms of a protective power that offered the only benefit for which they would fight. More unfortunate than guilty, they turned their arms against their fatherland . . . .

Such were the crimes of these blacks, which have earned them to this day the insulting titles of brigands, insurgents, rebels under the orders of Jean François. At that time I was one of the leaders of these auxiliary troops, and I can say without fear of contradiction that I owed my elevation in these circumstances only to the confidence that I had inspired in my brothers by the virtues for which I am still honored today.

Meanwhile, the Spanish, benefiting from the internal divisions to which the French part of St. Domingue had fallen prey and aided by the courage that gave to these same blacks the hope of imminent freedom, seized almost all of the North and a large part of the West. Le Cap, surrounded by them on all sides and beseiged by land and sea, was experiencing all the horrors of the cruelest famine. . . . The Republic that had just been proclaimed in St. Domingue was recognized only in the territory from Le Cap to Port-de-Paix, and the guilty excesses of its agents were not calculated to gain it adherents. But, following their departure for France, they [the Civil Commissioners] left the reins of power in the hands of General Laveaux, who lost no time endearing himself by a wise and paternal administration. It was sometime after this period that, having received the order to attack Le Cap and convinced by my information about the distressing state to which this city was reduced, of its powerlessness to resist the torrent that must engulf it, I went over to the Republic with the blacks under my command.

PROCLAMATION ON THE VILLATE AFFAIR. MARCH 1795 [3]

In the following proclamation Toussaint explains his actions during the Villate affair. He denies any prejudice against the people of color, but affirms his determination to destroy any disrup-

[3] From *Proclamations of Toussaint Louverture* (New York: New York Public Library, The Schomburg Collection); trans. Eleanor Johnson.

tive elements, whatever their color. Religion and nothing else, he insists, has served as his guide.

My heart and my feelings are rent upon learning every day of the new plots of the evil-doers, of these corrupt men, of these guilty men and greatly culpable toward the mother country. It is for you to prepare against their false declamations about which I am going to talk to you as a brother, friend and father; too happy I would be if I could get them to come back to themselves, oblige them to recognize and to renounce their errors, inspire them with wholesome remorse and finally put them back on the right path.

Ah my friends, my brothers, my children!—these men are guilty who try by a few quotations from my letters, to persuade you that I have sworn the Destruction of all men of color; they judge my heart by their own hateful and vindictive heart. It is not color that I am fighting; it is crime that I am pursuing and shall always pursue in whaever place it is hidden; this is the reason that:

Considering that it is my duty to enlighten you, I am going to do it, as briefly and as clearly as I possibly can; I am going to speak to you in the Language of reason, truth and religion.

I have written to certain chiefs to be on guard against men of color, because I knew, before the criminal arrest of the General in Chief, that some men of color were at the head of this infernal conspiracy; because I knew that in several quarters of the Colony, the emissaries of these bold chiefs were preaching disobedience, revolt against the lawfully constituted authorities; you have the proof of it today. Who arrested General Laveux? Who dared bring a heinous and sacrilegious hand upon the representatives of the Nation? Men of color; it was quite necessary then that I warn my subordinates to suspect these men. God forbid, however, that I confuse the Innocent ones with the guilty! No, my brothers, I am not prejudiced against any particular class; I know that there are men of color who are estimable and virtuous, irreproachable and I have the great satisfaction of having some of them near me, to whom I accord my Esteem, my Friendship and my Confidence; I love them, because, faithful to their duties, they have not participated in perfidious manoeuvres; I have several of them among my Officers, who have never strayed from the right path; and those as well as all faithful soldiers, can count on me; I cherish all virtuous men; I owe them protection, and they shall always obtain it, when they make themselves worthy of it.

When murders were being committed in the Mountain Port of Paix, in the name Etienne, did I not say that Black men were committing these crimes? Let us be just, when we want to accuse; but does calumny know any Limits?

Religion, I remind you, my brothers, is my Guide, it is the rule of my conduct, whatever others might say; Religion tells us, commands us to give back to Caesar that which belongs to Caesar, and to God that which belongs to God; it commands us to give the most complete subordination to our chiefs, to our superiors. A Colonel wishes his body officers to obey him, a Captain wishes his Lieutenants and second-lieutenants to obey him, the Lieutenant wishes his non-commissioned officers to obey him, and the Officers exact the same obedience from their Companies. Why? because they know that subordination is essential to armed Force; there can be no army without subordination.

Supposing that in the presence of a Captain, a Lieutenant, a second-lieutenant, some rebels were to insult, maltreat and arrest the Colonel; what shall they do? Shall they remain peaceful spectators of that criminal conspiracy? They would become guilty themselves, if they did not put forth their efforts to defend him, to snatch him from the hands of those wicked chiefs and they take it ill that I have hurried to the assistance of my chief, of my superior, of the representative of the Republic: they take it ill that I have arrested those who have participated in this Heinous plot. The French nation is going to judge us. I place into its hands those whom I believe guilty.

Officers, the least insubordination arouses you, you mete out severe punishment, sometimes you even stray from the Law in the severity of your punishments; remember that to command well, you must know how to obey.

And you Colonists, you the beloved Children of the Republic; you, whom this tender mother carries in her bosom, you whom she had overwhelmed with kindness, would allow yourselves to be drawn into the artificial suggestions of the wicked! Ah! my brothers, France has decreed, has sanctioned general Liberty; twenty-five million men have ratified this glorious and consoling Decree for humanity, and you fear that she may return you to your former state of Bondage, while she has so long been fighting for her own Liberty and for the Liberty of all Nations. How mistaken you are!

No, my Friends, you are being deceived, they are jealous of your happiness, they want to rob you of it, and you know the ones who are deceiving you; they are those who slander the intentions, the operations of the Governor general and myself, for we act together. Believe me then, my brothers, you know me, you know my Religion, you have regarded me up to this day as your Father, I believe I merit this title, I hope to always merit it, it is so near to my heart. I implore you for your happiness, shun the rebels, the wicked; busy yourselves with work, France, your good Mother, will reward you.

The mask is going to fall, the evil-doers feel that the Day of vengeance is approaching; they would like to have a great many accomplices so as to be assured of Impunity; but let them fall alone into the abyss they have dug under their Feet; the hand of God, the Avenger, is going to weigh down upon them, for one does not always defy the Supreme Being with impunity; they have scorned Religion; they have defied the terrible thunder bolts of a God in His Anger; they feel the earth falling in beneath their feet, and they would like to drag you along with them in the depths of their anguish.

Denounce then the wrong doers, those who slander my intentions and actions. I take God as my witness, who must judge us all, that they are pure; I long only for your happiness; one moment more and you will be convinced of it. Close your ears to the voice of the wicked and the Agitator; God lets him act a short while, but often in the midst of his course, He stops him. Look at the proud Haman, the favorite of Ahasuerus, he would like to have had the humble Mordecai perish unjustly. The Gallows, which he had had prepared for this faithful Israelite, served for himself.

Everywhere the Holy Bible (I am pleased to mention it because it consoles me) everywhere the Holy Bible, tells us of the proud being humbled and of the humble being elevated; everywhere it shows us terrible Examples of Divine Justice against great Criminals; now it is an Antiochus, who satiated with crimes, at the approach of death asks for mercy and does not obtain it: now it is a heinous son, an Absalom, urged to insurrection against the most tender of all Fathers and who died miserably; finally, everywhere it proves to us that great scoundrels are punished sooner or later.

Alas! we ask, in the Example of our Divine Master, only the conversion of the Sinner, that he may come back to himself, that he may recognize his mistakes, his errors, his crimes, that he may renounce them, that he may come back to us, and we are ready to give him the "kiss of peace and of reconciliation."

The present letter will be printed, read, published and posted everywhere where there will be need, in order that the wicked persuaded by my peaceable sentiments, may profit by the pardon that I offer them, and that the Good may be cautioned against the snares of Error and seduction.

3
Toussaint Defends the Revolution and His Race

Following the fall of the Jacobins in 1794, the revolu tion in France moved steadily to the right. From November 1795, the reactionaries who formed a large bloc in the French assemblies began clamoring for a "restoration of order" in the colonies. The elections of March 1797 brought even more of them into the assemblies. Led by Vienot Vaublanc, they deplored the situation in St. Domingue and condemned the policies of the Civil Commissioners. Their speeches were violently antinegro and openly questioned the capacity of the blacks for freedom. Toussaint himself was the victim of a scurrilous attack by Vaublanc. In September 1797, however, Vaublanc and his followers were arrested and deported from France because of their involvement in a royalist plot, and the rightward drift of the revolution was momentarily checked. Toussaint had been watching these events with mounting alarm. Fearful that Vaublanc's faction was having too much influence on public and official opinion in France and unaware that its members had been deported, Toussaint sent several letters to the Directory. Two of these eloquent statements on behalf of the freedom of the blacks are reproduced below.

In the first, Toussaint presents a stirring defense of the revolution and his race, cleverly attacking Vaublanc and his partisans as the real antirepublicans. Admitting the shortcomings of the blacks, which he attributes to slavery and the influence of evilminded whites, Toussaint insists that the cause of republicanism in St. Domingue can only be identified with that of the blacks. In defense of his brothers, he exposes the double standards by which colonial nations have always condemned the colonized people while justifying their own crimes and hypocrisy.

In the second reading, Toussaint reiterates more forcibly his dedication to the cause of freedom and the determination of his brothers to resist any attempt to deprive them of their natural rights.

Taken together, these selections constitute the most concise and compelling statement of Toussaint's commitment to the ideals of liberty and equality and to Republican France as long as she shared that commitment.

LETTER TO THE DIRECTORY, 28 OCTOBER 1797 [1]

Citizen Directors,

At the moment when I thought I had just rendered eminent service to the Republic and to my fellow citizens, when I had just proven my recognition of the justice of the French people toward us, when I believed myself worthy of the confidence that the Government had placed in me and which I will never cease to merit, a speech was made in the *Corps Legislatif* during the meeting of 22 May 1797 by Vienot Vaublanc . . . and, while going through it, I had the sorrow of seeing my intentions slandered on every page and the political existence of my brothers threatened.

A similar speech from the mouth of a man whose fortune had been momentarily wiped out by the revolution in St. Domingue would not surprise me, the loser has the right to complain up to a certain point, but what must profoundly affect me is that the *Corps Legislatif* could have approved and sanctioned such declamations, which are so unsuitable to the restoration of our tranquility; which, instead of spurring the field-negroes to work, can only arouse them by allowing them to believe that the representatives of the French people were their enemies.

In order to justify myself in your eyes and in the eyes of my fellow citizens, whose esteem I so eagerly desire, I am going to apply myself to refuting the assertions of citizen Vaublanc . . . and . . . prove that the enemies of our liberty have only been motivated in this event by a spirit of personal vengeance and that the public interest and respect for the Constitution have been continually trampled under foot by them. . . .

> *Second Assertion:* "Everyone is agreed in portraying the Colony in the most shocking state of disorder and groaning under the military government. And what a military government! In whose hands is it confined? In that of ignorant and gross negroes, incapable of distinguishing between unrestrained license and austere liberty." . . .

This shocking disorder in which the Commission found St. Domingue was not the consequence of the liberty given to the blacks but

[1] From *La Révolution française et l'abolition de l'esclavage,* 14 vols. (Paris, n.d.), 11:1–32; trans. George F. Tyson, Jr.

the result of the uprising of thirty Ventôse [the Villate affair], for, prior to this period, order and harmony reigned in all Republican territory as far as the absence of laws would allow. All citizens blindly obeyed the orders of General Laveaux; his will was the national will for them, and they submitted to him as a man invested with the authority emanating from the generous nation that had shattered their chains.

If, upon the arrival of the Commission, St. Domingue groaned under a military government, this power was not in the hands of the blacks; they were subordinate to it, and they only executed the orders of General Laveaux. These were the blacks who, when France was threatened with the loss of this Colony, employed their arms and their weapons to conserve it, to reconquer the greatest part of its territory that treason had handed over to the Spanish and English. . . . These were the blacks who, with the good citizens of the other two colors, flew to the rescue of General Laveaux in the Villate Affair and who, by repressing the audacious rebels who wished to destroy the national representation, restored it to its rightful depository.

Such was the conduct of those blacks in whose hands citizen Vienot Vaublanc said the military government of St. Domingue found itself, such are those negroes he accuses of being ignorant and gross; undoubtedly they are, because without education there can only be ignorance and grossness. But must one impute to them the crime of this educational deficiency or, more correctly, accuse those who prevented them by the most atrocious punishments from obtaining it? And are only civilized people capable of distinguishing between good and evil, of having notions of charity and justice? The men of St. Domingue have been deprived of an education; but even so, they no longer remain in a state of nature, and because they haven't arrived at the degree of perfection that education bestows, they do not merit being classed apart from the rest of mankind, being confused with animals. . . .

Undoubtedly, one can reproach the inhabitants of St. Domingue, including the blacks, for many faults, even terrible crimes. But even in France, where the limits of sociability are clearly drawn, doesn't one see its inhabitants, in the struggle between despotism and liberty, going to all the excesses for which the blacks are reproached by their enemies? The fury of the two parties has been equal in St. Domingue; and if the excesses of the blacks in these critical moments haven't exceeded those committed in Europe, must not an impartial judge pronounce in favor of the former? Since it is our enemies themselves who present us as ignorant and gross, aren't we more excusable than those who, unlike us, were not deprived of the advantages of education and civilization? Surrounded by fierce enemies, oft cruel masters; without any other support than the charitable intentions of the friends of freedom in France, of whose existence we were hardly aware; driven to excessive errors by opposing parties who were rapidly destroying each other; knowing, at first, only the laws of the Mother-Country that favored the pretensions of our enemies and, since our liberty, receiving only the semiyearly or yearly instructions of our government, and no assistance, but almost always slanders or diatribes from our old oppressors—how can we not be pardoned some moments of ill-conduct, some gross faults, of which we were the first victims? Why, above all, reflect upon unreproachable men, upon the vast majority of the blacks, the faults of the lesser part, who, in time, had been reclaimed by the attentions of the majority to order and respect for the superior authorities? . . .

> *Fourth Assertion:* "I believed upon my arrival here [in St. Domingue]," continues General Rochambeau, "that I was going to find the laws of liberty and equality established in a positive manner; but I was grievously mistaken; there is liberty in this land only for the commanders of Africans and men of color, who treat the rest of their fellows like beasts of burden. The whites are everywhere vexed and humiliated."

If General Rochambeau had reflected philosophically on the course of events, especially those of the human spirit, he would not find it so astonishing that the laws of liberty and equality were not precisely established in an American country whose connection with the Mother Country had been neglected for so long; he would have felt that at a time when Europeans daily perjured themselves by handing over their quarters to the enemies of their country, prudence dictated that Government entrust its defense to the men of color and blacks whose interests were intimately linked to the triumph of the Republic; he would have felt that the military government then ruling the colony, by giving great power to the district commanders, could have led them astray in the labyrinths of uncertainty resulting from the absence of laws; he would have recalled that Martinique, defended by Europeans, fell prey to the English, whereas, St. Domingue, defended by the blacks and men of color whom Rochambeau accuses, remained constantly faithful to France. More accurately, if he had made the slightest effort to familiarize himself impartially with the law before his pronouncement, he wouldn't have generalized on the intentions of the blacks in respect to some antirepublican whites; he wouldn't have been so certain that they were all vexed and humiliated. I shall not call upon those among the whites who remained faithful to the principles of the Constitution by respecting them regardless of men's color . . . : it was natural for the blacks to pay them the tribute of their gratitude; but it is to those who, openly declaring themselves the enemies of the principles of the Constitution, fought against them and whom a change of mind, more or less sincere, has brought back amongst us and reconciled with the country; it is these people whom I call upon to report the truth, to tell whether they weren't welcomed and protected and if, when they professed republican sentiments, they experienced the least vexation. When the proprietors of St. Domingue, when the Europeans who go there, instead of becoming the echoes of citizen Vaublanc by seeking to spread doubt about the liberty of the black people, show the intention of respecting this liberty, they will see growing in the hearts of these men the love and attachment that they have never ceased to hold for the whites in general and their former masters in particular, despite all of those who have tried to re-establish slavery and restore the rule of tyranny in St. Domingue.

> *Fifth Assertion:* "I believe," continues General Rochambeau, "it will be difficult to reestablish order amongst the squanderers because by pro-scribing the Africans they will push them to revolt when they want to reduce their influence and credit; I am not even afraid to predict that after having armed them it will one day be necessary to fight to make them return to work."

The prediction of General Rochambeau will undoubtedly be fulfilled should he reappear at the head of an army in order to return the blacks to slavery, because they will be forced to defend the liberty that the Constitution guarantees; but that this army may be necessary to force them to return to their rustic work is already flatly contra-dicted by what they have done in agriculture for the past year. . . . I will not be contradicted when I assert that agriculture prospers in St. Domingue beyond even the hopes of this colony's truest friends, that the zeal of the field-negroes is also as satisfactory as can be de-sired, and that the results of their rustic work are surprising when one reflects that in the middle of a war they were frequently obliged to take up arms in our own defense and that of our freedom, which we hold dearer than life; and, if he finds among them some men who are so stupid as not to feel the need for work, their chiefs have enough control to make them understand that without work there is no free-dom. France must be just toward her colonial children, and soon her

commerce and inhabitants will no longer miss the riches they will ex-
tract from their greatest prosperity; but, should the projects of citizen
Vaublanc have some influence upon the French government, it is reminded that in the heart of Jamaica—the Blue Mountains—there exists a small number of men [the Maroons] so jealous of their liberty as
to have forced the pride and power of the English to respect, to this
very day, their natural rights, which the French Constitution guaranteed to us. . . .

> *Eighth Assertion:* "A little after their arrival, the Agents had the im-
> pudence to welcome the negroes who had fought under the rebel chief
> Jean François, who had burned the plain and destroyed the greatest part
> of the colony. . . . These negroes had everywhere abandoned agricul-
> ture; their current cry is that this country belongs to them, that they
> don't want to see a single white man there. At the same time that they
> are swearing a fierce hatred of the whites, that is to say, the only true
> Frenchmen, they are fighting a civil war among themselves."

I swear to God, that in order to better the cause of the blacks,
I disavow the excesses to which some of them were carried; subterfuge
is far from me, I will speak the truth, even against myself. I confess
that the reproaches made here against the rebel band of Jean François
are justly merited. I haven't waited until today to deplore his blind-
ness; but it was the delirium of some individuals and not of all the
blacks, and must one confuse, under the same appellation of brigands,
those who persisted in a guilty conduct with those who fought them
and made them return to their duty? If, because some blacks have committed some cruelties, it can be deduced that all blacks are cruel, then
it would be right to accuse of barbarity the European French and all
the nations of the world. But the French Senate will not participate in
such an injustice; it knows how to repulse the passions agitated by the
enemies of liberty; it will not confuse one unbridled, undisciplined
rebel band with men who since the rule of liberty in St. Domingue have
given unquestionable proofs of loyalty to the Republic, have shed
their blood for it, have assured its triumph, and who, by acts of goodness and humanity, by their return to order and to work, by their
attachment to France, have redeemed a part of the errors to which
their enemies had driven them and their ignorance had led them.

If it were true that the blacks were so wrong to think that the properties on St. Domingue belonged to them, why wouldn't they make themselves masters by driving off men of other colors, whom they could
easily master by their numerical superiority? If they had sworn a fierce
hatred against the whites, how is it that at this moment the white pop-

ulation of Le Cap equals that of the blacks and men of color? How is it that more than half of the sugar planters of the Le Cap plain are white? If union and fraternity didn't reign among men of all classes, would whites, reds, and blacks be seen living in perfect equality? Without the union of all classes would European soldiers, along with blacks, be seen pursuing the same careers as their fellow citizens in Europe? Would one see them so lively in combat and often only to obtain the same triumphs as their noble rivals?

And then citizen Vaublanc proceeded to apply himself to inflaming the passions of the men of St. Domingue, to reviving barbarous prejudices, by proclaiming that the whites in St. Domingue are the only true Frenchmen! Does he include under this appellation the traitors paid by the English, those who following odious treachery introduced this perfidious nation into the territory of freedom? In this case, we retain the honor of not meriting this honorable name; but if the friends of freedom classify under this respectable denomination men submitting heart and soul to the French Constitution, to its beneficial laws, men who cherish the French friends of our country, we swear that we have, and will always have, the right to be called French citizens.

> *Ninth Assertion:* "Alternately tyrants and victims, they outrage the sweetest natural sentiments, they renounce the kindest affections and sell their own children to the English, an infamous traffic which dishonors both buyer and seller in the eyes of humanity."

I acknowledge with a shudder that the charge made against the black rebels in the mountains of Grand-Rivière, who are fighting under the English flag and are led by French *émigrés,* of having sold some blacks is unfortunately too well founded; but has this charge ever been made against the blacks loyal to the Republic? And haven't these miserable rebels been driven to these infamous acts by the whites, . . . partisans of the system citizen Vaublanc seems to want to restore to the colony? Against these misguided men, simultaneously guilty and victims, citizen Vaublanc pours all the odium merited by actions so criminal as to be equally reproved by the laws of nature and the social order; but why, at the same time, doesn't he apply himself to tarnishing the monsters who have taught these crimes to the blacks and who have all been, by a barbarous guild on the coast of Africa, wrenching the son from his mother, the brother from his sister, the father from his son? Why does he only accuse those who, kept in ignorance by unjust laws that he undoubtedly wishes to see revived, were at first un-

able to recognize their rights and duties to the point of becoming the
instruments of their own misfortune, while glossing over the outrages
committed in cold blood by civilized men like himself who were therefore even more atrocious since they committed evil knowingly, allowing the lure of gold to suppress the cry of their conscience? Will the
crimes of powerful men always be glorified? And will the error of weak
men always be a source of oppression for them and their posterity? No!
. . . I appeal to the justice of the French Nation. . . .

> *Thirteenth Assertion:* "It is impossible to ignore that the existence of
> the Europeans in the colony is extremely precarious. In the South, in
> the mountains of the East, when the blacks are in revolt it is always
> against their European managers. Since our arrival, a great number have
> perished in this manner, and we have the misfortune to see that we are
> without means to suppress them."

An unanswerable proof that these partial revolts were only the
effect of the perfidious machinations of the enemies of St. Domingue's
prosperity is that they were always suppressed by the authority of the
law, is that by executing those who were its leaders, the sword of justice
stopped their propagation. . . . But even supposing that the evils
brought about by these movements should be the work of some villainous blacks, must those who did not participate in them and trembled with horror at the news of these disasters also be accused? This,
however, is the injustice repeatedly done to black people; for the crime
committed by some individuals, people feel free to condemn us all.
Instantly forgotten are our past services, our future services, our fidelity
and gratitude to France. And what would citizen Vaublanc say if, because the French Revolution produced some Marats, Robespierres,
Carriers, Sonthonaxs, etc. etc. etc., the traitors who handed over Tou-
lon to the English; because it produced the bloody scenes of the Vendée, the September massacres, the slaughter of a great part of the most
virtuous members of the National Convention, the most sincere friends
of the Republic and Liberty in France and the colonies; if, because
some *émigré* troops took up arms against their country, which they had
previously sold to the foreign powers, a voice arose from St. Domingue
and cried to the French people:

> You have committed inexcusable crimes because you shunned those more
> informed and civilized than you. The discussions of the legislative bodies,
> their laws which were rapidly transmitted to you, the enlightened magis-
> trates charged with executing them, were before your eyes, at your side;
> you have ignored their voice, you have trampled upon your most sacred

duties, you have reviled the Fatherland. Men unworthy of liberty, you were only made for slavery; restore the kings and their iron scepture; only those who opposed revolution were right, only they had good intentions; and the ancien régime that you had the barbarity to destroy was a government much too kind and just for you.

Far be it from me to want to excuse the crimes of the revolution in St. Domingue by comparing them to even greater crimes, but citizen Vaublanc, while threatening us in the *Corps Legislatif,* didn't bother to justify the crimes that have afflicted us and which could only be attributed to a small number. . . . However, this former proprietor of slaves couldn't ignore what slavery was like; perhaps he had witnessed the cruelties exercised upon the miserable blacks, victims of their capricious masters, some of whom were kind but the greatest number of whom were true tyrants. And what would Vaublanc say . . . if, having only the same natural rights as us, he was in his turn reduced to slavery? Would he endure without complaint the insults, the miseries, the tortures, the whippings? And if he had the good fortune to recover his liberty, would he listen without shuddering to the howls of those who wished to tear it from him? . . . Certainly not; in the same way he so indecently accuses the black people of the excesses of a few of their members, we would unjustly accuse the entirety of France of the excesses of a small number of partisans of the old system. Less enlightened than citizen Vaublanc, we know, nevertheless, that whatever their color, only one distinction must exist between men, that of good and evil. When blacks, men of color, and whites are under the same laws, they must be equally protected and they must be equally repressed when they deviate from them. Such is my opinion; such are my desires.

LETTER TO THE DIRECTORY, 5 NOVEMBER 1797 [2]

The impolitic and incendiary discourse of Vaublanc has not affected the blacks nearly so much as their certainty of the projects which the proprietors of San Domingo are planning: insidious declarations should not have any effect in the eyes of wise legislators who have decreed liberty for the nations. But the attempts on that liberty which the colonists propose are all the more to be feared because it is with the veil of patriotism that they cover their detestable plans. We know that

[2] From C. L. R. James, *The Black Jacobins: Toussaint L'Ouverture and the San Domingo Revolution,* 2nd rev. ed. (New York: Vintage Books, Random House, Inc., 1963), pp. 195–97. Reprinted by permission of the author.

they seek to impose some of them on you by illusory and specious promises, in order to see renewed in this colony its former scenes of horror. Already perfidious emissaries have stepped in among us to ferment the destructive leaven prepared by the hands of liberticides. But they will not succeed. I swear it by all that liberty holds most sacred. My attachment to France, my knowledge of the blacks, make it my duty not to leave you ignorant either of the crimes which they meditate or the oath that we renew, to bury ourselves under the ruins of a country revived by liberty rather than suffer the return of slavery.

It is for you, Citizens Directors, to turn from over our heads the storm which the eternal enemies of our liberty are preparing in the shades of silence. It is for you to enlighten the legislature, it is for you to prevent the enemies of the present system from spreading themselves on our unfortunate shores to sully it with new crimes. Do not allow our brothers, our friends, to be sacrificed to men who wish to reign over the ruins of the human species. But no, your wisdom will enable you to avoid the dangerous snares which our common enemies hold out for you. . . .

I send you with this letter a declaration which will acquaint you with the unity that exists between the proprietors of San Domingo who are in France, those in the United States, and those who serve under the English banner. You will see there a resolution, unequivocal and carefully constructed, for the restoration of slavery; you will see there that their determination to succeed has led them to envelop themselves in the mantle of liberty in order to strike it more deadly blows. You will see that they are counting heavily on my complacency in lending myself to their perfidious views by my fear for my children. It is not astonishing that these men who sacrifice their country to their interests are unable to conceive how many sacrifices a true love of country can support in a better father than they, since I unhesitatingly base the happiness of my children on that of my country, which they and they alone wish to destroy.

I shall never hesitate between the safety of San Domingo and my personal happiness; but I have nothing to fear. It is to the solicitude of the French Government that I have confided my children. . . . I would tremble with horror if it was into the hands of the colonists that I had sent them as hostages; but even if it were so, let them know that in punishing them for the fidelity of their father, they would only add one degree more to their barbarism, without any hope of ever making me fail in my duty. . . . Blind as they are! They cannot see how this odious conduct on their part can become the signal of new disasters and irreparable misfortunes, and that far from making them regain what in their eyes liberty for all has made them lose, they expose themselves to a total ruin and the colony to its inevitable destruction. Do they think that men who have been able to enjoy the blessing of liberty will calmly see it snatched away? They supported their chains only so long as they did not know any condition of life more happy than that of slavery. But to-day when they have left it, if they had a thousand lives they would sacrifice them all rather than be forced into slavery again. But no, the same hand which has broken our chains will not enslave us anew. France will not revoke her principles, she will not withdraw from us the greatest of her benefits. She will protect us against all our enemies; she will not permit her sublime morality to be perverted, those principles which do her most honour to be destroyed, her most beautiful achievement to be degraded, and her Decree of 16 Pluviôse which so honors humanity to be revoked. *But if, to re-establish slavery in San Domingo, this was done, then I declare to you it would be to attempt the impossible: we have known how to face dangers to obtain our liberty, we shall know how to brave death to maintain it.*

This, Citizens Directors, is the morale of the people of San Domingo, those are the principles that they transmit to you by me.

My own you know. It is sufficient to renew, my hand in yours, the oath that I have made, to cease to live before gratitude dies in my heart, before I cease to be faithful to France and to my duty, before the god of liberty is profaned and sullied by the liberticides, before they can snatch from my hands that sword, those arms, which France confided to me for the defence of its rights and those of humanity, for the triumph of liberty and equality.

4
Toussaint Seizes Power

ON THE EXPULSION OF SONTHONAX: TOUSSAINT TO LAVEAUX,
22 May 1798 [1]

Toussaint's expulsion of Sonthonax has occasioned a good deal of historical controversy. Some have seen it as clear evidence of the black leader's determined ambition to become the sole authority in St. Domingue. Others claim that Sonthonax was an obstacle to Toussaint's desire to form a "common front" of mulattoes and blacks in the face of a threatened restoration of slavery by France. Hardly anyone accepts at face value Toussaint's own explanation—stated in the following selection—that Sonthonax wanted him to declare independence and to murder all the Europeans. In this letter to his cloest European friend, Toussaint emphatically denies his own ambitions by professing to want a European as ruler of a united and republican St. Domingue. He stresses that Sonthonax, who had always been a disruptive influence in the colony, did not conform to this ideal.

Citizen Representative,

I must say to you with my customary frankness, my dear and good friend, that I have learned with the greatest astonishment . . . that you have been one of the representatives of the people of St. Domingue most eager to favorably welcome the monster Sonthonax, who, you know without a doubt, following his arrival on his second mission, only concerned himself with arousing passions, vengeances, and trying to destroy the little order that you had established with such difficulty; who employed the precious resources conferred upon him by the government . . . solely to divide, subvert, revolutionize, attack, and war upon republicans, instead of pacifying the interior and fighting the English. Who, therefore, is this strange republican? What is this improper patriotism that still finds itself advocated by some virtuous souls? I call upon you, my dear General, to testify; weren't you to be one of the first victims of this perfidious agent's villainous ambition,

[1] Trans. George F. Tyson, Jr.

46

of this so justly hated disruptor? Isn't it within my heart, in the bosom of friendship, that you have lodged your grief, anxieties, and fears about his administration? Weren't the popularity and esteem you had acquired by your ardent love of general liberty obscured by his abominable projects? Didn't he refuse you the necessities of life while he gorged himself lavishly and insulted the public misery? What has been the fate of your economic administration? Didn't the insatiable monster Sonthonax exhaust everything by his disorderly conduct, by a combination of atrocious acts that bled the colony anew? . . . You, General, who know these truths, these crimes of Sonthonax, who know my heart, my sentiments, better than anyone, you are the one who does me injury when I learn that you believe Sonthonax more honest than me, a greater friend of the freedom of the blacks, when you doubt that Sonthonax proposed that I make the colony independent, when you say that the embarkation of Sonthonax was the work of Raymond and Pascal. . . . If you want to refer to those difficult times during your generalship, you will be convinced that I am incapable of being either the object or instrument of men. I have proven it to you several times, General. Remember the spurious maneuvers of the Spanish generals, the more enterprising ones of the English, sustained by the temerity and despair of the enemies of black freedom; you had given me full powers. Well! General, don't you know that without troops, almost without equipment or provisions, I destroyed their combined armies; I scattered them by opposing all their ruses and efforts with unbelievable ruses and efforts of my own? Didn't I emerge victorious and with honor? However, it is this circumstance of my life, which should shut the mouths of my calumniators, that Sonthonax scandalously slanders. In the midst of the representatives of the republican people he accuses me of having deceived two kings. Hah! How and why has no one questioned this assassin of liberty to ask in the name of what power I deceived two kings? His answer would have proven my love for liberty, for the courageous nation that proclaimed and defended it; it would have proven his infamy and my honor.

When I remind you of all this, believe me, General, it is less from ambition that I direct your attention to my past services than from the desire to justify myself before the indictments of a still deceiving villain; but what am I saying—he is at this moment exposed to shame, to scorn, weighed down by the curses of all the men he has afflicted in the two hemispheres. Let us speak of him no longer; on the contrary, let us endeavor, by mutual cooperation, to heal the profound wounds he has inflicted upon the country.

I renew, my dear General, the assurances of my respectful attachment and sincere gratitude to you. I embrace you with all my heart.

P.S. Recall, my dear General, how many times while talking with you I told you that it was politically expedient for the reins of the general administration of the colony to be in the hands of a single European leader, honest, sincere, friend of general liberty and the equal rights of citizens; I would desire one might find such a man, plus successors worthy of replacing him at the termination of each administration. I wanted only a single leader because I felt that in the hands of only one, the reins of the colony would be less subject to the whims of passion, that the colony would be less exposed to the internal wars that stem from party differences, differences which, once born, increase insensibly and so easily in St. Domingue, where passions favor one party, then another; from this derives acts of rivalry, of party discontents, and finally, of civil war. I wanted this leader to be European because I desire that the colony not lose the point of view of the country whose power rules it from a distance of two thousand kilometers. Certainly this desire could not be interpreted in my favor; I even excluded myself from this general administration for the invincible reason that I resided in the colony. I wanted him to be European because I still dreaded the prejudices, customs, private interests of those who, born in the colony and endowed with great talents, might be able to lay claim to this administration.

The results of the commission composed of four agents—among them the celebrated Sonthonax—proved that I was perfectly right in forming this desire for a single leader, because, as you know, these agents were divided from the start, even you were enveloped in their quarrels. . . .

In consequence of this perfect knowledge of the character of the agents, of the sentiments you have always known me to hold, how could you believe for one moment, my dear General, that I wanted to seize all power for myself when I sent Sonthonax back to France for having proposed to me that I declare independence and massacre the Europeans? I didn't want to endure authorities above me, nevertheless, under your orders I have provided you with plenty of proof to the contrary; it isn't power that I attacked, that I have returned, it is Sonthonax, assassin of liberty, infidel of his country, whom I arrested, disconcerted by his projects for independence. I respect and make respected the power in the hands of Raymond because he took no part in the criminal audacity of Sonthonax. I will furnish still further proof that I respect a superior power under the administration of the pacifier of the Vendée [Hédouville]; he merits that glorious title by his love for and observation of the laws of the Republic, upon which rests liberty and the equal rights of citizens, sacred rights that I swear to defend until the last moment of my life against those who attack them directly.

General, retract your enthusiasm for Sonthonax; he is not, I swear to you, the friend of his country; he wanted to make Republican France a second-class power by detaching one of her colonies, which would then have been divided up by the other powers in order to strengthen themselves. I am sincere, General, you know it; Sonthonax is not worthy of your friendship. I have examined him thoroughly; he has exposed himself to me; he believes me to have a corrupt, villainous heart; I have unmasked his. . . .

ADDRESS TO THE PEOPLE OF COLOR, 1800 [2]

This address was issued following the capture of the mulatto stronghold of Jacmel during the civil war between Toussaint and Rigaud. As in his address to the people of color concerning the Villate affair, Toussaint argues that he is not fighting against an entire caste but against criminal members of that caste who have led their fellow members astray. He depicts Rigaud as being an overly ambitious man, jealous of Toussaint's ascendancy. Rigaud alone is held responsible for the war and must be put down ruthlessly. However, Toussaint promises a full pardon to all of his followers who will surrender. The moderate tone of this statement should be compared to Toussaint's more strident speech to the people of color reproduced in the Duvalier-Denis selection (pp. 159–67), in which he suggests that the enduring color prejudice of Rigaud and the people of color against the blacks was the principal cause of the civil war.

Citizens:

By what fatality is it, that, hitherto deaf to my voice, which invites you to order, you have listened only to the counsels of Rigaud? How is it possible that the pride of a single person should be the source of your evils, and that to flatter his ambition, you are willing to destroy your families, ruin your property, and bring yourselves into disgrace in the eyes of the whole world?

I repeat to you for the third and last time, that my quarrel is not with the citizens of the South, but solely with Rigaud, inasmuch as he is disobedient and insubordinate; whom I wish to bring back to his duties, that he may submit to the authority of a chief whom he can no

[2] From Rev. John R. Beard, *Toussaint L'Ouverture: A Biography and Autobiography* (Boston, 1863), pp. 109–11.

longer disown. You ought not to have supported in his misdeeds a proud soldier who evidently raised the standard of revolt. You ought to have left me free to act, since I had a right to reprimand and even to punish him. This Rigaud knew well; but, too haughty to bow before the organs of the law, he has employed every means to seduce you and to retain you as accomplices. Consult your conscience; put away all prejudices; you will then easily know that Rigaud has desired to drive into revolt all men of color, in order to make them his partisans and coöperators. I need not remind you of the means he has taken for the purpose, and the resources he has employed to deceive you all. You know as well as I, perhaps better than I, his destructive projects, and all he has attempted to put them into execution; he pretended to command blacks and whites without being willing to be commanded by them. Yet the law is equal for all. Painful experience ought to have torn from your eyes the veil which hides the brink of the precipice. Give, then, close attention to what you are about to do, and the danger which you still run. Reflect on the perils and the calamities which threaten you, and hasten to prevent them. I am kind, I am humane, I open to you my fatherly arms. Come, all of you; I will receive you all; no less those of the South than those of the West, and of the North, who, gained over by Rigaud, have deserted your firesides, your wives, your children, to place yourselves at his side. And Rigaud himself— that ambitious man—if he had followed the advice which I gave him, to submit to his lawful superiors—would he not now be tranquil and peaceful in the bosom of his family? Would he not be firm and untroubled in the command which was intrusted to him? But, mastered by deadly passions, Rigaud has dug a gulf at your feet; he has laid snares which you could not avoid. He wished to have you as partisans in his revolt; and to succeed in his object he has employed falsehood and seduction. If you carefully examine this artful but very impolitic conduct you cannot but declare that Rigaud does not love his color, and that he had rather sacrifice it to his pride and ambition than labor for its happiness by good example and wise counsels. And in truth, citizens, the greater number of those whom he has misled have perished, either in battle, or on the scaffold. Must not the others who persist in this revolt expect a similar fate if they abjure not their culpable error? You may be well assured that if humanity did not direct the actions of a chief attached to his country as well as to his fellow-citizens, and more disposed to pardon than to punish, the calamity would be still greater. It belongs to you to prevent its augmentation. In consequence, I invite you, citizens, to open your eyes and to give serious attention to the future. Reflect on the disasters which may ensue from longer obstinacy. Submit to lawful authority, if you wish to preserve the South untouched. Save your families and your property.

But if, contrary to my expectation, you continue to support the revolt raised and propagated by Rigaud, in vain will you reckon on the fortifications he has constructed. The army of Toussaint L'Ouverture, led by generals whose bravery you know, will assail you, and you will be conquered. Then, not without grief, and in spite of my efforts, shall I see that you have been the unhappy victims of the pride and ambition of a single man. I will say more. Desiring to put an end to the evils which have already too long afflicted this unfortunate colony, and wishing to prove to the French nation that I have done everything for the safety and happiness of my fellow-citizens, if Rigaud—though the author of these troubles—presents himself in good faith, and without stratagem, and acknowledges his fault, I will still receive him. But if Rigaud persists, and if he refuses to profit by my offer, do you, fathers, mothers, families—do you all come. I will receive you with open arms. The father of the prodigal son received his child after he had repented.

FORCED LABOR DECREE, 12 OCTOBER 1800 [3]

This decree contains the essence of Toussaint's social and economic policy. It is intended to restore prosperity and domestic tranquility simultaneously. To this end the entire state is militarized. The estates become the units of local government, with the cultivators or field-negroes deprived of their freedom of movement and subject to a harsh military discipline. They are depicted as soldiers, whose duty is to serve the State and only the State. Severe penalties are imposed on all offenders. Vagrancy and idleness are crimes against the state. The publication of this proclamation throughout the colony marked the beginning of the erosion of Toussaint's hold over the black masses. For them, as for the new freemen everywhere in the West Indies following emancipation, freedom meant the freedom to dispose of their labor as they pleased. It meant the freedom to desert the hated plantations and to cultivate small plots in the hills. Toussaint understood the deep roots of this impulse, but he also knew that such a mass exodus would destroy the plantation system and thereby serve as a pretext for the reimposition of the ancien régime. This cruel contradiction was the malignancy at the heart of Toussaint's administration. The blacks had to be mobilized

[3] From *Supplement to the Royal Gazette* (Jamaica), 22, no. 47 (November 15–22, 1800): 9–10.

and disciplined, not in the name of an abstract principle, but in
order to preserve their hard earned gains. But to accomplish this
Toussaint had to set himself squarely against their most funda-
mental desires.

Regulations Respecting Field Labor

Citizens,

After putting an end to the war in the South, our first duty has been
to return thanks to the Almighty; which we have done with a zeal becoming so great a blessing: Now, Citizens, it is necessary to consecrate
all our moments to the prosperity of St. Domingo, to the public tranquillity, and consequently, to the welfare of our fellow citizens.

But, to attain this end in an effectual manner, all the civil and military officers must make it their business, every one in their respective
department, to perform the duties of their offices with devotion and
attachment to the public welfare.

You will easily conceive, Citizens, that Agriculture is the support of
Government; since it is the foundation of Commerce and Wealth, the
source of Arts and Industry, it keeps everybody employed, as being the
mechanism of all Trades. And, from the moment that every individual
becomes useful, it creates public tranquillity; disturbances disappear
together with idleness, by which they are commonly generated, and
everyone peaceably enjoys the fruits of his industry.

Officers civil and military, this is what you must aim at; such is the
plan to be adopted, which I prescribe to you; and I declare in the most
peremptory manner, that it shall be enforced: My country demands
this salutary step; I am bound to it by my office, and the security of
our liberties demands it imperiously.

But in order to secure our liberties, which are indispensable to our
happiness, every individual must be usefully employed, so as to contribute to the public good, and the general tranquillity.

Considering that the soldier, who has sacred duties to perform, as
being the safeguard of the people, and in perpetual activity, to execute
the orders of his Chief, either for maintaining interior tranquillity, or
for fighting abroad the enemies of the country, is strictly subordinate
to his superior officers; and as it is of great importance that overseers,
drivers and field-negroes, who in like manner have their superiors,
should conduct themselves as officers, subalterns, and soldiers in whatever may concern them.

Considering that when an officer, a subaltern, or a soldier deviates
from his duty he is delivered over to a court-martial to be tried and

punished according to the laws of the Republic, for in military service no rank is to be favoured when guilty: The overseers, drivers and field-negroes, as subject to constant labour, and equally subordinate to their superiors, shall be punished in like manner, in case of failure in their respective duties.

Whereas a soldier cannot leave his company, his battalion, or half-brigade, and enter into another, without the severest punishment, unless provided with a permission in due form from his Chief; field-negroes are forbidden to quit their respective plantations without a lawful permission. This is by no means attended to, since they change their place of labour as they please, go to and fro, and pay not the least attention to agriculture, though the only means of furnishing sustenance to the military, their protectors. They even conceal themselves in towns, in villages, and mountains, where, allured by the enemies of good order, they live by plunder, and in a state of open hostility to society.

Whereas, since the revolution, labourers of both sexes, then too young to be employed in the field, refuse to go to it now under pretext of freedom, spend their time in wandering about, and give a bad example to the other cultivators; while, on the other hand, the generals, officers, subalterns, and soldiers, are in a state of constant activity to maintain the sacred rights of the people. . . .

I do most peremptorily order as follows:

Art. 1. All overseers, drivers, and field-negroes are bound to observe, with exactness, submission, and obedience, their duty in the same manner as soldiers.

Art. 2. All overseers, drivers, and field-labourers, who will not perform with assiduity the duties required of them, shall be arrested and punished as severely as soldiers deviating from their duty. After which punishment, if the offender be an overseer, he shall be enlisted in one of the regiments of the army in St. Domingo. If a driver, he shall be dismissed from his employment and placed among the field-negroes, without ever being permitted to act as a driver again. And, if a common-labourer, he shall be punished with the same severity as a private soldier, according to his guilt.

Art. 3. All field-labourers, men and women, now in a state of idleness, living in towns, villages, and on other plantations than those to which they belong, with an intention to evade work, even those of both sexes who have not been employed in field labour since the revolution, are required to return immediately to their respective plantations, if, in the course of eight days from the promulgation of this present regulation, they shall not produce sufficient proof to the commanding officers in the place of their residence of their having some useful occupation or means of livelihood; but it is to be understood that being a servant is not to be considered a useful occupation; in consequence whereof, those amongst the laborers who have quitted their plantations in order to hire themselves, shall return thereto, under the personal responsibility of those with whom they live in that capacity. By the term "an useful occupation" is meant, what enables a man to pay a contribution to the State.

Art. 4. This measure, indispensable to the public welfare, positively prescribes to all those of either sex that are not labourers to produce the proofs of their having an occupation or profession sufficient to gain their livelihood, and that they can afford to pay a contribution to the Republic. Otherwise, and in default thereof, all those who shall be found in contravention hereto, shall be instantly arrested, and if they are found guilty they shall be drafted into one of the regiments of the army, if not, they shall be sent to the field and compelled to work. This measure, which is to be strictly enforced, will put a stop to the idle habit of wandering about, since it will oblige everyone to be usefully employed.

Art. 5. Parents are earnestly entreated to attend to their duty towards their children; which is, to make them good citizens; for that purpose they must instruct them in good morals, in the Christian religion, and the fear of God. Above all, exclusive of this education, they must be brought up in some specific business or profession to enable them not only to earn their living, but also to contribute to the expences of the Government.

Art. 6. All persons residing in towns and villages, who shall harbour labourers of either sex, all proprietors or tenants who shall suffer on their plantations labourers belonging to other estates, without immediately making it known to the Commandant of the district, or other military officers in the place of their residence, shall pay a fine of 200 or 800 livres, according to the abilities of the delinquent; in case of repetition of the offence, they shall pay three times as much; if the fine cannot be levied for want of effects, the offender shall be imprisoned for a month, and, in case of repetition for three months.

Art. 7. The overseers and drivers of every plantation shall make it their business to inform the commanding officer of the district in regard to the conduct of the labourers under their management; as well as of those who shall absent themselves from their plantations without a pass; and of those who, residing on the estates, shall refuse to work. They shall be forced to go to the labour of the field, and if they prove obstinate, they shall be arrested and carried before the military commandant, in order to suffer the punishment above prescribed, according to the expediency of the case.

The military commandants who shall not inform the commandants of districts, and those Generals under whose orders they act, shall be severely punished, at the discretion of the said General.

Art. 8. The Generals commanding the departments shall henceforth be answerable to me for any neglect in the cultivation of their districts. And when going through the several parishes and departments I shall perceive any marks of negligence, I shall proceed against those who shall have tolerated it.

Art. 9. I forbid all military men whatsoever, under the responsibility of the commanding officers, to suffer any women to remain in the barracks; those excepted that are married to soldiers, as well as those who carry victuals to men confined to their quarters; but these shall not be allowed to remain any time; plantation women are totally excluded. The commanding officers shall answer for the execution of this article.

Art. 10. The Commandants of the towns, or the officers in the villages, shall not suffer the labourers or field-negroes to spend the decades [a unit of time] in town; they shall also take care that they do not conceal themselves. Such officers as shall not punctually attend to this order shall be punished with six days confinement for the first time, a month for the second, and shall be cashiered for the third offence. They shall give information to the commandant of the district of such labourers as are found in the town during the decade, and the persons at whose houses they were taken up, that the said persons may be condemned to pay the fine imposed by article 6 of this present regulation. The plantation people, who shall in such cases be brought before the Commandant of the district, shall be sent back to their plantations after receiving the punishment, as above directed by article 2, with a strong recommendation to the commanding officer of their quarter that a watchful eye may be kept on them for the future.

Art. 11. All the municipal administrations of St. Domingo are requested to take the wisest measures, together with the Commandants of towns and of the districts to inform themselves whether those who call themselves domestics really are so, observing that plantation negroes cannot be domestics. Any person keeping them in that quality will be liable to pay the above-mentioned fine, as well as those who shall detain labourers of either sex for any kind of employment.

Art. 12. All commissaries of government in the municipalities will make it their duty to inform me of all the abuses repecting the execution of this regulation; and to give advice of the same to the Generals of department.

Art. 13. I command all the Generals of department, Generals, and other principal Officers in the districts to attend to the execution of this regulation, for which they shall be personally responsible. And I flatter myself that their zeal in assisting me to restore the public prosperity will not be momentary, convinced as they must be, that liberty cannot exist without industry.

ADDRESS TO THE MILITARY, 1801 [4]

The real basis of Toussaint's power lay in the Army. Accordingly, it came to enjoy far greater benefits and prestige than any other institution in the new St. Domingue. This address, issued following the defeat of Rigaud and the conquest of Santo Domingo, outlines the duties of soldiers during the reconstruction period. Toussaint renounces foreign conquest and pleads for the continued loyalty and unity of the troops in the difficult years ahead. In return he promises them substantial rewards. Implicit in the second-to-last paragraph is the idea that the loyalty of the military will be insured by sacrificing the interests of the cultivators, who will be forced to work in order to feed and maintain an army of twenty thousand.

Citizen Soldiers:

When the Government appointed me General-in-Chief I promised you, as well as my fellow citizens . . . to take no rest 'til I had forced the enemies of the Republic to evacuate our country. By the protection of the Almighty I have effected that point—you have been the useful witnesses of it—and your devotedness to second me has more than once merited the enlogiums [sic.] which I have given you with the effusion of a contented heart. The unhappy war of the South succeeded that victory. You have again fully demonstrated, by your sufferings, privations of every kind, and your love for the country, that you were worthy of being its children. Again the Conquerors of the pride and ambition of an individual [Rigaud], I brought you back peace; my time, my vigilance, my care, the sacrifice of my interests, nay everything, it has cost me to reestablish tranquillity and to conquer for

[4] From the Public Record Office (London), C.O. [Colonial Office] 137/106, enclosed in Nugent to Portland, 11 October, 1801. Crown copyright material appears by permission of the Controller of H. M. Stationery Office.

your rights; from the very dawn of the revolution I wished to be free, and my conduct has sufficiently shewn to you that I did not wish to be so alone. I have always treated you as my children, and as such, I have ever led you into the path of glory. You are all free. Do you forget so great a blessing? No. The soldier of the Republic is incapable of ingratitude. Dangers, battles, a family, children and a beloved wife, nothing has arrested my ardour. Days and nights you have always seen me, without taking the least repose, seeking the means to throw off the shameful yoke of slavery that debased us. Did there not also want the addition to this glory, seeing the former Spanish part reunited to the French part, in order to bridle forever the cupidity of the dealers in human flesh? This reunion has taken place. The island of St. Domingo is therefore under the same Government, it is entirely subject to the laws of the French Republic. What remains to be effected by you? The consolidation of liberty and the maintenance of order and public tranquillity, the restoration of peace, abundance and prosperity. My task is completed. To you, however, soldiers of every rank, it belongs to preserve this peace, the prelude of certain prosperity. We have vanquished the enemies of our repose; we have no more to contend with; we will not make war in other countries; we will limit ourselves to the guarding of our coasts and making them respected; we will cherish, we will protect, those who bring us the necessities of life; we will defend ourselves again those who, jealous of our rights, would again come to dispute them. Generals, officers, sub-officers and soldiers, it will be sufficient to bring to your recollection the evils you have suffered, that you may not again see them have existence. Union among yourselves will constitute your force; discipline, subordination and obedience to the laws will render you invincible. Exercise yourselves in them constantly, for the slightest disunion will again plunge you into incalculable calamities. Tho' we have silenced our enemies they will not be the less ready to watch your actions and to profit by your most trivial altercations to sow divisions among you and to light the torch of discord. Then would they wish to persuade you that darkness is light and light is darkness; that what is sweet is bitter and what is bitter is sweet. They would put you in arms, one against the other, and you will have only made a figure in the world for an instant, to be annihilated forever. Listen with attention to all that the wicked and evil-disposed would say to you, inform your Chiefs of it, who will render me an account of all. I shall act with severity against the disturbers of the public peace.

Until today, my friends, entirely occupied about the welfare of St. Domingo, I have only been able indirectly to procure you, with diffi-

culties, the necessities of life. But today, fixing my regards upon your
urgent wants, I am about to adopt *strong measures* to bring you relief.
Officers, sub-officers and soldiers, fulfill your duties incessantly and you
Generals, promote agriculture by every means in your power, maintain order and public tranquillity. I will promote commerce from
which abundance springs; consequently your subsistence and your
maintenance. Then shall everyone be enabled to procure his wants.
Military power shall return to its ordinary course and each Captain
shall be responsible to the Chief of a Corps for the cleanly appearance
of his Company. I am going again to sacrifice my time to bring this abundance, and I implore the assistance of the Almighty to second me. Rely
upon my care for this effect; I will use every effort to succor you. Soldiers . . . you may be happy, but you must overcome your passions
as you have overcome your enemies; be an army of brothers and you
will be so many heroes; if misery has weighted heavy upon you, the
result has been honor and glory. . . . Never turn your arms one
against the other. They are put in your hands to defend your rights,
liberty, equality and your country; be disciplined, subordinate, sub-
missive and steady to your Chiefs and you will be worthy of the honorable title of a French soldier. Love, cherish and practice the Christian
religion; be grateful in the sight of God and he will always protect
you; respect and cause to be respected persons and property; support
the weak against the powerful, the poor as well as the rich and you will
well deserve the gratitude of your country and your fellow citizens.

Such, soldiers, is what I wish you to become; arrive at this degree of
possible perfection and my recompense will be that of dying content.

TOUSSAINT'S DICTATORIAL DECREE, 25 NOVEMBER 1801 [5]

The following decree, which Victor Schoelcher has termed
"Toussaint's dictatorial decree," was issued immediately follow-
ing the Moise rebellion and the signing of the Peace of Amiens.
It shows Toussaint, confronted with grave internal and external
threats, tightening his control and severely restricting the free-
dom of his people. Faced with the crucial question of all post-
emancipation governments of how to make free labor productive
and disciplined, Toussaint clearly had opted for a policy of coer-
cion and violence. The imposition of virtual thought control,
the identification cards and stringent vagrancy laws, his efforts to
regulate family life and sexual mores, the harsh punishments for
offenders could only make a mockery of his professions of repub-

[5] From Schoelcher, *Vie de Toussaint-Louverture*, pp. 419–27; trans. George F.
Tyson, Jr.

licanism, while accelerating popular disenchantment with his rule. His efforts to explain the summary execution of Moise and his followers only begged the question of why, after being so generous to his white enemies, he was so unsparing with black men who had served him loyally since 1791. The strict obligations imposed upon local civil and military authorities reflect the deterioration of Toussaint's influence over this important segment of society and go far in explaining the loss of their support during the Leclerc invasion. However, those critics like Schoelcher who would condemn him for degenerating into a tyrant must take into account the critical foreign and domestic crises he was facing as well as the profound problems of law and order—the nature of which are indicated in the preface of this reading— inherent in every post emancipation West Indian society.

Since the revolution I have done everything in my power to restore the prosperity of our country in order to assure the liberty of my fellow citizens. Forced to fight the internal and external enemies of the French Republic, I made war with courage, honor, and loyalty. I never swerved from the rules of justice toward my greatest enemies; I have tried, as much as I could, to soften the horrors of war, to spare men's blood. . . . Often, after a victory, I welcomed as brothers those who the preceding day were under the colors of the enemy. By forgetting their errors and faults I wanted to make the cause of liberty legitimate and sacred to even its most ardent enemies.

I have constantly reminded my brothers-in-arms, generals and officers, that the grades to which they have risen are due to them only as the rewards of honor, bravery, and irreproachable conduct; that the more they have risen above their fellow citizens, the more all their actions and words must be irreproachable; that scandal among public men has consequences more fatal for society than that among average citizens; that the grades and offices which adorn them weren't given to them in order merely to serve their personal ambition but for the general welfare. . . .

It is up to the officers to give their troops good lessons and examples. Each captain must have the noble sense of rivalry of wanting his company to be the best disciplined, the most properly dressed, the best trained; he must think that the faults of his troops reflect upon him and believe himself degraded by the faults of those under his command. . . .

Such is the speech that I have given General Moise in private conversations over the past ten years; that I have repeated to him a thousand times in the presence of his comrades and generals; that I have repeated to him in my correspondence. On every occasion I sought to explain to him the sacred maxims of our religion, to prove to him that man is nothing without the power and will of God. . . . What haven't I done to restore his virtue, to change his wicked inclinations? Instead of listening to the advices of a father, of obeying the orders of a leader, he allowed himself to be driven only by his passions; following only his disastrous inclinations, he died a miserable death. Such is the fate reserved for all who imitate him. The justice of heaven is slow but infallible, and sooner or later it strikes down the evil ones. . . .

In one of my proclamations during the War of the South, I traced the duties of fathers and mothers toward their children, the obligation to foster in them a love and belief in God, always considering religion as the source of all virtue and the base of all goodness in societies. . . .

And yet, with what negligence have fathers and mothers raised their children, especially in the cities. They leave them in idleness and in ignorance of their primary duties; they seem to inspire in them contempt for agriculture, the most honorable and useful of all professions.

Hardly are they born before the same children are seen wearing jewels and earrings, indecently clad in dirty rags, wounding the eyes of decency by their nudity. In this manner they reach the age of twelve, without moral principles, without a trade, with a taste for luxuries and laziness in all education. And as bad impressions are difficult to correct, soon you have bad citizens, vagabonds, and thieves, and, if they are girls, prostitutes, each of them always ready to follow the first impulse of the first conspirator who will exhort them to disorder, assassination, and pillage. The people's magistrates must unceasingly watch for such worthless fathers and mothers and such dangerous pupils.

The same reproaches are equally applicable to field-negroes and negresses on the estates. Since the revolution, wicked men have said that liberty is the right to remain idle and follow only their whims. A similar doctrine would be welcomed by all bad subjects, thieves, and assassins. It is time to strike the callous men who persist in similar ideas.

As soon as a child can walk, he must be employed on the estates in some useful work, pursuing his skills, instead of being sent to the city where, under the pretext of an education he doesn't receive, he comes to learn vices and enlarges the mob of vagabonds and immoral women whose existence disturbs the tranquillity of decent citizens and is terminated by corporal punishment. It is necessary for the military commanders and magistrates to be inexorable toward this class of men; it is necessary to compel them, in spite of themselves, to be useful to a society that, without the strictest vigilance, they would otherwise plague.

Since the revolution it is evident that many more men than women perished in the wars; it is also found that the existence of the greatest number of the women in the cities is based solely on libertinism. Because of their prostitution they are entirely devoted to their appearance and want to do absolutely nothing useful. There are women who receive all the bad subjects and live off the fruit of their plunders. It is the duty of the magistrates, generals, and commanders not to leave a single one of them in the cities; . . . the least negligence here would render them deserving of public denunciation.

Moise, it is true, was the spirit and leader of the last conspiracy, but he would never have been able to consummate his infamy if he hadn't found accomplices.

As for domestics, each citizen should have only as many as are necessary to take care of indispensable services. The persons in whose houses they live must be the primary supervisors of their conduct and tolerate nothing from them contrary to good manners, to obedience, and to good order; if they are thieves, to denounce them to the military commanders for punishment conformable to the laws; and, since under the new order all work merits payment, all payment must require work. Such is the invariable and firm will of the government.

There is another object worthy of its attention; it is the surveillance of foreigners arriving in the colony. Some among them, knowing only from enemy reports of the new order, of the changes which are brought about, hold opinions all the more dangerous because they are eagerly welcomed by those who, basing their hopes upon disorders, ask only for pretexts. Such disrupters must be so much the more severely punished; carelessness by public functionaries in this regard would jeopardize the confidence they need and would make them justifiably regarded as accomplices of the enemies of liberty.

The most sacred institution among men living in society, that from which the greatest blessings flow, is marriage. . . . Therefore, a wise government must always take care to surround good marriages with honor, respect, and veneration; it can rest only after extirpating the last root of immorality. Military commanders, public authorities especially, are inexcusable when they display the scandal of vice publicly. Those who, having legitimate wives, admit concubines into their homes or, unmarried, live publicly with several women are not worthy of their command and will be discharged.

Idleness is the source of all disorders, and if it is tolerated by a single individual I will take him to the military commanders, persuaded that those who tolerate parasites and vagabonds are secret enemies of the government.

No one, under any pretext, must be exempted from a task of which he is capable. Creole fathers and mothers who have children and property must live there in order to work there, to make their children work, or to supervise the workers and in moments of relaxation to instruct them themselves, or with teachers, in the precepts of our religion. . . .

By these means they will become useful and respectable citizens, and the horrible events which we must never forget will be forever banished from this colony.

In consequence, I decree the following:

I. All commanders who, during the late conspiracy, had knowledge of the disorders that erupted and tolerated pillage and assassinations, who could have prevented or arrested the revolt, allowing the law which declares "life, property, and refuge of all citizens sacred and inviolable" to be broken, will be tried before a special court and punished according to the law. . . . All military commanders who, by imprudence or negligence, failed to stop the disorders will be discharged and punished by a year in prison. A rigorous inquiry will be made into their conduct, after which the government will pronounce upon their fate.

II. All generals, commanders of districts or quarters, who in the future neglect to take all necessary measures to prevent or stop sedition will be tried before a special tribunal and punished according to the law. . . .

III. In case of disorder, or indications of it, the national guard of each quarter or district will be under the orders of those military commanders who request it.

All military commanders who will not have taken all necessary measures to prevent disorders in their quarter or the spreading of disorders from a neighboring quarter into theirs, all military personnel, be they of the line or national guard, who will refuse to obey lawful orders WILL BE PUNISHED BY DEATH.

IV. All persons, men or women, whatever their color, who are convicted of having made serious remarks tending to excite sedition *will be tried before a court martial* and punished according to the laws.

V. All creoles,[6] men or *women,* convicted of having held ideas tending to disrupt the public tranquillity but who are not to be *sentenced to death* will be sent to the fields *with a chain attached to one foot for six months.*

---

[6] This term refers to all individuals born in the colony and to Africans.

VI. All foreigners who fall under the preceding article will be deported.

VII. All citizens, men and women, whatever their rank or condition, living in the communes of the colony where there are municipal administrators *are required to obtain an identification card.*

This card will show the given names, surnames, residence, circumstances, profession, title, age, and sex of its bearer.

It will be signed by the mayor and the police commissioner of the quarter in which lives the person to whom it will be issued.

It will be renewed *every six months* in exchange for a *gourdin* paid by each individual into the communal treasury.

VIII. Municipal administrations are expressly ordered to issue identification cards only to those persons who will have a well-known position or trade, *unreproachable conduct,* and assured means of existence. All those unable to fulfill rigorously the conditions necessary to obtain it will be sent back to agriculture, if creoles, or deported, if foreigners.

IX. Fifteen days after the publication of this decree, all persons found without an identification card will be returned to agriculture, if creole, if foreigner, deported WITHOUT TRIAL, *if they don't want* to serve with the troops of the line. . . .

XI. All domestics who, by leaving the house in which they served, will not be judged worthy of receiving a certificate of good conduct *will be declared ineligible for an identification card.* Anyone who issues one to them as a favor will be punished by one month in prison.

XII. Within fifteen days after the publication of this decree, all managers or overseers of estates will send to the commanders of their quarter an exact list containing the ages and sexes of all their field-negroes, under penalty of eight days in prison. All managers or overseers, as the principal supervisors of their estate, are declared personally responsible for all types of disorders committed because of the idleness or vagrancy of their field-negroes. . . .

XIV . . . The final lists deposited in the governmental archives will serve, in the future, as *unchangeable foundations for fixing the field-negroes upon their estates.*

XV. All managers or overseers of estates on which a foreign field-negro takes refuge will be responsible for denouncing him to the sectional captain or commander within twenty-four hours, under penalty of eight days imprisonment.

XVI. All section captains or commanders who negligently leave a foreign field-negro in his section *more than three days* will be discharged.

XVII. Vagrant field-negroes, once arrested, will be taken to the quarter commander, who will have the police return them to their estates. It is recommended that managers and overseers closely supervise them and *deprive them, for three months, of passes to leave their estates.* . . .

XIX. *All soldiers are forbidden to enter an estate except to see their fathers or mothers* and with the expressed permission of his leader. If he fails to return to his corps at the fixed hour, he will be punished according to the requirements of the case, in conformity with the military ordinances.

XX. *All persons convicted of having disturbed or attempting to disturb a household will be denounced to the civil and military authorities, who will report it to the governor,* who will decide their fate according to the requirements of the case. . . .

5

Toussaint's Memoir

Written in prison to vindicate himself against the charges of treason made by Napoleon and Leclerc, this document is the closest thing to an autobiographical sketch available to students of Toussaint. It must, however, be read with extreme caution, since it is primarily designed to win sympathy and a pardon for its author. In the first part, Toussaint strongly affirms his unwavering loyalty to France, disclaiming any inclination toward independence. He explains his resistance to Leclerc as caused by the Frenchman's suspicious and improper behavior, and he denies plotting an insurrection after his surrender. His arrest and deportation are recounted in a tone of anger and dismay over the uncivilized behavior of supposedly civilized men. In the second part, Toussaint summarizes his career in the service of France and defends his administration. He portrays himself as a loyal, dedicated, honest, humane man devoted to France and Napoleon. He does, however, acknowledge that his Constitution was an error.[1]

It is my duty to render to the French Government an exact account of my conduct. I shall relate the facts with all the simplicity and frankness of an old soldier, adding to them the reflections that naturally suggest themselves. In short, I shall tell the truth, though it be against myself.

The colony of Saint Domingo, of which I was commander, enjoyed the greatest tranquillity; agriculture and commerce flourished there. The island had attained a degree of splendor which it had never before seen. And all this—I dare to say it—was my work. . . .

[Then] Gen. Leclerc came. Why did he not inform me of his powers before landing? Why did he land without my order and in defiance of the order of the Commission? Did he not commit the first hostilities? Did he not seek to gain over the generals and other officers under my command by every possible means? . . .

In regard to the Constitution, the subject of one charge against me:

[1] From Beard, *Toussaint L'Ouverture*, pp. 295, 307–8, 321–26.

Having driven from the colony the enemies of the Republic, calmed the factions and united all parties; perceiving, after I had taken possession of St. Domingo, that the Government made no laws for the colony, and feeling the necessity of police regulations for the security and tranquillity of the people, I called an assembly of wise and learned men, composed of deputies from all the communities, to conduct this business. When this assembly met, I represented to its members that they had an arduous and responsible task before them; that they were to make laws adapted to the country, advantageous to the Government, and beneficial to all—laws suited to the localities, to the character and customs of the inhabitants. The Constitution must be submitted for the sanction of the Government, which alone had the right to adopt or reject it. Therefore, as soon as the Constitution was decided upon and its laws fixed, I sent the whole, by a member of the assembly, to the Government, to obtain its sanction. The errors or faults which this Constitution may contain cannot therefore be imputed to me. At the time of Leclerc's arrival, I had heard nothing from the Government upon this subject. Why today do they seek to make a crime of that which is no crime? Why put truth for falsehood, and falsehood for truth? Why put darkness for light and light for darkness? . . .

If Gen. Leclerc went to the colony to do evil, it should not be charged upon me. It is true that only one of us can be blamed; but however little one may wish to do me justice, it is clear that he is the author of all the evils which the island has suffered, since, without warning me, he entered the colony, which he found in a state of prosperity, fell upon the inhabitants, who were at their work, contributing to the welfare of the community, and shed their blood upon their native soil. That is the true source of the evil.

If two children were quarreling together, should not their father or mother stop them, find out which was the aggressor, and punish him, or punish them, if they were both wrong? Gen. Leclerc had no right to arrest me; Government alone could arrest us both, hear us, and judge us. Yet Gen. Leclerc enjoys liberty, and I am in a dungeon.

Having given an account of my conduct since the arrival of the fleet at St. Domingo, I will enter into some details of previous events.

Since I entered the service of the Republic, I have not claimed a penny of my salary; Gen. Laveaux, Government agents, all responsible persons connected with the public treasury, can do me this justice, that no one has been more prudent, more distinterested than I. I have only now and then received the extra pay allowed me; very often I have not asked even this. Whenever I have taken money from the treasury, it has been for some public use; the governor (*l'ordonnateur*) has used it as the service required. I remember that once only, when far from home, I borrowed six thousand francs from Citizen Smith, who was governor of the Department of the South.

I will sum up, in a few words, my conduct and the results of my administration. At the time of the evacuation of the English, there was not a penny in the public treasury; money had to be borrowed to pay the troops and the officers of the Republic. When Gen. Leclerc arrived, he found three millions, five hundred thousand francs in the public funds. When I returned to Cayes, after the departure of Gen. Rigaud, the treasury was empty; Gen. Leclerc found three millions there; he found proportionate sums in all the private depositories on the island. Thus it is seen that I did not serve my country from interested motives; but, on the contrary, I served it with honor, fidelity, and integrity, sustained by the hope of receiving, at some future day, flattering acknowledgments from the Government; all who know me will do me this justice.

I have been a slave; I am willing to own it; but I have never received reproaches from my masters.

I have neglected nothing at Saint Domingo for the welfare of the island; I have robbed myself of rest to contribute to it; I have sacrificed everything for it. I have made it my duty and pleasure to develop the resources of this beautiful colony. Zeal, activity, courage—I have employed them all.

The island was invaded by the enemies of the Republic; I had then but a thousand men, armed with pikes. I sent them back to labor in the field, and organized several regiments, by the authority of Gen. Laveaux.

The Spanish portion had joined the English to make war upon the French. Gen. Desfourneaux was sent to attack Saint Michel with well-disciplined troops of the line; he could not take it. General Laveaux ordered me to the attack; I carried it. It is to be remarked that, at the time of the attack by Gen. Desfourneaux, the place was not fortified, and that when I took it, it was fortified by bastions in every corner. I also took Saint-Raphaël and Hinche, and rendered an account to Gen. Laveaux. The English were intrenched at Pont-de-l'Ester; I drove them from the place. They were in possession of Petite Rivière. My ammunition consisted of one case of cartridges which had fallen into the water on my way to the attack; this did not discourage me. I carried the place by assault before day, with my dragoons, and made all the garrison prisoners. I sent them to Gen. Laveaux. I had but one piece of cannon; I took nine at Petite Rivière. Among the posts gained at Petite Rivière, was a fortification defended by seven pieces of cannon, which I attacked, and carried by assault. I also conquered the Spaniards intrenched in the camps of Miraut and Dubourg at Verrettes. I gained a famous victory over the English in a battle which lasted from six in the morning until nearly night. This battle was so fierce that the roads were filled with the dead, and rivers of blood were seen on every side. I took all the baggage and ammunition of the enemy, and a large number of prisoners. I sent the whole to Gen. Laveaux, giving him an account of the engagement. All the posts of the English upon the heights of Saint Mare were taken by me; the walled fortifications in the mountains of Fond-Baptiste and Délices, the camp of Drouët in the Matheux mountains, which the English regarded as impregnable, the citadels of Mirebalais, called the Gibraltar of the island, occupied by eleven hundred men, the celebrated camp of l'Acul-du-Saut, the stone fortifications of Trou-d'Eau, three stories high, those of the camp of Decayette and of Beau-Bien—in short, all the fortifications of the English in this quarter were unable to withstand me, as were those of Neybe, of Saint Jean de la Maguâna, of Las Mathas, of Banique and other places occupied by the Spaniards; all were brought by me under the power of the Republic. I was also exposed to the greatest dangers; several times I narrowly escaped being made prisoner; I shed my blood for my country; I received a ball in the right hip which remains there still; I received a violent blow on the head from a cannon-ball, which knocked out the greater part of my teeth, and loosened the rest. In short, I received upon different occasions seventeen wounds, whose honorable scars still remain. Gen Laveaux witnessed many of my engagements; he is too honorable not to do me justice: ask him if I ever hesitated to endanger my life, when the good of my country and the triumph of the Republic required it.

If I were to record the various services which I have rendered the Government, I should need many volumes, and even then should not finish them; and, as a reward for all these services, I have been arbitrarily arrested at St. Domingo, bound, and put on board ship like a criminal, without regard for my rank, without the least consideration. Is this the recompense due my labors? Should my conduct lead me to expect such treatment?

I was once rich. At the time of the revolution, I was worth six hundred and forty-eight thousand francs. I spent it in the service of my country. I purchased but one small estate upon which to establish my wife and family. To-day, notwithstanding my disinterestedness, they seek to cover me with opprobrium and infamy; I am made the most unhappy of men; my liberty is taken from me; I am separated from all that I hold dearest in the world,—from a venerable father, a hundred and five years old, who needs my assistance, from a dearly-loved wife, who, I fear, separated from me, cannot endure the afflictions which overwhelm her, and from a cherished family, who made the happiness of my life.

On my arrival in France I wrote to the First Consul and to the Minister of Marine, giving them an account of my situation, and asking their assistance for my family and myself. Undoubtedly, they felt the justice of my request, and gave orders that what I asked should be furnished me. But, instead of this, I have received the old half-worn dress of a soldier, and shoes in the same condition. Did I need this humiliation added to my misfortune?

When I left the ship, I was put into a carriage. I hoped then that I was to be taken before a tribunal to give an account of my conduct, and to be judged. Far from it; without a moment's rest I was taken to a fort on the frontiers of the Republic, and confined in a frightful dungeon.

It is from the depths of this dreary prison that I appeal to the justice and magnanimity of the First Consul. He is too noble and too good a general to turn away from an old soldier, covered with wounds in the service of his country, without giving him the opportunity to justify himself, and to have judgment pronounced upon him.

I ask, then, to be brought before a tribunal or council of war, before which, also, Gen. Leclerc may appear, and that we may both be judged after we have both been heard; equity, reason, law, all assure me that this justice cannot be refused me.

PART TWO

TOUSSAINT VIEWED BY HIS CONTEMPORARIES

6

Frenchmen React to Toussaint

Frenchmen were greatly divided in their opinions about Toussaint. The very real contributions made by the ex-slave in defense of their richest colony were appreciated by all republicans; his fantastic career seemed to confirm the universality of the doctrines of liberty and equality. Between 1794 and 1797 his bravery, intelligence, and dedication were widely heralded in the French press and legislative assemblies. However, as the revolution veered rightward after Thermidor, and as Toussaint himself became more defiant of the French government, this praise was transformed into violent denunciation, which took on strong racial overtones. Criticism was leveled at his arrogance, ambition, hypocrisy, duplicity, and tendencies toward independence. His influence over the blacks, once considered a virtue, was now condemned as sinister and dangerous. By 1800 the voices of the defamers had all but silenced Toussaint's friends and provided an ideological underpinning for Napoleon's decision to depose "the gilded African." The following selections give some indication of the nature of this anti-Toussaint literature and the official Napoleonic interpretation of his crimes.

General Hédouville's report of 1798, submitted in the wake of his expulsion from St. Domingue, stresses Toussaint's deceitfulness, ambition, and desire for independence. This opinion was confirmed by the extremely influential report of General Kerversau three years later. Kerversau, who served in St. Domingue for several years and participated in the Leclerc expedition, makes an appeal to European pride as a reason for deposing Toussaint. To offset such attacks, Toussaint sent a French engineer, Colonel Vincent, to France to argue on his behalf. Vincent underlined Toussaint's prodigious energies and his charismatic hold over the black population of the colony. He urged Napoleon to trust in Toussaint's devotion to France and to rule through him rather than risk an uncertain invasion. The short portrait by Pascal, one

of Toussaint's five secretaries, also emphasizes Toussaint's ener-
gies and ubiquity but shows him to be distrustful and ambitious.
Louis Dubroca's Life of Toussaint Louverture *draws liberally*
and uncritically from these unfavorable reports to present the
official Napoleonic interpretation. Released in Paris at the same
time Leclerc was invading St. Domingue, this book depicts Tous-
saint as a bloodthirsty black savage, a hypocritical traitor, an
ambitious schemer, who could never be trusted by the French
government. His Constitution of 1801 is cited as evidence of an
unquenchable thirst for power and independence. His criminal
activities forced the hitherto tolerant French government to
intervene in the name of France and the black population that
Toussaint had betrayed. Dubroca's account is full of distortions,
falsehoods, and specious arguments. It is reproduced here not
only because it is so representative of the entire range of anti-
Toussaint literature, but also because it demonstrates that
throughout the ages there has been no shortage of scholars wil-
ling to justify and obscure the most blatant aggressions and
treacheries in the name of reason, justice, peace, and freedom.
The excerpts from the letters of General Leclerc reveal French
fears of Toussaint's powerful influence over the blacks, even after
his surrender. In these letters Leclerc virtually requests the mur-
der of Toussaint. Pamphile de Lacroix, an officer in Leclerc's
army, has left us one of the most detailed portraits of Toussaint
and his life-style as ruler of St. Domingue. Although reflecting the
official Napoleonic view, Lacroix bases his account on authentic
documents and firsthand observations by French colonists and
thereby manages a much more sysmpathetic evaluation than most
Frenchmen of his generation. Finally, there is the opinion of the
exiled Napoleon Bonaparte, who acknowledges his error in over-
throwing Toussaint and attempting to restore the colonial ancien
régime.

GENERAL HÉDOUVILLE, DECEMBER 1798 [1]

The facts I have related show that all Toussaint's protestations
of attachment to the Republic were false; that his sole aim has been
to preserve that arbitrary authority usurped before my arrival in the
colony; and that even before that time he had been secretly negotiat-
ing with Maitland for the evacuation of the English posts on conditions that assured the return of the *émigrés,* free trade with the English
and Americans, and his *de facto* Independence; covering his ingratitude, meanwhile, by oaths of fidelity.

[1] Quoted by T. Lothrop Stoddard, *The French Revolution in San Domingo* (Boston, 1914), p. 275.

But presently, Toussaint Louverture will deceive all those enemies of ours whose tool he may at this time appear, and in the end he will oppress and cover with humiliation those whites whom he fears as much as he hates; yes, even those among them who are especially bound to him and who have encouraged him in his measures. . . . Toussaint Louverture now receives the *émigrés* with open arms: yet at the same time he never ceases to fill the cultivators with suspicion against all white men, to the end that these may never succeed in destroying his despotism. He is heaping up great wealth by the sale of colonial products to the English and Americans, and to-day San Domingo is practically lost to France. If the Directoire cannot take the very strong necessary measures, the sole hope of checking Toussaint Louverture even for the moment lies in sedulously fostering the hate which exists between the mulattoes and negroes, and by opposing Rigaud to Toussaint Louverture.

GENERAL KERVERSAU, 1801 [2]

I have shown Toussaint elevating himself from the bosom of slavery to supreme domination, advancing step by step along tortuous paths, taking on all the colors and forms that suited his ambition, in turn caressing and threatening; finally, emboldened by impunity, expelling by open force the depositories of national authority, oppressing the whites he had flattered by recalling the *émigrés;* exterminating men of color to the chant of sacred hymns and to the clamor of his proclamations of clemency; ruling over the blacks after having done away with their ex-chiefs whose influence or attachment to the Republic he feared; making treaties of alliance and commerce with the enemies of the State, receiving their agents and ships in his ports, and for each new outrage sending a special deputation to France to affirm his devotion and fidelity. I have shown him using the most odious means and the most absurd pretexts to wrest from the Consul's Agent the order to usurp the only portion of St. Domingue that the protection of an allied power had preserved for the Republic [Santo Domingo]. Then, furious at seeing this prize snatched from his covetous ambitions but concealing his anger, he deceived the Spanish government by solemn promises and the people by perfidious caresses and deposed the trustee of national power [Commissioner Roume] because he dared to annul the decree that had been extorted from him. Thereafter, he arrogated all power to himself, made laws, seized the terrible right of life and

---

[2] From Paul Roussier, "Introduction," in *Lettres du Général Leclerc* (Paris, 1937), pp. 22–24; trans. George F. Tyson, Jr.

death, and grasped in his hands the liberty, welfare, and life of all citizens. I have shown him alledging revolts in order to exercise vengeance or divert attention from his own movements, arresting the Agent in order to stifle his voice, . . . next, suddenly pouncing upon the Spanish part that he had lulled into a fatal sense of security, seizing it by guile and force; finally, as silent master of the entire island, coining money and creating a phantom colonial assembly in order to legitimate all his crimes and sanction the code of his tyranny in the name of the people.

What remains for him in order to consummate his grand work of independence but to dare to proclaim it? Who established the duties? Who gives laws to St. Domingue? Who disposes of the public coffers? Who regulates the number of troops and creates new regiments at his will? Who appoints all civil and military employees and even creates administrators, generals, and judges? Who negotiates on equal terms with foreign nations and makes treaties of neutrality and even alliance with the enemies of the Mother Country? Who expelled from the colony proprietors arriving with passports from the Mother Country, functionaries appointed by the Mother Country, Commissioners sent by the Mother Country? Who incarcerated the agent of the Mother Country? . . .

Let there be no mistake, as long as he remains in the colony he alone will be the sovereign; he may, perhaps, rule in the name of France as long as she is willing to bow to his domination; a kind of order will exist, but it will be one that he will have established; some laws will exist, but they will be his will; there will be an authority, but it will be his. Should he consent to receive the representatives of the Mother Country, they will be like pashas of the Porte in Egypt, honored captives without power as long as he will allow them there and ignominiously expelled at the first suspicion they will awake in this suspicious and touchy spirit. It is up to the Republic to consider whether after having given laws to all the monarchs of Europe, it suits its dignity to allow a rebellious negro in one of its colonies. Even if this humiliating and precarious criminal ceased to exist, it is necessary to be careful; there will be successors no less formidable. For they will not have those discretions which always accompany a new born rule and that inspired him—his advanced age and his naturally timid and temporizing character. The military anarchy that Bonaparte destroyed in Egypt exists in full force in St. Domingue: an uneasy militia that only desires disorder and only recognizes its chiefs; the rapacious and ambitious beys of a shiek Elbalad; an absolute master whom everyone envies and who distrusts everyone; a brutalized and oppressed popu-

lace, always blindly carried away by their strongest impulse; a mob of
merchants and travelers, almost all passing through the island and taking no other interest in the revolutions in government than that of
avoiding becoming its victims; finally, some civil magistrates, placed
in complete dependence upon the highest district commander and
passive instruments in the hands of the chiefs. Such is the spectacle presented by this colony and the elements that compose it.

COLONEL VINCENT, 1801 [3]

Toussaint, at the head of his army, is the most active and inde-
fatigable man of whom we can form an idea; we may say, with truth,
that he is found wherever instructions or danger render his presence
necessary. The particular care which he employs in his march of always deceiving the men of whom he has need and who think they enjoy
a confidence he gives to none, has such an effect that he is daily expected in all the chief places of the colony. His great sobriety, the
faculty, which none but he possesses, of never reposing, the facility
with which he resumes the affairs of the cabinet after most tiresome
excursions, of answering daily a hundred letters, and of habitually tir-
ing five secretaries, render him so superior to all those around him
that their respect and submission are in most individuals carried even
to fanaticism. It is certain that no man, in the present times, has obtained such an influence over a mass of ignorant people as General
Toussaint possesses over his brethren in St. Domingue.

PASCAL[4]

Toussaint-Louverture knew neither love nor hate nor the lines
of blood. If he didn't always strike, he never pardoned. His unknown,
resolute, terrible will was the supreme law without appeal. His spies,
who were everywhere, around his generals, on the estates, in the huts of
the blacks, were the mutes of this suspicious despot. He succeeded, so
to speak, in making himself invisible wherever he was and visible
where he wasn't; he seemed to have stolen the spontaneity of his movements from a tiger. When he was thought to be in Le Cap, he was in
Santo-Domingo, or frequently he arrived alone at night to surprise
the troops and people; a few days later, when he was believed to be

³ Quoted in Schoelcher, *Vie de Toussaint-Louverture*, p. 384; trans. George F.
Tyson, Jr.
⁴ From J. de Norvins, *Souvenirs d'un historien de Napoléon* (Paris, 1896), 2: 362–
63; trans. George F. Tyson, Jr.

sick at home with his secretaries, he appeared at Port-au-Prince. Speedy horses were placed along all his routes, facilitating these sudden appearances, which were frequently punctuated by his vengeance. Thus there was neither thought of betrayal nor time for treason. Impenetrable in his designs, which he confided to no one, Toussaint dictated separately in creole to each of his secretaries, who translated it into French; what one of them had begun under his dictation was constantly continued by another, and to prevent all communication between them—which was punishable by death—the one to whom he had made the first dictation was sent sixty or eighty leagues from his residence for an indefinite period. Cruelty or clemency, violence or justice, were only political instruments to him. He was more patient than insensible, more prudent than passionate; from his slave background he preserved frugality and vigor. His pride was insatiable; he proved it well by writing to Napoleon: "The first of the blacks to the first of the whites . . ." and by naming himself dictator for life. Independently of his passion to dominate St. Domingue alone, not the least of the causes of his rebellion was the desire to fight against the vanquisher of Italy and Egypt.

DUBROCA[5]

Jean François and Toussaint Louverture . . . endeavoured to shew . . . an unlimited devotion to the interests of the Spanish government. The war they made upon the French Republicans was a war of cannibals. It was no uncommon thing for them to move with horror and disgust, even those whose instruments they were become. Every Frenchman, of whatever colour he was, if he was in the service of the Republic, was certain, in falling into their hands, to find death in the midst of unexampled tortures. Surrounded with a crowd of priests and emigrants, whose counsels increased their ferocity, these two Negro Chiefs believed themselves charged with executing the vengeance of the altar and the throne. Their zeal was distinguished by the most frightful of character—fanaticism which murders without remorse in the name of heaven; and that extreme barbarism for which the sacred laws of nature, consanguinity, and humanity have no restraint.

When the history of this war shall be written, before the eyes of the reader will be placed the horrible picture of men sawn in two, or mutilated in every limb, or burnt over a slow fire, or hung by the feet to a tree and flayed alive. La Vendée alone offers some resemblance

[5] From Louis Dubroca, *The Life of Toussaint Louverture* (London, 1802), pp. 9–14, 18–22, 45–50, 62–65.

of the war, which for two years Toussaint made on the Republicans of the colony. It was in vain, during this time, that the commissaries of the French government at St. Domingo . . . endeavoured to lead him back to his duty to the mother country, in whose name they offered him, as well as to Jean François, peace, liberty, and protection. These offers were answered by new and greater acts of atrocity. Toussaint, thinking proper to state the motives of his conduct, wrote with his own hand to the commissaries a letter, dated the 28th of August, 1793, in which are these remarkable expressions:

> We cannot obey the will of the nation because we have been accustomed to execute that only of a king. The King of France is lost to us, but we are honoured with marks of distinction and favour by the King of Spain. For these reasons we cannot acknowledge you commissaries of the French nation till you have placed a king on the throne. . . .

The victories and success of the French Republic began to disgust Spain with the confederacy. Toussaint foresaw the end of his employment in the Spanish service; and perhaps apprehended that he should be made a sacrifice at the peace between France and Spain. He therefore prepared to change his party, and his new treachery was accompanied with circumstances of horror. When he had joined the Spaniards he presented himself with his hands stained in republican blood: to efface the remembrance of this, if possible, he resolved on returning to the Republicans, to offer the same trophy, and to sacrifice to them the blood of Spaniards as an atonement! . . .

Toussaint Louverture was made General of Division, and Lieutenant Governor of Saint Domingo; and thus elevated, saw himself in a condition successfully to prepare the way for his own usurpation. He had already made some progress in this great work by propagating through every possible channel the expectation of the future independence of the colonies in the West Indies, when the arrival of new agents from France, commissioned by the Executive Directory to proclaim the constitution of . . . [1795] opportunely for his purposes, added greatly to his influence, and furnished new arms to his ambition.

These agents had instructions to express, in the strongest terms, to Toussaint, the good will and respect of the French Government, and to acknowledge by new favours the services he had rendered the Republic, in rescuing General Laveaux, protecting the constituted authorities, and saving the colony from the internal factions which threatened its destruction.

The Commissioners of the Executive Directory had scarcely landed in Saint Domingo when they hastened to fulfil the wishes of the French Government toward Toussaint. They received him with marks of the most distinguished favour, and invited him to render further services to the mother country by driving the English from the colony. . . . Strengthened by the confidence of the French Government, and aided with the counsels of able men in the colony, Toussaint, after several affairs in which he displayed great military talents and uncommon personal courage, at length wrested from the English, Le Mirblais, Les Grand Bois, and other places which they had seized. His conduct during this war was brilliant and without stain; and that epoch of his life would be truly great, if the services he rendered the Republic at that time had not been, like all that preceded, subservient to his ambition. It was not as yet his interest to conduct the war feebly against the English, or to act in concert with them: his projects demanded that he should first give every pledge of fidelity to the French Government, to possess its entire confidence; and obtain new honours and power, to facilitate the execution of his designs.

Toussaint seldom deceived himself: the Commissioners of the Executive Directory, grateful for his services, and desirous of giving new proofs of their satisfaction, declared him General in Chief of the Armies of Saint Domingo. . . .

But even this was not the whole advantage he derived from his victories. The report of his splendid actions passing rapidly from the new world to France, spread the greatest glory round the name of Toussaint Louverture. In the tribune of the Council of Ancients his exploits were vaunted with the utmost enthusiasm. He was spoken of as the Saviour of the colony, and as one of the most faithful and strenuous partisans of the French Republic. His various atrocities were no longer called to mind. His apparent zeal for the welfare of France imposed upon the nation; and the hypocritical assumption of virtuous and noble sentiments, which then and now seemed to direct his conduct, as they grace his proclamations and discourse, completely blinded even those who were inclined to fear him. . . .

Toussaint, rendered absolute master of the Island, and without rival, has never ceased to exercise a tyranny almost as intolerable in its means as in its object. At the conclusion of the late troubles, which agitated the northern part of the Island, in which near 600 White people were slain, together with all the Black domestics of the estates on which they resided, the Negro Chief caused his own nephew, General Moyse, to be shot; the same who had been the secret agent of his dark intrigues.

There wanted but one formal act to add to the splendour of the successful ambition of this perfidious African; this was solemnly to dissolve the ties which united the colony to the mother country; to proclaim his independence by public acts, and constitute himself the supreme head of the Island. This last enterprise, so long meditated, and so steadily prepared, in the midst of so many treasons, characterized with the blood of so many victims, was executed. . . . The constitution which the French colony of St. Domingo assumed at that period affected to preserve some relations between the mother country and the colony; but, in fact, entirely annihilated all such. It is the name of Toussaint Louverture, that man grown old in the execution of crimes, the assassin of his benefactors, hypocritical and perjured, and abhorred of all nations, which is placed at the head of this constitution! But the inhabitants of St. Domingo, and above all those Blacks who owe to France the inexpressible benefit of liberty, who have often shed their blood for the mother country, who by their valour have signalized their restoration to their natural rights, and who are characterized as much by attachment to their friends as hatred to their oppressors, can never have consented to a constitution which separates them from their benefactors, cuts them off from a country of which they are the children, and delivers them into the hands of a tyrant, whose fury they have so often experienced. This constitution is not their work; it is the contrivance of a factious party, who, in arms, uniting themselves to their Chief, after spreading terror by their cruelties through all bosoms, have dared to call their will by the sacred name of the will of the people, and present to the world the code which guarantees the personal ambition of the majority of the citizens.

The interval which has passed between the publication of the act we are speaking of [the evidence of the treason of Toussaint Louverture] and the commencement of the expedition prepared by France against the traitor speaks too plainly in favour of the French government to permit me to endeavour, by my own reflections, to add to the universal sentiment which proclaims that government the pacificator of the world. What has the First Consul left unattempted to lead back to honour and his duty, to the interests of the mother country, and even his own proper interest, this man, who perhaps had the stupidity to take for the language of fear that of clemency and humanity? Till all means of conciliation had been tried, the expedition had never been resolved on; and then, how much in the spirit of peace was even this attempt begun! Those vessels that bore with them the thunder of the Republic, to chastise a rebel, carried also the most sacred pledges to the mildness and magnanimity of the French government. The ministers of public vengeance were instructed, rather than crush the culprit with force, to endeavour to reclaim him, by a benefaction, the most touching to the heart of a man who had not abjured all the sentiments of nature, by restoring to him his two sons, so long separated from their father, and so carefully and generously educated in the midst of a nation which he betrayed!

But neither the clemency of the French Government, nor the unbounded proofs of its kindness, could subdue this ferocious Negro: too much accustomed, doubtless, to plunder, and to the enjoyment of unqualified tyranny to enter into a just and civilized order of things, which must have restrained his ruinous ambition. Toussaint Louverture has completed his crimes; and by his audacious resistance put a term to the pacific dispositions of the French Government. It belongs now to the courage of the French troops to finish this disgraceful contest. May victory, so long the ally of the French Republic, continue faithful to her in this enterprise! May the happy genius of the great Chief of the nation hover over the operations of this war, to accelerate its conclusion, and to spare the blood of the French people, which so many secret enemies, no doubt, wish to see entirely shed! . . .

This celebrated Negro is of the middle stature. He has a fine eye, and his glances are rapid and penetrating. Extremely sober by habit, his activity in the prosecution of his enterprises is incessant. . . .

His disposition is dark and taciturn. He seldom speaks the French language, and that very ill. All his actions are covered with such a profound veil of hypocrisy, that, although his entire life has been a series of treachery or crimes, all who approach him are betrayed into an opinion of the purity of his intentions. The Marquis D'Hermona, that intelligent and distinguished Spanish officer . . . said of him, "If God descended on earth he could not inhabit a heart more apparently good than that of Toussaint Louverture."

His character is a strange and frightful mixture of fanaticism and fierce passions. He passes without remorse from the altar to premeditated carnage, and from devotion to the darkest contrivances of perfidy. He appears always surrounded by priests, for whom he affects uncommon veneration. Priests generally draw up his proclamations. . . .

But all this exterior of devotion is no other than a mask, with which he finds it useful to cover the depraved passions of his heart, more successfully to direct the blind credulity of the Negroes. If he were still further to extend his hypocrisy and his influence over them, of which he is capable, if he sees need, it cannot be doubted that with the extravagant ideas the Blacks have formed of him, seconded by the priests, who are devoted to his service, he might assume the character of an inspired personage, and be obeyed in his commands to his followers, to commit all crimes in the name of heaven.

Toussaint Louverture is not sincerely attached to the liberation of the Negroes, and detests the dominion of Europeans. He loathes with a mortal hatred the Mulattoes, whose race in the colony he has almost rooted out. He despises his own brethren, the Negroes, whom he employs merely as instruments of his ambition, and whose death he coldly commands by thousands, when his power is in the least menaced.

He abused the confidence of his first benefactors. He betrayed his own faction, the Spanish, English, Mulattoes, White people, France under royal government, Republican France, his own blood, his country, and the religion he professes to respect.

Such is the portrait of Toussaint Louverture, whose life, when there shall be opportunity of writing it with more ample circumstances, will furnish a striking example of the crimes to which ambition will lead, when education, integrity, and honour, do not check its natural progress.

GENERAL LECLERC'S LETTERS [6]

5 May 1802: General Toussaint has surrendered here. He left perfectly satisfied with me and ready to carry out all my orders. I believe that he will carry them out because he is persuaded that if he did not I would make him repent it.

6 June 1802: My position grows worse from day to day. Disease takes my men. Toussaint Louverture is playing false—just as I expected. However, I have gained from his submission what I had intended—the winning over of Dessalines and Christophe with their troops. I have just ordered his arrest, and I think I can count on Dessalines (whose spirit I have mastered) to hunt him down if he escapes. At the same time, do not be astonished if I fail. For the last two weeks this man has been very suspicious: not that I have given him cause, but the fact is, he regrets his former power, and these regrets have engendered the idea of re-forming his party.

11 June 1802: In one of my last despatches I told you of the pardon granted General Toussaint. This ambitious man, however, from that very moment never ceased to conspire in secret. He surrendered only because Generals Christophe and Dessalines told him that they saw he had deceived them and that they were resolved no longer to

[6] Quoted in Stoddard, *The French Revolution*, pp. 327–29.

make war upon us. But no sooner had he seen himself thus abandoned than he sought to organize a great insurrection among the cultivators. The reports which came to me from Dessalines on Toussaint's
conduct since his submission left no doubt on this point. I intercepted
letters written to his agent at Le Cap which proved that he was trying
to regain his former influence. Under such circumstances I could not
allow him time to carry out his criminal projects. I ordered his arrest.
The thing was not easy, but it is done. I am now sending to France
with all his family this man so dangerous to San Domingo. Citizen
Minister, the Government must put him in some fortress in the centre
of France, so that by no possibility can he escape and return to San
Domingo, where he has the power of a religious leader. For if, three
years from now, this man were to reappear at San Domingo, he might
well destroy everything that France had done.

11 June 1802: Toussaint Louverture must not be at liberty. Im-
prison him far within the Republic, that he may never see San Domingo again.

July 1802: You cannot keep Toussaint at too great a distance from
the sea nor in a place too sure. The man has fanaticised this country to
such a degree that his appearance would set everything once more
aflame.

PAMPHILE DE LACROIX [7]

He welcomed, without familiarity, the old colonists who had
proven themselves most imbued with color prejudice. Old memories
were catered to. . . .

He took into his service those subaltern officers of the *émigré*
legions who remained in the colony and offered a special protection to
those who didn't want to serve.

He was even more affected in the scrupulous respect he paid the
priests. This veneration was calculated; it gave the appearance of
saintliness to the man who had once sent an agent to the Director to
assure him that his religion was only a political façade.

Abandoning himself to his fortune, he was humble only in his personal dress; but all his public deeds, all his actions, were designed to
increase his power; and he became more powerful than any of his
predecessors as Governor General of St. Domingue.

He surrounded himself with a large bodyguard in which he arro-
gantly placed the distinguished names of the ancien régime. To denote

[7] From Pamphile de Lacroix, *Mémoires pour servir à l'histoire de la révolution de Saint-Domingue*, 2 vols. (Paris, 1819), 1:394–410, 2:204–7; trans. George F. Tyson, Jr.

the brilliance of his rank he gave his horseguard the colors and insignia of the bodyguard of the old order and would appear only with great military pomp. Preceded by two trumpeters dressed in silver helmets, red caps, and a tunic, he enveloped himself in all the trappings of absolute power. Finally, in order to win their favor, he ostensibly allowed the proprietors to reason with him.

Fearing nothing from the blacks, whose enthusiasm he had aroused and who obeyed him like slaves, he pretended to welcome eagerly the complaints made against them and seemingly disregarded those of the blacks against the whites.

If, however, these complaints reflected public opinion, he made it easy for those attacked to export from the colony the illegal fortune they had been accused of making. All who dominated by virtue of rank or property became the marked objects of his affections.

By such methods Toussaint soon gained many long-winded advocates throughout the world; that was what he wanted and it was his chief preoccupation. . . .

In the North and West prosperity had returned, despite the war in the South. . . . The first fruit of the organization of these resources had been sufficient to cover the expenses of the colony.

The retreat of General Rigaud and the men of color of the South threw new territorial riches into Toussaint-Louverture's eager hands. He profited from them, and the glitter of his prosperity reached to foreign shores. The scattered colonists vegetating there caught sight of a glimmer of hope, and despite the painful feeling that the new order —the predominance of the blacks—elicited in them, they would . . . accept with gratitude the reinstatement of their property and their return to the colony.

From every country came their letters expressing their complete confidence in the authority and kindness of the General-in-Chief of St. Domingue, in the justice and excellence of his administration, all of which effectively strengthened and inflated the pride of Toussaint-Louverture. The following anecdote illustrates this well:

The manager of the Bréda estate, where Toussaint-Louverture had been a slave, was vegetating in the United States. Having learned of this, Toussaint-Louverture wrote asking him to return to St. Domingue to take charge of the interests of "their former good master." . . . The manager quickly returned; he disembarked at Port-au-Prince; the first persons he saw confirmed that the General-in-Chief spoke of him with interest; the same evening he was invited to his circle; he rushed there wanting to throw himself into the arms of his benefactor, but this remote benefactor drew back and in a solemn voice shouted for everyone to hear: "Slowly, Mr. Manager, today a greater distance exists from me to you than formerly existed from you to me. Return to the Bréda estate, be just and unbending, make the blacks work hard, so as to add by the prosperity of your small interests to the general prosperity of the administration of the first of the blacks, the General-in-Chief of St. Domingue."

In these circles, to which no one dared refuse an invitation, the behavior of Toussaint-Louverture was truly something admirable. There were two kinds of circles.

You had to be invited to the "great circles." Toussaint-Louverture wore the undress uniform of a general officer. His simple dress in such a brilliant gathering contrasted with the dignified manner he kept.

When he appeared in the grand hall where his guests had gathered in advance, everyone, without distinction of sex, had to rise. He required that they maintain a highly respectful attitude and especially liked the whites to address him with decent manners. Careful to judge the correctness of these manners, whenever someone impressed him he would cry out: "Well done! That is how one should present himself." Then, turning to the black officers around him: "You other negroes," he said to them, "strive to assimilate these manners and learn to present yourselves as is required. That is what it means to have been raised in France; my children will be like that."

He wanted the women, especially the white ladies, to dress as if they were going to church, and their bosoms had to be completely covered. Several times they saw him divert his eyes and exclaim that "he couldn't conceive how honest women could be so lacking in decency." Another time he was seen throwing his handkerchief over the bosom of a young girl, while telling her mother in a stern voice "that modesty must be the ornament of her sex."

In these circles he affected to speak only to the wives of old colonists; in the same way he always referred to the wives of foreigners as "Madame." If he spoke to the women of color, and what was more unusual, to the black women, he called them "Citizeness." All white women were received in these circles by right. As for the others, he accepted only the wives of high officials. After speaking to everyone, having made a tour of the room, and returning to the door by which he had entered, he made a dignified bow, turned his head right and left, saluted with both hands, and slowly retired with his officers.

The "small circles" were public audiences that took place every evening. Toussaint-Louverture appeared there dressed like the old proprietors on their plantations, that is, in white pants and vest of very fine linen, with a madras headcloth. All citizens entered the grand hall and he spoke to them all. He enjoyed embarrassing the blacks who attended these audiences. He pretended a kindness for those whose confusion derived from the respect and admiration they felt in his presence, but when a black replied to him with some assurance, he sternly questioned him on the Catechism or agriculture, to which the disconcerted black did not know how to respond. Then he did not fail to add to his confusion by severely reproaching him for his ignorance and incapacity. In the same manner he was heard saying to the blacks and men of color who asked him for positions as judges: "I greatly desire it since I presume you know Latin." "No, my General." "How then, can you want to be a judge if you don't know Latin?" Then he reeled off a series of Latin words he had learnt by heart from the psalm book or elsewhere and which had no relevance to the present situation. The whites restrained their laughter because no one laughed at Toussaint-Louverture, and the negroes retired, consoled at not being made judges and convinced that their General-in-Chief knew Latin.

After touring the grand hall during the small circles, Toussaint-Louverture invited people with whom he desired to spend the evening into the small chamber outside his bedroom that served as his study. The greatest number of these people were always the principal whites of the colony. There he seated everyone, including himself, and spoke of France, his children, religion, his old masters, his thanks to God for his freedom and for granting him the necessary qualities to fulfill the position in which he had been placed by France. He also spoke of the progress of agriculture and commerce, but never of the new politics; he questioned each person, with an air of concern, about his particular affairs and family; he conversed with the Mothers Superior about their children's schools, asking if the children were being prepared for their first communion; and, if he found some young people there, it pleased him to question them on the Catechism and the Gospel.

When he wanted to conclude this audience, he rose up and made a deep bow. They retired, while he accompanied them to the door, assigning particular appointments to those who requested them, and then shut himself up with his secretaries, with whom he worked strenuously into the night. Like all extraordinary men, his weakness was wanting to hide the circumstances of his mysterious and unbelievable eminence. A Capuchin had taught him to read as a youth, but he would not admit it; with a good-natured and secretive air, he sometimes said:

> From the outset of the troubles in St. Domingue I felt that I was destined for great things. When I received this divine opinion I was fifty-

four years old; I didn't know how to read or write; I knew some Portugese words and spoke them to a noncommissioned officer stationed at Le Cap, and, thanks to him, in a few months I knew how to sign my name and read fluently. The St. Domingue revolution was taking its course; I saw that the whites would be unable to endure because they were divided and ruined; I congratulated myself at being black.

It was necessary to begin my career; I went to the Spanish part of the island where protection and asylum were given to the first troops of my color. This protection and asylum led nowhere; I was thrilled to see Jean François make himself a Spaniard at the moment when the powerful French Republic proclaimed the general emancipation of the blacks. A secret voice told me: "Since the blacks are free, they need a leader," and that I must be this leader predicted by Abbé Raynal. With this sentiment I quickly returned to the service of France, and the voice of God hasn't deceived me.

Surrounded by a guard of fifteen to eighteen men, brilliantly dressed, with several hundred horses in his personal service, Toussaint-Louverture had the radiance of a Prince. . . .

In every village he had old black godmothers, who prepared the *calaloo* that he ate alone in his room. They were also the trustees of his wine, which had been bottled and sealed in his presence; but when, as often happened, Toussaint-Louverture was not in the villages, he limited his nourishment to a glass of water every twenty-four hours and, in the absence of a biscuit, one or two bananas, or better two or three sweet potatoes.

He slept only two or three hours; the uncurbed passion to dominate everything was the source of his life.

Placed in the midst of insurgent slaves from the beginning of the St. Domingue revolution, outwitted by the Spanish and English, attached to France, fighting with everyone and believing himself betrayed by everyone, Toussaint-Louverture felt, at an early moment, the need of becoming inscrutable. Although his age contributed to this, it was also his nature. Hypocrisy was the essence of his character. One never knew what he was doing, if he was leaving or staying, where he had gone, from whence he had come. Often it was announced that he was at Le Cap, and he was really in Port-au-Prince. When he was thought to be in Port-au-Prince, he was in Cayes, the Môle, or St. Marc. . . .

No one knew better than Toussaint-Louverture the theater of his operations and the character of the individuals under his command. In order to captivate the old masters, he flattered their particular vanity and their proprietary interests; he assisted them by virtue of his moral credit with the blacks.

The soldiers revered him as an extraordinary being, and the field-negroes prostrated themselves before him as if he were divine. All his generals trembled before his gaze (Dessalines dared not look him in the face), and everyone trembled before his generals.

Never was a European army subject to a sterner discipline than that observed by Toussaint-Louverture's troops. Each rank commanded with a pistol in his hands and had the right of life or death over his subordinates.

The system of agriculture had assured the well-being of the general officers and their superiors; it was with words that the junior officers and soldiers were kept in an obedience differing little from slavery. They were told that they were free, and they believed it because a series of adroit insinuations placed them above the field-negroes and because a soldier was always right when he complained against a black civilian. This supremacy of the black soldier insured that he was always feared and obeyed.

After Toussaint-Louverture had established and assured his military supremacy, he was unafraid of arming the field-negroes. The money he spent to procure arms and ammunition reached unbelievable sums. . . .

He never ceased repeating to the field-negroes that the liberty of the blacks consisted in the preservation of these arms and ammunition, whose good condition he himself assured by frequent reviews.

It was at these reviews that he appeared to be inspired and became the idol of the blacks who listened to him.

He spoke to them in parables in order to be better understood; he frequently used the following one. Into a glass vase filled with kernels of black corn he mixed a few white kernels and said to those around him: "You are the black kernels, the whites who would reenslave you are the white kernels." Then he shook the vase and, presenting it to their fascinated eyes, exclaimed, as if inspired, "See the white ones only here and there?"—that is to say, consider the whites in proportion to yourselves.

It is from his own mind, rather than circumstances or the counsel of others, that Toussaint-Louverture drew the inspiration of his political progress. While riding throughout the colony with the speed of lightning, seeing everything for himself, he prepared his administrative decisions; he planned as he galloped; he even planned when he pretended to pray.

Cabinet work—he had to respond to one to three hundred letters each day, a duty apparently alien to him—seemed to be as keen a pleasure for him as sensual satisfaction is to the rest of mankind. . . .

Judged by the interest of the moment, through the prism of passions, Toussaint-Louverture has in turn been represented as a fierce brute, or the most astonishing and best of men, more often as an execrable monster or saintly martyr; he was not at all like that.

Gifted with great talents, he owed his elevation to a multitude of accidental circumstances. The selfish calculus of politics contributed more to making him a leader of his caste than the continuous meditations of his taciturn ambition. Foreign greed and proprietary interests opened the door for him; he rushed past superior men, using to his advantage the art of warfare that he understood so well. The enthusiasm of the blacks maintained him by force of arms in the position he had achieved, but the mask of hypocrisy with which he covered himself during his rise to supreme power became, when he was attacked, the fetter of his warlike resolutions and the cause of his defeat.

Flattery, whose vulgarity intoxicates those placed in the highest positions, had strongly reinforced his own self-love and kept Toussaint-Louverture persuaded that he was the destined avenger of the outrages committed against his race foretold by Abbé Raynal.

In the catastrophe that befell the first of the blacks, as with all powerful men since, one divines the hand of God, who is so often pleased to humiliate the dreams of human pride.

A spirit of vanity, which momentarily led him out of his character, sufficed to deprive Toussaint-Louverture of the elevated position his genius had earned him. If this genius wasn't vast in acquired knowledge, it was immense in supernatural thoughts and inspirations. . . .

The idea of attaining supreme power came to him only after a long period and by imitation; he had shown himself attached to the principles of France when England wanted to make him king, but when Toussaint-Louverture saw men whose former follies threatened the new institutions passing from Napoleon's salons to high positions of State, he willingly allowed himself to be misled by foreign suggestions. He was fearful that they would revoke the liberty of the blacks by calling for the reestablishment of the old colonial order. If his confidential assertions can be believed, it was solely to conserve the means of maintaining these rights by force of authority that led him to declare himself governor for life. "I have taken up again the calendar of the Republic," he said, "in order to show that I do not aim at independence, but the means of guaranteeing to my threatened caste the rights which it had conceded to them."

In order to achieve this goal, he pushed the blacks to those cruel excesses that humanity, particularly France, came to deplore.

NAPOLEON BONAPARTE [8]

"I have to reproach myself with the attempt made upon the colony during the consulship. The design of reducing it by force was a great error. I ought to have been satisfied with governing it through the medium of Toussaint. Peace with England was not sufficiently consolidated, and the territorial wealth I should have acquired by its reduction would have served but to enrich our enemies." He had, he observed, the greater reason to reproach himself with the attempt, because he had foreseen its failure, and it was executed against his inclination. He had solely yielded to the opinion of the council of state and his ministers, hurried along, as they are, by the clamours of the colonists, who formed a considerable party at Paris, and were, besides, he said, either nearly all royalists, or in the pay of the English faction.

The Emperor assured us, that the army which had been sent out, consisted but of sixteen thousand men, and was quite sufficient. The failure of the expedition was solely to be attributed to accidental circumstances, such as the yellow fever, the death of the Commander-in-Chief, a new war, etc., etc.

"Toussaint," observed the Emperor, "was not a man destitute of merit; but he certainly was not so highly gifted as was attempted in his time to describe him. His character, besides, was ill calculated to inspire real confidence; he had given us serious causes of complaint. It would have been necessary to be always distrustful of his sincerity. He was chiefly guided by an officer of engineers or artillery. That officer had come to France before Leclerc's expedition, and conferences were, for a long time, held with him. He exerted himself very much to prevent the attempt, and described with great precision, all its difficulties, without pretending, however, that it was impossible." The Emperor thought that the Bourbons might succeed in reducing Saint-Domingo by force; but on that subject the result of arms was not to be calculated upon; it was rather the result of commerce and of grand political views. Three or four hundred millions of capital swept away from France to a remote country; an indefinite period for reaping the fruits of such a sacrifice; the very great certainty of seeing them engrossed by the English, or swallowed up by revolutions, etc., etc.: those were the points for consideration. The Emperor concluded with saying, "The colonial system, which we have witnessed, is closed for us, as well as the whole continent of Europe; we must give it up, and henceforth confine ourselves to the free navigation of the seas, and the complete liberty of universal barter."

[8] From Count de Las Cases, *Journal of the Private Life and Conversations of the Emperor Napoleon at Saint Helena* (Philadelphia, 1823), 4:114–15.

7

Englishmen React to Toussaint

*The international repercussions of Toussaint's ascend-
ancy in St. Domingue following the expulsion of the British are
clearly evident in the official correspondence of the Governor of
Jamaica, Earl Balcarres. Having just terminated an exhausting
war against the Jamaica Maroons and plagued after 1797 by
hordes of runaway slaves who had infested the mountains vacated
by the exiled Maroons, Balcarres was quick to perceive the extreme danger Toussaint posed to the security of Jamaica. His
initial response was to request more troops, while attempting to
"manage" Toussaint. But after being outmaneuvered diplomati-
cally by Toussaint for several months, he could only conclude
that it was Britain that was being used. The selection by Edward
Corbet provides a comprehensive description of Toussaint's government in 1801 by the British agent on the scene.*

EARL BALCARRES, GOVERNOR OF JAMAICA

4 July 1798:[1] St. Domingo can only henceforward be considered
as a Brigand island.

That, Jamaica, being under the *lee* of a great and powerful country,
lies open to her arms, and—what is ten time worse—her opinions.

That, the successes of the Brigands there, holds forth such an example to our Negroes here, as to place Jamaica in a new point of view,
and to render her safety much more precarious and problematical than
at any former period.

That, this colony can only be maintained by a force so combined,
and so judiciously disposed of, as to keep the slaves in the greatest possible subjugation.

That, this island is so vulnerable in the greatest degree for its proximity to St. Domingo and Cuba, and it is easily in the power of the
enemy to throw in Banditti, by means of boats and canoes, who would
find no great difficulty in securing themselves in the fastness.

[1] From the Public Record Office, London, C.O. 137/100; Balcarres to Portland,
4 July 1798. Crown copyright material appears by permission of the Controller of
H. M. Stationery Office.

The interior of this island must therefore be possesesd by our troops, *coute que coute:* those woods and fastenesses must be ranged by companies of woodsmen posted there, living there, and constantly patrolling. . . .

I think the military constitution of this island greatly changed by the new lights which have been infused into the minds of the slaves; which, to my judgement, has the effect that the active services of the Militia are, in a great measure, tied up: and I conceive that the most judicious disposition of the Militia is to allow most of them to remain at their homes and to watch over the conduct of the Negroes on the several estates and plantations. . . .

30 October 1798:[2] Toussaint cannot keep very long in any terms with the Directory of France. If we manage with him the rupture may be earlier, because being well with us, he will the less fear the Directory. By our bringing him forward . . . the Directory will quarrel with him, appoint a successor, and he will of course throw himself under the *protection* of England. Or the contrary, if we don't support him, he must throw himself entirely into the arms of the Directory. That, it is surely the interests of the British government, of its trade, and the Colony of Jamaica to take measures with Toussaint, and even our safety requires it, for it is well known to Toussaint that in forty-eight hours they can fell the . . . large cotton tree, build boats of it, each to contain thirty men and within sixty hours of the cutting down of the tree, land in Jamaica some five hundred men. That these men are to be considered as lost, but they would succeed in destroying the plantations. . . .

That, Great Britain has everything to gain and nothing to lose by a trading connexion with Toussaint. That the strict meaning of the connexion is a *trading connexion;* that, Toussaint has laid aside all his gunboats, having no hostile intention against Jamaica, if it can be avoided. That, Toussaint can have no interest in the destruction of Jamaica.

7 December 1799:[3] There seems great reason to suppose that Toussaint may, [before] long, acquire an ascendancy over the whole island of Saint Domingo. From what I have observed of his general conduct, I must suspect that he is playing a game, not only with us, but with the Directory; and that his aim is Independence. If that is established, of which there is a probability, his next object will naturally be the

[2] From the Public Record Office, London, C.O. 137/100; Balcarres to Portland, 30 October 1798.

[3] From the Public Record Office, London, C.O. 137/103; Balcarres to Portland, 7 December 1799.

loss of Jamaica to the Crown of Great Britain; such an event would so establish his Dominion, that no circumstance could afterwards shake him. But, he will never regard his power as absolutely established while the British Navy can avail themselves of the harbours of Jamaica. That independence, and consequently the destruction of Jamaica is his ultimate aim appears to me evident. . . .

THE BRITISH AGENT IN ST. DOMINGUE, MARCH 1801 [4]

The pay of his troops, officers I am assured, as well as men, is a bit per day or two Dollars and three quarters per *month,* they finding themselves in everything but arms. The officers have some extra allowances, but not considerable. They aim at a good discipline and are in some degree successful. . . .

All the towns have some troops, more or less, according to their size and importance, and besides, military posts of different descriptions over the country, and no person is permitted to travel without a passport from the General commanding in the Arrondissement in which he is.

Altho' I have stated the military force under General Toussaint's command at about fourteen thousand men, he can bring any further number into the field, as far as he may have arms, or circumstances require it.

In his department of Finance, he has, by very heavy imposts on imports & exports (ten per cent *ad valorem* on the one and twenty per cent on the other), and other taxes, acquired a very respectable revenue. I am pretty well satisfied from the different information I have received, that the amount of duties & other taxes exceed one hundred thousand Dollars per *month,* and that he has always in his Treasury *here* a sum not inferior to that which I have mentioned.

In his military establishment, altho' he brings forward his own colour to the situations of the first rank, he nevertheless assimilates a certain number of whites & people of colour; of the latter, however, the number now in the island is inconsiderable, having either emigrated or been destroyed in the course of the war with Rigaud.

He is compelling by the most rigorous measures, everyone, except such as are employed in military service, to return to their *former* plantations & carry on a system of cultivation as formerly, for which they receive a certain portion of the productions, one fourth divided

---

[4] From The Public Record Office, London, C.O. 137/105; Edward Corbet to Balcarres, 31 March 1801. Crown copyright material appears by permission of the Controller of H. M. Stationery Office.

amongst them. There is a certain officer in each parish, who fixes their proportion of this fourth to be paid to each person, or, as they are called here *cultivateurs,* according to their respective capabilities.

Coffee, cotton & cocoa are what is produced here in greatest quantities. Their means are not adequate to restoring the many sugar works destroyed during the state of warfare which this Island has, from a variety of parties & combinations, for eleven or twelve years experienced.

Your Lordship I presume may have observed that General Toussaint's government is perfectly despotic (but, I must at the same time say aims at being just), altho' he has recourse at times to the appearance of Legislation. There is now assembling here what is called a Colonial assembly which will finally consist of six or eight persons, and the purpose for which they are supposed to be called together is, to give their sanction to such public acts as he may deem advisable to require it.

Your Lordship will also have observed that he does every thing in the *name* of the French Republic. . . .

The white people that remained or have returned since His Majesty's Government was withdrawn from this island, have experienced, as far as I learn or perceive, good treatment, conforming however to all laws & regulations that are made.

A considerable number are in possession (under certain restrictions), of their former properties.

In regard to the trade of this island, which is not inconsiderable, I have to observe that the Americans, it appears to me, have acquired a degree of ascendancy that perhaps it was not originally intended they should enjoy, and while it not only militates against the fair pretentions and interest of the British trader, it gives them a degree of political influence which I do not hold it altogether proper they should possess, conceiving, my Lord, that while we permit an intercourse with the peculiar description of government that exists in this island, we should be principals in the business, and that they should feel they are solely indebted to *British* connection for the benefits they derive from a certain freedom of commerce.

8
Americans React to Toussaint

*Despite the ideals expressed in the Declaration of In-
dependence, Americans were never enthusiastic over the creation
of a sister republic in the hemisphere, particularly as it was governed by blacks. Official U.S. recognition of Haiti had to wait
until 1862. As early as 1791 George Washington urged that the
U.S. render every possible aid to France to help "crush the alarm
ing insurrection of the negroes in St. Domingo." Eight years later
an anxious Thomas Jefferson referred to Toussaint and his fel
low freedom fighters as "the cannibals of the terrible Republic."
Other distinguished Americans expressed a similar abhorrence
for the Haitian Revolution and called for greater vigilance over
the black population in the U.S. Nor was this pervasive uneasiness without foundation. Like a later struggle for national liberation in Vietnam, events in St. Domingue had not only raised serious questions about the nature of the national ideology but had
exposed and aggravated deeply rooted class and racial tensions at
the core of American life. After 1791 slave unrest increased
sharply throughout the South, much of it directly stimulated by
news from St. Domingue. The upshot was that in order to prevent a repetition of events in St. Domingue, the slave trade was
abolished in 1807, and controls were tightened over the slaves and
free colored population. Moreover, the question of establishing
commercial relations with Toussaint's government occupied a
prominent place in the national debates of 1798–1801, simultaneously clarifying and acerbating the conflict between agrarian
and commercial interests—which was also a sectional conflict
between North and South—that characterized American politics
of the period. One of the most concise expressions of the racial
and class fears aroused by the Haitian Revolution can be found
in the speech of Albert Galletin, soon to become Jefferson's Secretary of the Treasury, in the Congressional Debates of 1799. Speaking against a Federalist bill to exempt Toussaint's St. Domingue
from the trade embargo imposed against French shipping, Galletin makes it clear that, in the name of National Interest, he
opposes extending the right of national self-determination to
other peoples, especially if they are colored. Despite Galletin's
impassioned oratory, the bill, backed by the Adams Administration and New England commercial interests was passed by a substantial majority. This important victory for Toussaint was*

93

*largely the result of his handling of the American representative
to St. Domingue, Edward Stevens. Convinced of Toussaint's sincerity, Stevens sent home glowing reports, praising the Haitian
leader's abilities, moderation, and eagerness for a special trading
relationship with the United States. The following extracts from
his letters offer a detailed description of Toussaint's situation on
the eve of the war with Rigaud and indicate how Toussaint was
able to obtain American aid by the lure of a rupture with France.
The correspondence between Rufus King, the American ambas-
sador to England, and Timothy Pickering, the American Secretary of State, in early 1799 demonstrates the deep concern of
American and British statesmen over the impact of the St. Domingue revolution upon the slave societies of the Western hemisphere. In the face of this threat to the old colonial system, the
determination of both nations to pursue a common policy toward
Toussaint's government foreshadowed the subsequent pattern of
cooperation and joint economic exploitation that came to char-
acterize Anglo-American policy toward the new nations of Latin
America and the Carribbean during the nineteenth and twentieth
centuries.*

ALBERT GALLETIN [1]

Mr. G[alletin] conceived, therefore, that the question comes to
this: Is it proper to give power to the President, under our present circumstances, to stipulate with certain agents, that in case they will dis-
obey their Government, by declaring themselves independent, or by
throwing themselves into other hands, we will renew our commercial
intercourse with you? No man, said Mr. G., will deny that a trade of
this kind would be advantageous to the United States; he believed it to
be one of the most lucrative branches of our commerce; but it was
nevertheless thought proper, at the last session, to suspend it, in order,
as then supposed, to effect a greater good. Therefore, this commerce
being advantageous to the United States, is not a sufficient reason why
this measure should be taken, if it be wrong in itself, and may produce
greater mischiefs than the trade can do us good.

What, said Mr. G., are the inconveniences which would arise from
a measure of this kind? It must be allowed, in the first place, that it
would give the lie to all our former declarations of abhorrence against
the attempts of other countries to divide the people of a nation from
their Government; for we here, said he, assume the ground that it is
proper to negotiate and stipulate with a part of the people, with a certain district of a country, with any person who shall choose to say that

[1] From the *Annals of Congress*, 10, 5th Cong., January 1799, pp. 2749–52.

he claims the right of governing in any place. We abandon the general ground of treating with a foreign Government, and determine to treat with any individual who may either have, or claim to have, authority. Mr. G. believed a principle of this kind at all times improper; and it would be peculiarly improper in us to act upon it, with respect to a nation, against which we have so many grounds of complaint of this kind. He had already stated, that it could only be justified in a state of war, if then, to hold out encouragement to insurrection and rebellion to the colonies of another country.

But, provided the act be justifiable, would it be our interest to do it; and what would be the probable effect of such a measure? To be able to speak upon this point with perspicuity, it would be necessary to investigate the real object of this section a little more closely. . . .

Mr. G. said he knew that the independence of St. Domingo had been a favorite theme with gentlemen, and they had made an appeal upon it to the avarice of the people of the United States, that, in case of war, this independence would be of advantage to the United States, and that, during a time of peace, the minds of the people ought to be prepared for this event. . . .

. . . This section is inserted in the bill to encourage Toussaint to declare the island independent. Nay, his views, if he is a man of sense, must go further; he must not only secure a temporary trade, but he would also desire to know whether it be the wish of this country that St. Domingo should become independent; because he should suppose that if the Government of the United States was opposed to such an event, a temporary trade would not be a sufficient inducement to him to throw off his present allegiance.

To me, however, said Mr. G., if it be the intention of the General to declare it, the independence of St. Domingo is a very problematical event. It would certainly be the interest of Great Britain to oppose an attempt of this kind; since it could not be her interest to have a black Government there. But supposing the event possible, he should consider it as extremely injurious to the interests of the United States. Suppose that island, with its present population, under present circumstances, should become an independent State. What is this population? It is known to consist, almost altogether, of slaves just emancipated, of men who received their first education under the lash of the whip, and who have been initiated to liberty only by that series of rapine, pillage, and massacre, that have laid waste and deluged that island in blood; of men, who, if left to themselves, if altogether independent, are by no means likely to apply themselves to the peaceable cultivation of the country, but will try to continue to live, as heretofore, by plunder and depredations. No man, said Mr. G., wishes more than I do to see an abolition of slavery, when it can be property effected; but no man would be more unwilling than I to constitute a whole nation of freed slaves, who had arrived to the age of thirty years, and thus to throw so many wild tigers on society. If the population of St. Domingo can remain free in that island, he had no objection; but, however free, he did not wish to have them independent, and he would rather see them under a government that would be likely to keep them where they are, and prevent them from committing depredations out of the island. But if they were left to govern themselves, they might become more troublesome to us, in our commerce to the West Indies, than the Algerines ever were in the Mediterranean; they might also become dangerous neighbors to the Southern States, and an asylum for renegadoes from those parts.

This being the case, Mr. G. said, he must deprecate every encouragement which may be held out to produce such an event. Did not gentlemen recollect what an alarm was sounded last year, with respect to the probability of an invasion of the Southern States from the West Indies; an alarm upon which some of the strongest measures of the last session were grounded? Mr. G. could not help hoping, there would be a general wish not to take any measure which may imbody so dangerous a description of men in our neighborhood, whose object may be plunder, and who might visit the States of South Carolina and Georgia, and spread their views among the negro people there, and excite dangerous insurrections among them. He did not wish, therefore, to see this black population independent; and that the interest will be wholly black is clear. The General is black, and his agent here is married to a black woman in this city. Mr. G. did not mean by this to throw any reflection upon the General. He believed he had behaved well to Americans. His remarks were general, and were only intended to show that it would be with a black population we must treat.

EDWARD STEVENS [2]

Stevens to Pickering, L'Archahaye, June 24th, 1799

My Apprehensions of an immediate Rupture between the rival Chiefs of this Colony have been realised. Rigaud has actually commenced Hostilities and taken forcible Possession of *petit* and *grand Goave,* two Districts which formerly appertained to the Department of Toussaint. At the latter Place he is encamped with an Army of

[2] From "Letters of Toussaint Louverture and Edward Stevens, 1798–1800," *American Historical Review,* 26 (October 1910), 76–80, 93.

4000 Men. Toussaint is now at Leogane with 20,000. Rigaud's Army is well fed, well clothed, and well paid. The uninterrupted Trade he has carried on from the South with St. Thomas, the Continent of America, and The Island of Jamaica, has supplied him with Plenty of Provisions, Clotheing, and Ammunition. The arbitrary and oppressive Contributions he has levied from the Inhabitants of the South, and the Application of all the publick Revenue, for several Years past, to his own private Purposes, have given him a great Command of Money. His Infantry are well disciplined, and his Cavalry the best in the Colony. The former consists of black Troops that have served under him since the Commencement of the Revolution, and a few of the Cultivators whom he has deceived and induced to espouse his Cause, by Misrepresentation and Bribery. The latter is composed entirely of Mullattoes. These are the best Horsemen in the Colony. From Indolence and Pride these People seldom travel on foot, and being accustomed to ride from their Infancy, they acquire a Facility of managing a Horse, which renders them superior to the Negroes. Add to this that they are allways much better mounted.—Toussaint's Army, on the contrary, is in want of every Thing. He has but little Ammunition, and few Military Stores. There is not, at present, a Barrel of Flour or Salt Provisions in this Port of the Island, and his Troops are but indiffirently clad. All these Circumstances have induced him, hitherto, to remain on the defensive, and have enabled Rigaud to gain ground. He is only waiting for the Supplies he momently expects from Jamaica, to put his Forces in Motion and strike a vigorous Blow. When he commences his Operations the Contest will be but short. Toussaint has on *his* Side most of the Blacks, and all the Whites of the Colony. His humane and mild Conduct has render'd him respectable to the latter, and they now look up to him as their only Shield against the cruel Tyranny of Rigaud. When the latter had got Possession of Petit Goave, all the whites in Port au Prince rose in a Mass, and desired Permission to march against him; but Toussaint objected to it, observing that they had already suffered Misfortunes enough by the Revolution, and that he had Men enough to finish the Contest, and protect *them*, without subjecting them again to the Horrors of War. Besides this decided Support of the Inhabitants in his Favor, Toussaint acts *apparently* under the Sanction of the french Republic, while the other is considered as a Rebel and Outlaw. All the public Acts of the Agent are in favor of Toussaint, and hostile to his Rival. In this Line of Conduct will Roume continue as long as he is invested with any public Authority. The fact is, that he dare not do otherwise. He is, at present, no better than a dignified Prisoner at the Cape, from whence he is not permitted to depart. Possessing only the

Semblance of Power, he will be tolerated for a Time, as useful in signing such Edicts as Toussaint dictates, and giving an Appearance of
Legality to his Proceedings. As soon as Rigaud falls, Roume will be
sent off, and from that Moment the Power of the Directory will cease in
this Colony. I hinted to you, some Time ago, my suspicion that Rigaud
was privately supported by the french Government, from the cruel
Policy of weakening both Mullattoes and Negroes, by fomenting and
keeping up a Contest between them. Every Day confirms me more in
this Opinion, and I have now no doubt that the Agent is the secret and
diabolical Instrument employed by them for this Purpose. He certainly is privately in the Interests of Rigaud, and Toussaint seems well
acquainted with this Fact. . . .

The Causes that have brought on this Contest . . . may be partly
attributed to the Jealousy which naturally exists between two rival
Chiefs, whose Theatre of Acting is limited. The one *proud, haughty*
and *cruel,* and agitated by a restless Ambition, views with Impatience
a Negro at the Head of Affairs and in Possession of that Power, which
he thinks is due alone to his superior Talents. The other more mild
and humane thinks that the Interests of human Nature require this
Man to be deposed, and that the Authority he himself possesses is justly
merited by the Services he has render'd the Colony. Both wish to reign,
but by different means, and with different Views. Rigaud would del-
uge the Country with Blood to accomplish this favourite Point, and
slaughter indiscriminately whites, blacks, and even the leading Chiefs
of his own Colour. The Acquisition of Power, with him, is only desir-
able because it would enable him to indulge, without Restraint, his
cruel and sanguinary Passions. Toussaint, on the contrary, is desirous
of being confirmed in his Authority by the united Efforts of all the Inhabitants, whose Friend and Protector he wishes to be consider'd, and,
I am convinced, were his Power uncontroled he wd: exercise it in protecting Commerce, encouraging Agriculture and establishing useful
Regulations for the internal Government of the Colony.—'Tho' the
Dissension between these Chiefs is of an old Date, and Rigaud has been
long making Preparations to force the supreme Command from the
Hands of Toussaint, yet I do not imagine that the Explosion would
have taken place so soon, had it not been for the Circumstances that
have recently occurred. The Publication of Gen: Maitland's Treaty at
the Mole, and the many injudicious Paragraphs that were inserted in
the english Papers gave an Air of Plausibility to a Tale, which Rigaud
studiously propagated, that the Colony of St: Domingo was to be sold
to the british Government, and once more brought under the Yoke of
Slavery. But when the *Camilla* appeared off the Cape and British Offi-

cers were seen landing in their Uniform, even the Friends of Toussaint were stagger'd. . . . The secret Conferences of Gen: Maitland with Toussaint at Decataux, excited Suspicions in the Minds of the Cultivators, and added a Force to the Insinuations of his Enemies, which all the Efforts of his Friends were unable to resist. Rigaud triumphantly appeals to these Facts in a Declamation he lately published against Toussaint. Mutiny, Desertion and Treachery were the immediate Effects of Rigaud's Intrigues and Toussaint's unsuspicious Conduct. Several Bodys of his Troops deserted to the South, and a few subaltern Officers, whom he thought strongly attached to him, went off to his Rival. By vigorous and decided Measures, however, he quieted these Disturbances, and every Thing was reduced to order when the *Camilla* again made her Appearance at L'Arcahaye, where she has continued from the 11th: Inst: until this Day. The same Suspicions, the same Intrigues of his Enemies have been renewed, and 'tho' I believe Toussaint will again suppress them, yet you would scarcely credit the Mischief that has been done. This last Visit has thrown many Obstacles in the Way of Gen: Maitland's Negotiation, and prevented Toussaint from doing many things which he was well inclined to do, but which the critical Situation of his Affairs would not admit of. . . . My Efforts in favour of the british Interests will become more difficult, and my Situation be rendered more unpleasant. You may be assured, however, Sir, that I shall not omit any Thing that lays in my Power to promote the joint Interests of both Countries.

With respect to the Issue of the Contest between Toussaint and Rigaud, I own I am not apprehensive. As far as I can judge . . . as soon as the former has furnished his Army with what it wants and taken the Field, the latter must yield. Toussaint runs no Risk from open Force. He is too powerful. His only Danger is from internal Treason; but as he is now on his guard, and has taken every necessary Precaution to prevent it, I believe he is tolerably safe, even from that Hazard.

It will readily occur to you, Sir, that if Toussaint should prove unsuccessful, all the Arrangements we have made respecting Commerce must fall to the Ground. The most solemn Treaty would have little Weight with a Man of Rigaud's capricious and tyrannical Temper. This Circumstance points out the absolute Necessity of supporting Toussaint by every legal Measure, and it was this which induced me to consent to the small temporary Supply which he is to receive from Jamaica. I hope it will come in Time to serve him until the Ports are open'd, which I have given him every Reason to believe would be done on the Day appointed. I beg Leave here to repeat what I have already hinted in all my Letters, that it might be prudent to direct some of the American

Ships of War to cruise on the south Side of the Island, and about Jeremie, in order that they might cooperate with the British in cutting of all Supplies of Provision and Ammunition.

I am sorry to inform you that the present civil War will have a considerable Influence on the Agriculture of this Island, and diminish the Exports of the present Year not a little. The Cultivators began to be industrious, and the Expectation of selling their Produce, made them labour with alacrity; but a great many of them have of late been drafted for the Army. Most of the Horses, Mules, Oxen and Carts belonging to the different Plantations have also been put in Requisition. The Proprietors of Estates, therefore, can neither bring in the Produce which is already prepared for Market, nor prepare more.

Stevens to Pickering, Cap François, Feby. 13th, 1800

The political State of this Colony is approaching rapidly towards a very important Crisis. Even the nominal Power of the Agent and his Adherents is now nearly annihilated. The flying Artillery which has cost near half a Million of Dollars, and which was to have laid the flourishing Colony of Jamaica in Blood and Ashes, is disbanded. The Command of the Treasury and a control of the civil as well as military Departments has been openly assumed by the Genl: in Chief and his subordinate Officers. Every Thing announces a speedy Dissolution of those Ties, which once connected this important Colony with the Mother Country.

While I was uncertain of the real Intentions of *Toussaint,* I was loth to say any Thing to you about them. Now that I think I know them, it is my Duty to announce them to you. *He* is taking *his measures slowly* but *securely. All connection with France* will *soon* be *broken off. If he is not disturbed he will preserve appearances a little longer. But as soon as France interferes with this colony he will throw off the mask and declare it independent.*

RUFUS KING AND TIMOTHY PICKERING (1799)[3]

R. King to the Secretary of State, London, Jany. 10, 1799

The situation *of St. Domingo*[4] having on repeated consideration appeared to me to be likely materially to affect certain great interests *of the U.S.* and consequently to require of them a comprehensive as well as cautious Policy to protect those interests and to turn to profit if

---

[3] From Charles R. King, ed., *The Life and Correspondence of Rufus King* (New York, 1896), 2: 499–505, 557–58.
[4] Italics in cipher.

possible the changes *of which the Independence of Saint Domingo* is the forerunner, *I went* some days since *to Lord Grenville, and after* stating *to him my reflections* upon this subject, observed *that the principle motive that led me* to submit them *to him was in order to ascertain his opinion whether* it would not be of great *and mutual benefit that we should act in concert* as well in respect *to the present as the expected* condition of this *Important Island. He could best* decide the advantages and disadvantages *which they* were likely *to expect from the emancipation of that Colony. With regard to us we had to* apprehend some inconveniences *from the Influence of the example upon our slaves in the Southern States,* and it would be incumbent *upon us to pursue such measures as* should promise security *against,* and, if practicable, *effectually prevent the depredations and Piracy to be apprehended should St. Domingo become the Resort and Asylum of Buccaneers & rovers. We had* never attempted *to foment insurrections among our neighbours,* nor to persuade *the Colonies near us to throw off their allegiance; but we* should neglect what *we owe to ourselves,* if *in the present case* and in others which may be like it, *we did not adopt* such measures as should seem best calculated not only to render *them harmless,* but as far as possible to make *them beneficial to us.* What *those measures* would be, it was not possible *for me* to form an opinion; but that *they and we* should take care not to embarrass *each other,* and so disappoint *the views of both,* appeared *to me* very plain.

Ld. Grenville said that it seemed highly probable *that St. Domingo would become independent,* and *that he* entirely agreed in the *opinion I had* expressed in reference to the Policy and advantage *of a concert of* measures between *them and us.* At present *they had not* formed any distinct views on that head; the late engagements *of himself and colleagues in Parliament had* delayed the Business, *but they were then* engaged in the consideration *of the subject which* in a variety of lights *they considered* an important one; . . .

That they desired to secure *their colonies* from the influence *of the example of St. Domingo* and to prevent the existence of a new *Barbary power* in that *quarter of the world. They* moreover had it in view to propose *to Toussaint to put the Trade* upon such a footing as might afford *to him the supplies* that he should require, and at the same time guard against the mischiefs *that they and we desire to prevent: that he had* thought of an *exclusive company* composed jointly *of British and American subjects;* that the Idea had not been examined, and that as soon *as he had more* fully considered the subject, *he would* invite *me to meet him and his Colleagues* for the purpose of considering it. . . .

I asked Ld. [Lord] *Grenville if the Independence of St. Domingo must* not inevitably have a great influence *upon Jamaica and the other Islands? he* answered that certainly *it must; must it not be soon* followed, *notwithstanding all your viligance, by the abolition of the whole Colony System in that quarter of the world?* the *Colony System* must fall to the ground, *we have* foreseen it, and nothing remains but to *postpone it* as long as possible and to employ such measures as seem best adapted to diminish *the Evils of the event* when it arrives, and *I have no reserve,* added *his Ld.Ship,* in saying *that* in whatever *we do, we must act in Harmony with you.*

Last evening I received a letter from *Lord Grenville,* a copy of which and of the enclosed *Minute* are annexed, and according to *his Ld.Ship's* invitation I met *him and his Colleagues* this morning. *The Conference* began *by my* saying that before *I* made any observation *upon our present equivocal situation in regard to France,* or upon the division *of the Trade between us and them,* as proposed, I ought to express my belief *that the Plan* would be objected to as well on account of the general *unpopularity of monopolies in America,* as on the score of a defect *of power in Congress to* create an *Exclusive Corporation* for the Purposes *of Trade.* Such *a Power is* not expressly given, and if it exists must be taken by inference *from Powers* which are distinctly given. Questions of this sort are liable to much debate, and in this case would perhaps be opposed by some who might think *the Power* exists, but who dislike *monopolies.* Besides *our merchants are* numerous and full of enterprize, and no way has suggested itself by which a limited *number of them* could without undue preference be selected to compose a company. In respect to the proposed *Division of the trade between us and them, I said,* that the distinction *in the supplies* seemed plain and natural enough, but there *were articles supply'd to St. Domingo not of their manufacture nor of our production,* such as Wines, Brandies, nankeens & probably other commodities that did not occur, in respect to which *it might be agreed that such articles might be supplied by either.* In regard to *our situation with France* it is easier to say what it is not, than what it really is, & I could only express my hope that it might soon become less doubtful & better defined.

Mr. Pitt observed that it would be presumptuous *in a stranger* to give an opinion *on the Powers* given *to Congress by our Constitution,* wh. possibly were not as *large as we might* find to *our* advantage *that they should be,* but the *present case* was of great strength, and the mischiefs with which *we were menaced* were such that it wd. be singular indeed, if an adequate *Power* did not exist to guard against them. *Our Southern States* were open *to Emissaries of St. Domingo,* and perhaps all things considered it was not stating it too widely *to say that we had* as much or more *to apprehend* than *they had from St. Domingo becoming the Resort and Refuge of Buccaneers & Pirates. If the proposed project* affords a fair probability of preventing those Evils, it would be unfortunate that it should *fail from a defect of Power in Congress:* and perhaps *we* should think it expedient in that case to refer *the Plan to the* respective *States for their confirmation.* In respect to the *articles not of growth or manufacture of either,* it will, *said Mr. Pitt,* be best to divide *the supply between us in* some equitable and convenient manner, betraying *to my* apprehension, *a fear of an open competition.*

Ld. Grenville after making several observations explanatory *of the minute he had sent me, asked* what other *plan could* be devised that would be likely to avoid the objections *which I had suggested* and which would secure the principal *objects in view.*

I reply'd that if it should *turn out Congress had not the Power,* or were unwilling to erect an *exclusive Commercial Company, the Power, to form Treaties* and to regulate *Trade with foreign nations, were* expressly given, *and under them in the shape of Treaties and Laws, we could* establish such regulations *as our Interest and Safety, & those of our friends should require;* going upon the idea of the *entire Independence of St. Domingo, we and they might form Treaties with Toussaint, by* which it should be agreed *that the citizens of the United States and the subjects of G. Britain alone should trade to that Island. These Treaties might* contain such special stipulations relative to the particular *Ports of Trade—the coasting Vessels* to be employ'd *between these Ports—the supplies* which should or should not *be carried there—emigrations—*the suppression *of Privateers,* and all such other *points* as may suggest *themselves* upon a full consideration of the Question.

A Convention might likewise be made *between the United States and G. Britain* that should prescribe *the regulations* to be observed *by Each* in carrying *on the trade* which should be open *to all the subjects of the two* Countries. *This Convention to be valid when* Laws conforming *and providing for the execution of its stipulations sho'd be enacted by the Legislatures of both nations—*these regulations *might be as minute* and extensive *as the various objects to be attained* shou'd require.

Lord Grenville made several objections *to this Plan,* grounded upon the insecurity *there would be in enforcing the* observance of the requisite regulations *when the Trade should be* open to all *the People of the two Countries. Mr. Pitt appeared* less decided on this Point and agreed *as they all did in my* observation *that concert in this business between us and them,* was on many accounts *of the first importance* that if the best Plan was inconsistent *with concert, one* must be devised that will secure *this primary object* and as many others as possible; and that the more *liberal the terms* were in respect *to Toussaint,* the more advantageous the *connexion* would be to the *Inhabitants of St. Domingo,* and the less likely to be defeated by the instigation *of Emissaries. I asked* what probability there was *that Toussaint would agree to a Plan* that should leave *him but a* limited *Independence; Mr. Dundas reply'd* that taking *all their* information together, *he thought it* quite probable *that Toussaint would consent,* and with respect *to his* intentions *he had told one of their officers* lately *returned, that he would throw off the yoke of France, if he* could be supported.

It was remarked that something must be done *immediately. I replied that I could* see no objection *to Col. Grant's going* forward according *to their first* intention. *He might open the Plan to Toussaint and* state the difficulties likely to exist *against its* adoption *by the United States* —that whatever should be agreed upon *between Toussaint and G. Britain* should be open *for the accession of the United States,* and also *open to* such modifications *as should* enable *the U.S. to* become *a party in case they* decline or are *unable to agree to the* proposed *Plan* —that full information *should be given to the President thro' me,* as well as *by Ld. Grenville thro' Mr. Liston,* with the assurance *that G. Britain* desires *the cooperation of the U.S., and will agree* on such equitable *commercial stipulations,* as shall be compatible with the attainment *of the principal objects they have in view* in respect *to their Colonies. To this Ld. Grenville and his Colleagues assented and the conference* ended with the suggestion *that the President would think it* adviseable *to send some person to join Col. Grant* in settling the arrangements *with Toussaint.*

This is *a subject that merits* deliberate and extensive consideration. Whatever *we do, should be* done with a view as well to the present *Colony system,* as to future events still more important than the present. It is certain *that Great Britain* desires *to act with us, and we* may be sure *of her cooperation if we* will concur in *her Plans. She will* even risk something *to obtain our concurrence, but she* will act *without us* in case *we* disagree as to the terms of *a joint cooperation. We also* can act *without her* and should, *as she* undoubtedly does, balance the advantages & disadvantages *of a separate and a joint negotiation.*

T. Pickering to R. King, Philadelphia, March 12, 1799

Private and Confidential. In Cipher.

My public letter of this date will inform you of the Proceedings of our Government respecting St. Domingo. We meddle not with the politics of the Island. T[oussain]t will pursue what he deems the interest of himself and his countrymen; he will probably declare the Island independent. It is probable that he wished to assure himself of our commerce as the necessary means of obtaining it. Neither moral nor political reasons could induce us to discourage him; on the contrary both would warrent us in urging him to the Declaration. Yet we shall not do it. We go no further than the Act of Congress directs. We shall never receive from the French Republic indemnification for the injuries she has done us. The commerce of St. Domingo presents the only means of compensation, and this I have no doubt we shall obtain. We fear no rivals. Toussaint respects the British; he is attached to us; he knows our position, but a few days' sail from St. Domingo, and the proptitude with which we can supply his wants. He cannot form a black (Colony); the blacks are too ignorant. The Government must be military during the present war, and perhaps for a much longer period. The commerce of the United States and of other nations (for you will observe we aim at no exclusive privileges) will amply supply all their wants, and take off all their produce. So that there will not, and ought not to be, any inducements to withdraw the Blacks from the cultivation of the Island to navigation; and confined to their own Island they will not be dangerous neighbours. Nothing is more clear than, if left to themselves, that the Blacks of St. Domingo will be incomparably less dangerous than if they remain the subjects of France; she could then form with them military corps of such strength in a future war, as no European or other white force could resist. France with an army of those black troops might conquer all the British Isles and put in jeopardy our Southern States. Of this the Southern Members were convinced, and therefore cordially concurred in the policy of the Independence of St. D., if T[oussain]t and his followers will it. Mr. Read was the only exception to this opinion, and his opinions are sometimes unaccountable. Mr. Liston appears to be also equally convinced of the policy of that independence, as it would respect the British Isles. For as he observes, the radical evil is already done, and becomes irremediable, in France making the Blacks free. T[oussain]t will command 50 or 60,000 Black troops, if necessary; they are jealous of France, that she intends, if possible, to bring them back to their former slavery. This jealousy is incurable. We, therefore, confidently reckon on the Independence of St. Domingo. *Rigaud* is a subordinate chief, and a Mulatto. This race in the Island are but a handful, not above one eighth of the population of the Blacks, and must be crushed if they resist the will of T[oussain]t. . . .

9
Haitians React to Toussaint

The following three selections give the views of three Haitian contemporaries. The first is by Henri Christophe, one of Toussaint's ablest generals and later King of Haiti. In his account Christophe remains loyal to the memory of his chief but chastizes him for his pro-French, antiblack policies. Christophe's attitude is expanded by his official propagandist, the Baron de Vastey. Tormented by fears, characteristic of all Haitians in the years following the declaration of independence, of a new French attempt to recapture the colony, de Vastey's writings are violently antiwhite and anti-French. He argues that all civil and racial conflicts that have plagued his country were the results of white intrigues and machinations. Toussaint is condemned for allowing himself to be misled by white colonists and priests, who inflamed his ambitions and persuaded him to pass laws oppressive to his black brothers. The third selection is by Beaubrun Ardouin, a noted historian and politician, whose views reflect those of the liberal, western-oriented, mulatto class that has generally ruled Haiti after the death of Christophe. Ardouin, whose family suffered greatly as a result of Toussaint's war with Rigaud, severely criticizes the black leader for his ambition, his treatment of the people of color, and for failing to act in the "general interest of his race."

HENRI CHRISTOPHE [1]

Under the administration of Governor-General Toussaint L'Ouverture, Hayti arose from her ruins, and everything seemed to promise a happy future. The arrival of General Hédouville completely changed the aspect of affairs, and struck a deadly blow to public tranquillity. We will not enter into the detail of his intrigues with the Haytian General, Rigaud, whom he persuaded to revolt against the legitimate chief. We will only say, that before leaving the island, Hédouville had put everything into confusion, by casting among us the firebrands of discord, and lighting the torch of civil war.

[1] From Beard, *Toussaint L'Ouverture*, pp. 331–34.

Ever zealous for the reëstablishment of order and of peace, Toussaint L'Ouverture, by a paternal government, restored their original energy to law, morality, religion, education, and industry. Agriculture and commerce were flourishing; he was favorable to white colonists, especially to those who occupied new possessions; and the care and partiality which he felt for them went so far that he was severely censured as being more attached to them than to people of his own color. This negro wail was not without reason; for some months previous to the arrival of the French, he put to death his own nephew, General Moise, for having disregarded his orders relative to the protection of the colonists. This act of the Governor, and the great confidence which he had in the French Government, were the chief causes of the weak resistance which the French met with in Hayti. In reality, his confidence in that Government was so great, that the General had disbanded the greater part of the regular troops, and employed them in the cultivation of the ground.

Such was the state of affairs whilst the peace of Amiens was being negotiated; it was scarcely concluded, when a powerful armament landed on our coasts a large army, which, attacking us by surprise, when we thought ourselves perfectly secure, plunged us suddenly into an abyss of evils.

Posterity will find a difficulty in believing that, in so enlightened and philosophic an age, such an abominable enterprise could possibly have been conceived. In the midst of a civilized people, a horde of barbarians suddenly set out with the design of exterminating an innocent and peaceable nation, or at least of loading them anew with the chains of national slavery.

It was not enough that they employed violence; they also thought it necessary to use perfidy and villainy,—they were compelled to sow dissension among us. Every means was put in requisition to carry out this abominable scheme. The leaders of all political parties in France, even the sons of the Governor Toussaint, were invited to take part in the expedition. They, as well as ourselves, were deceived by that *chef-d'œuvre* of perfidy, the proclamation of the First Consul, in which he said to us, "You are all equal and free before God and the Republic;" such was his declaration, at the same time that his private instructions to General Leclerc were to reëstablish slavery.

The greater part of the population, deceived by these fallacious promises, and for a long time accustomed to consider itself as French, submitted without resistance. The Governor so little expected the appearance of an enemy that he had not even ordered his generals to resist in case of an attack being made; and, when the armament arrived, he himself was on a journey toward the eastern coast. If some few generals did resist, it was owing only to the hostile and menacing manner in which they were summoned to surrender, which compelled them to respect their duty, their honor, and the present circumstances.

After a resistance of some months, the Governor-General yielded to the pressing entreaties and the solemn protestations of Leclerc, "that he intended to protect the liberties of every one, and that France would never destroy so noble a work." On this footing, peace was negotiated with France; and the Governor Toussaint, laying aside his power, peaceably retired to the retreat he had prepared for himself.

Scarcely had the French extended their dominion over the whole island, and that more by roguery and deceit than by force of arms, than they began to put in execution their horrible system of slavery and destruction.

To hasten the accomplishment of their projects, mercenary and Machiavellian writers fabricated fictitious narratives, and attributed to Toussaint designs that he had never entertained. While he was remaining peaceably at home, on the faith of solemn treaties, he was seized, loaded with irons, dragged away with the whole of his family, and transported to France. The whole of Europe knows how he ended his unfortunate career in torture and in prayer, in the dungeon of the Château de Joux.

Such was the recompense reserved for his attachment to France, and for the eminent services he had rendered to the colony.

BARON POMPÉE DE VASTEY [2]

The first civil war was produced by the ambition of Rigaud: and the second, which was only the reaction of the former, by that of Pétion. Both of these Generals were merely the instruments employed by the French to divide and destroy us.

In this war, destructive to the Haytians, and profitable only to the Whites, these last sided, *some* with General Toussaint, and *others* with General Rigaud. On both sides they were the warmest advocates for civil war, and the most zealous promoters of massacre and carnage. Incalculable were the mischiefs resulting from their perfidious councils. . . .

After Rigaud's departure the WHITES, both *Royalists and Republicans, Great Planters,* and *Inferior Whites,* all rallied around General Toussaint. Rigaud failed in overthrowing Toussaint, as Hédouville

[2] From Baron Pompée de Vastey, *An Essay on the Causes of the Revolutions and Civil Wars of Hayti* (Exeter, 1823), pp. 24–27.

had proposed; the Ex-colonists took other means to accomplish this end: aided by the non-conformist (*non-concordatistes*) priests who swayed the mind of General Toussaint, they surrounded this unfortunate chieftain, lavishing upon him the most sumptuous entertainments, and the basest flattery. He was a second Spartacus, the illustrious hero predicted by the Abbé Raynal, and at the same moment they were both in France and in the country plotting fresh contrivances for his destruction.

To accomplish their perfidious projects, they recommended to General Toussaint the establishment of a system of police nearly as rigorous as that of the ancient regíme, in order thus to alienate from him the affections of the Blacks. They led him to sacrifice his own nephew, Gen. Moyse, upon the pretext of a conspiracy against the Whites. They suggested to him the formation of a Constitution which should render Hayti *nearly* independent of France; which he should have done completely or not at all; for such a measure admitted of no medium: it was necessary to be either *dependent* or *independent,* the one or the other; and Gen. Toussaint, by rendering himself partially independent of France, exposed himself to her vengeance, without giving himself the means of resisting her. The Ex-colonists likewise suggested to him the idea of granting furloughs to a large part of the troops in order to send them back to agricultural pursuits. Nay, they went still further, and carried their assurance to the extent of persuading him to repair and improve the roads, so as to facilitate the transportation of artillery and the march of the French troops. Thus, while really adopting the most erroneous measures, the unfortunate Toussaint believed he was only promoting the welfare of his brethren and country: a mistake of which he was but too clearly convinced.

Whilst the ex-colonists were thus paving the way within the country for Gen. Toussaint's downfall, those who were in France, were busied in exerting their influence with Bonaparte; whom they supplied with pecuniary aid, and gave him those perfidious counsels, which speedily brought upon us the expedition under the command of Leclerc.

Then all joined against the unfortunate Toussaint. *White Royalists, White Republicans, Great Planters* and *Inferior Whites, Lawyers, Conformist* and *Nonconformists Priests* . . . all were now *for once* unanimous: the cause was common; *the Restoration of Slavery or the extermination of the Blacks,* was the question at issue: and upon such a subject no diversity of opinion could prevail.

And *we* too—infatuated that we were! how did *we* act? We rushed in crowds with frantic impatience to meet the iron yoke prepared for our necks.

We are French, said they:—France had bestowed freedom upon us:—France could not now bring us new fetters, after having burst the old: the mere suspicion was criminal:—the mention of it unpardonable.

The whole of the Department of the South submitted without firing a shot. This was one of the consequences of the war of Rigaud. Men of Colour and Blacks, both those who had been originally free, and those whom the Revolution had enfranchised, were to be seen hastening in crowds to throw themselves into the arms of the French, of *their brethren before God and before* the *Republic*. Never was conquest more easy: hardly did a twentieth part of the population oppose a feeble resistance. . . .

BEAUBRUN ARDOUIN [3]

To our mind, Toussaint Louverture not only had been struck by the hand of man, he had been struck especially by the hand of that divine Providence whose sacred laws he had so often ignored. . . . [Providence] desired that [Toussaint] expiate in a dungeon all his wrongs, all the crimes he had committed while all-powerful, in order to present an example to his contemporaries, to posterity. . . .

Let us cast a retrospective glance over the career of Toussaint Louverture in order to examine whether he observed the moral and religious precepts which he so constantly made use of as a window dressing before the eyes of the multitude to better control it and to assure the success of his views against his opponents.

Did this man, whom nature had endowed with incontestable talents, a true genius whom the circumstances of the times so favored, did he really follow *the best methods* to attain the high position that he occupied in his country? We say *no*, for to our eyes *success does not suffice* to legitimate the march of a man toward supreme power; it will not justify the *means* employed by such a man if they are visibly in disagreement with moral principles. . . . *The base of politics or social art must be honesty and justice*. . . . Let us apply these principles to the political life of Toussaint Louverture.

The unhappy condition into which he was born—that of slavery imposed on the black race by the white—required, so to speak, some natural vices; among them dissimulation held the first rank because of the servitude of the slave toward his master. Toussaint Louverture had been taught to read and write by his godfather, Pierre Baptiste, a black of Haut-du-Cap, who had been educated by the Jesuits. . . . It ap-

[3] From Beaubrun Ardouin, *Études sur l'histoire d'Haiti*, 6 vols. (Paris, 1853), 5: 50–51; trans. George F. Tyson, Jr.

pears that the neophyte acquired that for which the Jesuits have always been reproached—*a consummate hypocrisy* that affects the appearance of religion and devotion in order to better conceal its views.

Who better than Toussaint Louverture combined *dissimulation* and *hypocrisy?* These vices were undoubtedly the effect of his condition and his education before the revolution.

The revolution erupted in St. Domingue, and it is to this man, forty-eight years of age, knowing how to read and write imperfectly, already possessing an experience acquired by the attention that his pensive spirit gave to the daily conversations of the counter-revolutionary nobles under his master's roof; it is to him that they addressed themselves in order to circulate counter-revolutionary views among the slaves. It was at that time that his *political* education commenced . . . We have already seen . . . how he then disseminated these ideas among the slaves in order to realize the plan of the counter-revolutionaries of whom he was the chief agent.

It is to this plan, executed with uncommon audacity and resolution, that we must attribute his downfall. It is evident that the political organization of his government and, above all, the misuse of his authorized power, was so contradictory *to the real interests of the black race* as to arouse the invincible repugnance of his brothers. . . . On the other hand, this *organization,* and not the *misuse* of his authority, was so contrary to the *sovereignty* of France as to attract to his head the thunder hurled by the consular government when circumstances were favorable. Without the support of the black race which he had violated he had to succumb in this struggle.

We have already identified all the *vices* and *virtues* which distinguished Toussaint Louverture. His vices were: dissimulation, hypocrisy, cunning, deceit, machiavellianism, vanity, pride, suspicion, egotism. His virtues were: audacity, energy, resolution, firmness, love of order, prodigious activity, an insatiable ambition which was the height of his genius. . . .

Nevertheless, if we have identified the mistakes he committed, the wrongs he did, if we have tarnished his crimes, let us still remember what his passage in power left that was *good and remarkable* in his country. Aren't the people compelled to accept almost all their governors as a composite of good and evil? Where is the perfect man found?

Toussaint Louverture bequeathed to his country a military organization and a civil, financial, and judicial administration that have been conserved almost completely by the various governments that have succeeded his. . . . Without a doubt, all these institutions were derived from those of France, but he applied them with intelligence.

As an enlightened man, he made his brothers understand that although they descended from Africans and must honor that origin, they must also free themselves from all their coarser superstitions, notably *Voodoo,* because even if they had lived in the deepest ignorance in Africa that was no reason to adopt beliefs that degrade and brutalize man and only bring him scorn. By making the cult of the true God prevail over these ridiculous beliefs, in honoring the Christian religion, which, unhappily, he himself didn't observe sufficiently, he indicated to them, nevertheless, that it is through Christianity that they will attain a social state in conformity with the civilization of the Old World.

In forcing his brothers to work by measures of too much severity, he wanted them to learn that the obligation imposed upon man by his needs is one of the most essential means of prosperity, stability, order, and liberty that the people can practice in order to avoid wallowing in barbarism. Elsewhere, these measures have incurred our lively reproaches; we will uphold them while acknowledging that his wrongs may be attenuated in consideration of the influence his age exercised over his ideas, of the influence of the despotic education that he received, . . . and especially of the demoralized state in which he found the population *at that time,* also, by the revolutions, the incessant agitations, and the vicious habits he had acquired as a brigand. . . .

While on this subject, let us not forget, not to *justify* or even *excuse,* but *to explain the cruel acts* of Toussaint Louverture's domination, the example exercised over the revolutionaries of St. Domingue by those who led the French Revolution in the fatal and horrible period of the Terror. With this spirit of emulation that he will display next by modeling himself in certain respects after the person of the First Consul (since many of the colonists had persuaded him that he was the Bonaparte of St. Domingue), he was allowed to believe what he himself imagined, that he had to adopt the cruel system of the Terrorists in order to overcome all resistance and reestablish order and tranquillity in the colony. Since he had reconciled these ideas to those making up his naturally despotic character, it is not astonishing that he abused his power.

Finally, his war with France (caused by his arrogance and in order to conserve his position) served as an example to the men of his race to undertake a war which would deliver them from their bondage. In this he rendered an immense service to his country. Even by becoming a victim of his task of reconstructing the old colonial order, he served it, for he was sacrificed by France. The injustice France committed against him in consideration of what he had accomplished for her and her colonists, his agony, his sadness would finally contribute to enlighten his brothers as to the course they had to take up. Henceforth, they knew they could no longer count upon the good feelings of the mother country, that a struggle to the death yawned between them, and that in order to preserve their liberty it was necessary to free themselves completely from France's domination.

10
Romantics React to Toussaint

The story of Toussaint has always appealed to the literary and poetic imagination. Lamartine wrote a major play about his life, Harriet Martineau a three-volume novel. The romantics, always fascinated by the tragedy of great men locked in a titanic struggle with vast impersonal forces, were quite naturally attracted to Toussaint. Two famous poems, one by an Englishman, the other by an American, each associated with the romantic movement in his respective country, are reprinted below. William Wordsworth's sonnet, written after Toussaint's arrest and imprisonment, urges the ex-slave to find solace in his immortality, while the lengthier work of John Greenleaf Whittier reflects this great Quaker's involvement in the abolitionist crusade.

WILLIAM WORDSWORTH [1]

Toussaint, the most unhappy man of men!
Whether the whistling rustic tends his plough
Within thy hearing, or thy head be now
Pillowed in some deep dungeon's earless den;
Oh, miserable chieftain! where and when
Wilt thou find patience? Yet die not: do thou
Wear rather in thy bonds a cheerful brow;
Though fallen thyself, never to rise again,
Live and take comfort. Thou hast left behind
Powers that work for thee: air, earth, and skies.
There's not a breathing of the common wind
That will forget thee: thou hast great allies:
Thy friends are exultations, agonies,
And love, and man's unconquerable mind.

JOHN GREENLEAF WHITTIER [2]

'Twas night. The tranquil moonlight smile
With which Heaven dreams of Earth shed down
Its beauty on the Indian isle,—
    On broad green field and white-walled town;

[1] From Beard, *Toussaint L'Ouverture*, p. 346.
[2] From Beard, *Toussaint L'Ouverture*, pp. 358–65.

And inland waste of rock and wood,
In searching sunshine, wild and rude,
Rose, mellowed through the silver gleam,
Soft as the landscape of a dream,
All motionless and dewy wet,
Tree, vine, and flower in shadow net:
The myrtle with its snowy bloom,
Crossing the nightshade's solemn gloom,—
The white cecropia's silver rind
Relieved by deeper green behind,—
The orange with its fruit of gold,—
The lithe paullinia's verdant fold,—
The passion-flower, with symbol holy,
Twining its tendrils long and lowly,—
The rhexias dark, and cassia tall,
And proudly rising over all,
The kingly palm's imperial stem,
Crowned with its leafy diadem,
Star-like, beneath whose sombre shade,
The fiery-winged cucullo played!
Yes,—lovelier was thine aspect, then,
    Fair island of the Western Sea!
Lavish of beauty, even when
Thy brutes were happier than thy men,
    For they, at least, were free!
Regardless of thy glorious clime,
    Unmindful of thy soil of flowers,
The wasting negro sighed, that Time
    No faster sped his hours;
For by the dewy moonlight still
He fed the weary-turning mill,
Or bent him, in the chill morass,
To pluck the long and tangled grass,
And hear above his scar-worn back
The heavy slave-whip's frequent crack;
While in his heart one evil thought
In solitary madness wrought,—
One baleful fire surviving still
    The quenching of the immortal mind,—
    One sterner passion of his kind,
Which even fetters could not kill,—
The savage hope, to deal, erelong,
A vengeance bitterer than his wrong!

Hark to that cry!—long, loud and shrill,
From field and forest, rock and hill,

Thrilling horrible it rang,
  Around, beneath, above;—
The wild beast from his cavern sprang,—
  The wild bird from her grove!
Nor fear, nor joy, nor agony
Were mingled in that midnight cry;
But, like the lion's growl of wrath,
When falls that hunter in his path,
Whose barbèd arrow, deeply set,
Is rankling in his bosom yet,
It told of hate, deep, full, and strong,—
Of vengeance kindling out of wrong;
It was as if the crimes of years,—
The unrequited toil,—the tears,
The shame, and hate, which liken well
Earth's garden to the nether hell,—
Had found in Nature's self a tongue,
On which the gathered horror hung;
As if, from cliff and stream and glen,
Burst on the startled ears of men
That voice which rises unto God,
Solemn and stern,—the cry of blood!
It ceased; and all was still once more,
Save ocean chafing on his shore,
The sighing of the wind between
The broad banana's leaves of green,
Or bough by restless plumage shook,
Or murmuring voice of mountain brook.

Brief was the silence. Once again
  Pealed to the skies that frantic yell,—
Glowed on the heavens a fiery stain,
  And flashes rose and fell;
And, painted on the blood-red sky,
Dark, naked arms were tossed on high;
And, round the white man's lordly hall
  Trode, fierce and free, *the brute he made;*
And those who crept along the wall,
And answered to his highest call,
  With more than spaniel dread,—
The creatures of his lawless beck,—
Were trampling on his very neck!
And on the night-air, wild and clear,
Rose woman's shriek of more than fear;
For bloodied arms were round her thrown
And dark cheeks pressed against her own!

Then, injured Afric!—for the shame
Of thy own daughters, vengeance came
Full on the scornful hearts of those
Who mocked thee in thy nameless woes,
And tho thy hapless children gave
One choice,—pollution, or the grave!
Where then was he whose fiery zeal
Had taught the trampled heart to feel,
Until Despair itself grew strong,
And Vengeance fed its torch from wrong?
Now,—when the thunderbolt is speeding;
Now,—when oppression's heart is bleeding;
Now,—when the latent curse of Time
   Is raining down in fire and blood,—
That curse, which, through long years of crime,
   Has gathered, drop by drop, its flood,—
Why strikes he not, the foremost one,
Where murder's sternest deeds are done?

He stood the aged palms beneath,
   That shadowed o'er his humble door,
Listening, with half-suspended breath,
To the wild sounds of fear and death,—
   Toussaint L'Ouverture!
What marvel that his heart beat high!
   The blow for freedom had been given;
And blood had answered to the cry
   That earth sent up to Heaven!
What marvel that a fierce delight
Smiled grimly o'er his brow of night,
As groan and shout and bursting flame
Told where the midnight tempest came,
With blood and fire along its van,
And death behind!—he was a man!

Yes, dark-souled chieftain!—if the light
   Of mild Religion's heavenly ray
Unveiled not to thy mental sight
   The lowlier and the purer way,
In which the Holy Sufferer trod
   Meekly amidst the sons of crime,—
That calm reliance upon God
   For justice, in his own good time,—
That gentleness to which belongs
   Forgiveness for its many wrongs,
Even as the primal martyr, kneeling

For mercy on the evil-dealing,—
Let not the favored white man name
Thy stern appeal with words of blame.
Has *he* not, with the light of heaven
   Broadly around him, made the same,
Yea, on his thousand war-fields striven,
   And gloried in his ghastly shame?—
Kneeling amidst his brother's blood,
To offer mockery unto God,
   As if the High and Holy One
   Could smile on deeds of murder done!—
As if a human sacrifice
Were purer in His holy eyes,
Though offered up by Christian hands,
Than the lone rites of Pagan lands!

         *   *   *

Sternly, amidst his household band,
His carbine clasped within his hand,
   The white man stood, prepared and still,
Waiting the shock of maddened men,
Unchained and fierce as tigers when
   The horn winds through their caverned hill;
And one was weeping in his sight,—
   The sweetest flower of all the isle,—
The bride who seemed but yesternight
   Love's fair embodied smile,
And, clinging to her trembling knee,
Looked up the form of infancy,
With tearful glance in either face,
The secret of its fear to trace.

"Ha,—stand or die!" The white man's eye
   His steady musket gleamed along,
As a tall negro hastened nigh,
   With fearless step and strong.
"What, ho, Toussaint!" A moment more,
His shadow crossed the lighted floor.
"Away," he shouted; "fly with me;
The white man's bark is on the sea;
Her sails must catch the seaward wind,
For sudden vengeance sweeps behind.
Our brethren from their graves have spoken,
The yoke is spurned, the chain is broken;
On all the hills our fires are glowing,
Through all the vales red blood is flowing!

No more the mocking White shall rest
His foot upon the Negro's breast;
No more, at morn or eve, shall drip
The warm blood from the driver's whip;
Yet, though Toussaint has vengeance sworn,
For all the wrongs his race have borne,—
Though for each drop of Negro blood
The white man's veins shall pour a flood;
Not all alone the sense of ill
Around his heart is lingering still,
Nor deeper can the white man feel
The generous warmth of grateful zeal.
Friends of the Negro! fly with me,—
The path is open to the sea;
Away for life!"—He spoke, and pressed
The young child to his manly breast,
As, headlong, through the crackling cane,
Down swept the dark insurgent train,—
Drunken and grim, with shout and yell
Howled through the dark, like sounds from Hell!

Far out in peace the white man's sail
Swayed free before the sunrise gale.
Cloud-like that island hung afar
   Along the bright horizon's verge,
O'er which the curse of servile war
   Rolled its red torrent, surge on surge.
And he,—the Negro champion—where
   In the fierce tumult, struggled he?
Go trace him by the fiery glare
Of dwellings in the midnight air,
The yells of triumph and despair,
   The streams that crimson to the sea!

Sleep calmly in thy dungeon-tomb,
   Beneath Bensaçon's alien sky,
Dark Haytian!—for the time shall come,
   Yea, even now is nigh,
When everywhere thy name shall be
Redeemed from color's infamy;
And men shall learn to speak of thee,
As one of earth's great spirits born
In servitude and nursed in scorn,
Casting aside the weary weight
And fetters of its low estate,
In that strong majesty of soul

Which knows no color, tongue, or clime,
Which still hath spurned the base control
    Of tyrants through all time!
For other hands than mine may wreathe
The laurel round thy brow of death,
And speak thy praise as one whose word
A thousand fiery spirits stirred,—
Who crushed his foeman as a worm,
Whose step in human hearts fell firm:
Be mine the better task to find
A tribute for thy lofty mind,
Amidst whose gloomy vengeance shone
Some milder virtues all thine own,—
Some gleams of feelings, pure and warm,
Like sunshine on a sky of storm,—
Proof that the Negro's heart retains
Some nobleness amidst its chains,
That kindness to the wronged is never
    Without its excellent reward,—
Holy to humankind, and ever
    Acceptable to God.

PART THREE

TOUSSAINT IN HISTORY

11
The Abolitionists

The following selections by four leading figures in the abolitionist movements of England, France, and the United States demonstrate the highly favorable reaction of the generality of abolitionists to Toussaint. In part, this was because the ex-slave's intelligence and achievements validated the abolitionist argument that blacks were capable of becoming the equals of whites under conditions of freedom. But in part their uncritical enthusiasm was due to their eagerness to dodge the explosive questions of the objectives and tactics of liberation raised by the Haitian Revolution. For abolitionists everywhere were determined that emancipation should come peacefully, as a gift from above, rather than as a revolution from below. Moreover, the successful rebellion of the slaves had dealt a devastating blow to the incipient abolitionist movements in England, France, and, particularly, the United States. And subsequent Negro rule in Haiti frequently proved an embarassment. Toussaint offered a way out of this dilemma. He could be counterpointed against the ignorant savagery of the black masses and the incompetency of the rulers of independent Haiti. In their studies, therefore, abolitionists took great pains to disassociate Toussaint from the bloody excesses of his black brothers at the beginning of the revolt, while emphasizing his devotion to his white master. Nor did they find fault with the authoritarian features of his government. His loss of contact with the masses was considered a point in his favor. Finally, Toussaint's unwavering loyalty to France suggested that he recognized that his race could not progress without the assistance and guidance of sympathetic white men. Clearly then, Toussaint had a great appeal to the elitist and conservative tendencies in abolitionist thought. Furthermore, a homily on the greatness of the black leader enabled the writer to eschew critical analysis, while still scoring a propaganda point about the Haitian Revolution. Toussaint's rule was effusively praised for its wisdom and moderation, his character for its religiousness (Christian, of course), loyalty, dedication, honesty, gratitude, and humanity.

*The exaggeration of Toussaint's virtues for propagandistic
reasons is apparent in the piece by James Stephen, a prominent
English abolitionist. The observation of Wylie Sypher about
Stephen's biography—that in it Toussaint becomes the incarna-
tion of the Oroonoko legend of the westernized, white/black
man that had pervaded European consciousness since the 17th
century—holds true of most abolitionist literature about Toussaint. Written in 1802, when Stephen was urging the English
government to support Toussaint against the French, the biography was reissued in 1814 in an effort to persuade Czar Alexander I of Russia to aid the antislavery cause at the Congress of
Vienna. Stephen initially sought to compare a virtuous Toussaint
to a wicked Bonaparte, but in the later edition he seeks to have
Alexander identify with Toussaint as a man who also coura-
geously defied the French Emperor. The next two selections are
by American abolitionists: Wendell Phillips from a speech made
in December 1861 and Rev. John R. Beard from his 1863 biography. In both, Toussaint becomes a paradigm of the ideal black
man with Phillips stressing his "courage, purpose and endurance"
while Beard glorifies his Christianity. The final reading is by the
foremost French abolitionist, Victor Schoelcher. Schoelcher has
been called "a superior breed of abolitionist," and the validity of
this observation can be found in his biography of Toussaint. Although his study catalogues the standard set of virtues, it is a
serious attempt to present a complete portrait of the man, thereby
reflecting Schoelcher's deep concern with the colonized peoples
themselves as well as with abstract principles of morality. Schoelcher quotes at length from Toussaint, his contemporaries, and
official documents. A true French liberal, he sees Toussaint as
an essentially good man corrupted by too much power and ambition. This failing he attributes to the dehumanizing nature of his
slave experience rather than to changing historical circumstances
or any inherent racial characteristic.** *

JAMES STEPHEN [1]

To: His Imperial Majesty Alexander, Emperor of All the Russias

That illustrious African well deserved the exalted names of Christian, Patriot, and Hero. He was a devout worshipper of his God, and
a successful defender of his invaded country. He was the victorious

---

* For the reaction of black abolitionists, see the following section, pp. 137–47.

[1] From [James Stephen], *The History of Toussaint Louverture* (London, 1814), pp.
iii–v, 1–2, 6–9, 15–20.

enemy, at once, and the contrast of Napoleon Buonaparte, whose arms he repelled, and whose pride he humbled, not more by the strength of his military genius, than by the moral influence of his amiable and virtuous character: by how many ties, then, of kindred merit and generous sympathy must he not be endeared to the magnanimous Liberator of Europe!

In nothing, however, will your Imperial Majesty more sympathize with the brave Toussaint, than in his attachment to the great cause in which he fell—the cause, not of his country only, but of his race; not merely of St. Domingo, but of the African continent.

How would it have cheered the gloom of that solitary dungeon in which this great man resigned his gallant spirit, had he been assured that an arm more powerful than his own would shortly vindicate on his oppressor, the rights of suffering humanity! But could he also have foreseen that with that arm would be found a heart, the seat of every generous affection, a soul ennobled by every elevated sentiment, the unhappy hero would perhaps have lost the remembrance of all his sorrows, while he indulged the animating hope now cherished by every friend to the same sacred cause—the hope that Alexander, the great and the good, having been guided by Providence to restore freedom, justice and peace to one Continent, may, through his powerful influence, soon dispense the same blessings to another. . . .

We have no distinct account of the conduct of Toussaint while a slave, but may safely conclude that he was sober, honest, humble, and industrious, because it is certain that he was a favorite with his master, which without possessing those good qualities, especially the two latter, in a high degree, no slave could possibly become. It is also pretty certain that he was a good husband, and a good father; for it appears that he had, in opposition to the relaxed system of morality prevalent in that country, early joined himself to one woman, by whom he had several children, the objects of his tender affection; and we shall find that the mother continued to live with him when they were both advanced in years, and to share with him all the dangers and hardships of war, down to the time when he fell into the hands of his treacherous and bloody enemies, and was sent to perish in one of Buonaparte's dungeons.

Toussaint, by the uncommon kindness of his master, or as some say, by his own unassisted pains, learned to read and write; and it appears from his letters and other writings, as well as from his wise conduct, that he made good use of these talents. He probably owed to them in a great measure, the power which he afterwards obtained over the minds of his poor ignorant countrymen; and this, when we find to what good purposes he used his power, will seem an instance of God's gracious providence; for not one Negro slave in ten thousand has the same advantage.

This great man was also prepared for public life by a good quality more important than all others put together: he was a devout man, and a sincere disciple of Christ. . . .

Toussaint first rose to notice when the fury of the struggle between master and slave was over; and his first labours were to protect the white people, who were now in their turn the feeble and oppressed party, from the revenge of his brethren. During the first troubles of the island, our hero appears to have remained quietly at home in his master's service. Perhaps he expected a peaceable change of the state of his brethren from the French Convention; or perhaps he was too pious and humane to join in the means by which the rest broke the galling chains of their private bondage, though he might see no other way of deliverance. Certain it is, that he was no enemy to the grand cause of general freedom; as might be proved, not only from the great sacrifices he has since made to it, but from the confidence that was soon after reposed in him by the Negroes at large. It is probable that he was led to remain so long inactive in the war, not only from the mildness and piety of his disposition, but from affection and gratitude to his master; and that these motives being generally known, helped, as virtue will always do in the main, to gain him confidence and support when he entered on public life. . . .

On our hero's first rising to power among the Negroes, he gave to this master one very pleasing earnest of his future character, which it would be wrong to pass over in slience. The white people, especially the planters, were so odious, both from their former tyranny, and the blood they had cruelly shed in the struggle to preserve their power, that the Negroes, when they gained the ascendant, were disposed to give them no quarter, and happy were those among them who could escape from the island, though it were to go with their families into a foreign country without any means of subsistence. The master of Toussaint, now his master no more, was one of the unfortunate planters who, not having escaped in good time, was on the point of falling into the hands of the enraged Negroes, and would in that event certainly have been put to death; but his former kindness to Toussaint was not forgotten. Our hero, at the great risk of bringing the vengeance of the multitude on his own head, delivered his unhappy master privately out of their hands, and sent him on board a ship bound for America, then lying in the harbour. Nor was this all; he was not sent away without the means of subsistence; for this brave and generous Negro found means to put on board secretly for his use a great many hogsheads of sugar, in order to support him in his exile till the same grateful hands should be able to send him a larger supply.

Let this story redden the cheeks of those, who are wicked and foolish enough to say that Negroes have no gratitude. Small is the debt of gratitude which their best treatment under the iron yoke of West India slavery can create; but a noble mind will not scrupulously weigh the claims of gratitude or mercy. Toussaint looked less at the wrong of keeping him in a brutal slavery, than to the kindness which had lightened his chain: . . .

Toussaint seems to have risen by degrees till he came to the chief command, by the growing love and esteem of the people, founded on his good qualities, which unfolded themselves more and more as his power increased. He did not flatter the common people, or encourage them in their crimes, like *Boukmant, Biassou,* and the rest of their leaders.

These chiefs, who were always urging them to revenge and slaughter, and telling them, perhaps, that their freedom was in danger so long as a White Man was suffered to live in the island, appeared at first to be their truest friends; but Toussaint, who was always trying to teach them mercy, industry, and order, was ultimately found to be the man they could best depend upon; and happy had it been for them had they always followed his councils. . . .

But events arose, which made it impossible for Toussaint, as a wise man and a true patriot, longer to refuse his adherence to the existing government of France. The cause of royalty having failed in that country, little could be done to serve the royal family by prolonging the miseries of civil war in a West India Island, while the great stake of Negro liberty might be lost by further opposition to the parent state. It was probably a deciding consideration with our hero, that the Planters and Loyalists of St. Domingo, with whom he was now allied, began openly to intrigue for the assistance of Great Britain, and to invite us to invade the island; for their object, however friendly to French royalty, was certainly adverse to Negro freedom; and it was less for the sake of restoring the sceptre of France to the Bourbons, than for that of recovering the iron sceptres of their own plantations, that most of these men desired to have the British flag flying at St. Domingo —they were staunch royalists then for the same reason that makes them now staunch friends to a Corsican usurper. Toussaint knew this, and saw that he must either make terms with the French commissioners, or engage himself on the same side with foreign invaders, and with Frenchmen who were sworn foes to the liberty of his race. For these and other reasons he found it necessary to give peace to the republican party whom he had already conquered, and to acknowledge the authority of the Convention.

From this time he was a faithful servant of France during every change in its government, though often molested and embarrassed in his plans for the public good by the folly and wickedness of the persons in authority in the mother country. . . .

It was a great mercy to many unfortunate white people who remained on the island, that a man like Toussaint possessed the chief power. He protected them from being massacred, and restored them to the property of which they had been deprived. When he found himself strong enough, and so well known to his followers as not to be afraid of slander, he even invited the banished planters to return from America, and other places to which they had fled for refuge; and such of them as returned, were restored by him to their estates. . . .

And here I must notice the greatest difficulty which Toussaint had to struggle with in his labours for the public good. The cruel and brutal method of driving, naturally makes the poor negroes regard their agricultural work with incurable dislike. Toussaint took unwearied pains to remove this difficulty, and to restore the tillage of the soil, upon which, under God, he knew that the happiness of every country chiefly depends. To this end, he encouraged the labourers by giving them a third part of the crops for their wages; a large compensation, in a country where sugar and coffee are the chief productions. He also made laws to restrain idleness, and oblige people to labour upon fair terms for their own livelihood; and to enforce these laws, he made use of his power as a general.

Some people have found fault with him, because he did not employ the civil power for this purpose, instead of the military; but in truth he had no civil power to employ. People in this happy land are apt to forget, that laws, and magistrates, and courts of justice, all exactly fitted to produce peace, order and public happiness, with the utmost possible regard to the liberty of the subject, are blessings that grow with the oak, and not with the mushroom. Human wisdom can no more make them on a sudden, or renew them in a moment when madly destroyed, than it can raise a tall tree in a single night from an acorn. As to Toussaint and his Negroes, they had every thing which belongs to civil life, to learn. In their former state they could know nothing of it; for a slave has no country; the breath of his master is his law, and the overseer is both judge and jury: the driver is both constable and beadle, as well as car[t]man, to the human cattle. During the war, there was no place for any but military institutions, and Toussaint therefore, when it was necessary to enforce laws for the public good, had no officers of civil justice to whom he could resort.

WENDELL PHILLIPS [2]

Ladies and gentlemen: I have been requested to offer you a sketch, . . . of one of the most remarkable men of the last generation, —the great St. Domingo chief, Toussaint l'Ouverture, an unmixed negro, with no drop of white blood in his veins. My sketch is at once a biography and an argument,—a biography, . . . of a negro soldier and statesman, which I offer you as an argument in behalf of the race from which he sprang. I am about to compare and weigh races; indeed, I am engaged tonight in what you will think the absurd effort to convince you that the negro race, instead of being that object of pity or contempt which we usually consider it, is entitled, judged by the facts of history, to a place close by the side of the Saxon. . . .

In the hour you lend me to-night, I attempt the Quixotic effort to convince you that the negro blood, instead of standing at the bottom of the list, is entitled, if judged either by its great men or its masses, either by its courage, its purpose, or its endurance, to a place as near ours as any other blood known in history. . . .

Some doubt the courage of the negro. Go to Hayti, and stand on those fifty thousand graves of the best soldiers France ever had, and ask them what they think of the negro's sword. And if that does not satisfy you, go to France, to the splendid mausoleum of the Counts of Rochambeau, and to the eight thousand graves of Frenchmen who skulked home under the English flag, and ask them. And if that does not satisfy you, come home, and if it had been October, 1859, you might have come by way of quaking Virginia, and asked her what she thought of negro courage.

You may also remember this,—that we Saxons were slaves about four hundred years, sold with the land, and our fathers never raised a finger to end that slavery. They waited till Christianity and civilization, till commerce and the discovery of America, melted away their chains. Spartacus in Italy led the slaves of Rome against the Empress of the world. She murdered him, and crucified them. There never was a slave rebellion successful but once, and that was in St. Domingo. Every race has been, some time or other, in chains. But there never was a race that,

[2] From Wendell Phillips, *Speeches, Lectures, and Letters* (New York, 1884); reprinted by Greenwood Press, Inc., Negro Universities Press (Westport, Conn., 1968), pp. 468–69, 491–94.

weakened and degraded by such chattel slavery, unaided, tore off its own fetters, forged them into swords, and won its libery on the battlefield, but one, and that was the black race of St. Domingo. God grant that the wise vigor of our government may avert that necessity from our land,—may raise into peaceful liberty the four million committed to our care, and show under democratic institutions a statesmanship as far-sighted as that of England, as brave as the negro of Hayti!

So much for the courage of the negro. Now look at his endurance. In 1805 he said to the white men, "This island is ours; not a white foot shall touch it." Side by side with him stood the South American republics, planted by the best blood of the countrymen of Lope de Vega and Cervantes. They topple over so often that you could no more daguerrotype their crumbling fragments than you could the waves of the ocean. And yet, at their side, the negro has kept his island sacredly to himself. It is said that at first, with rare patriotism, the Haytian government ordered the destruction of all the sugar plantations remaining, and discouraged its culture, deeming that the temptation which lured the French back again to attempt their enslavement. Burn over New York to-night, fill up her canals, sink every ship, destroy her railroads, blot out every remnant of education from her sons, let her be ignorant and penniless, with nothing but her hands to begin the world again,—how much could she do in sixty years? And Europe, too, would lend you money, but she will not lend Hayti a dollar. Hayti, from the ruins of her colonial dependence, is become a civilized state, the seventh nation in the catalogue of commerce with this country, inferior in morals and education to none of the West Indians isles. Foreign merchants trust her courts as willingly as they do our own. Thus far, she has foiled the ambition of Spain, the greed of England, and the malicious statesmanship of Calhoun. Toussaint made her what she is. In this work there was grouped around him a score of men, mostly of pure negro blood, who ably seconded his efforts. They were able in war and skilful in civil affairs, but not, like him, remarkable for that rare mingling of high qualities which alone makes true greatness, and insures a man leadership among those otherwise almost his equals. Toussaint was indisputably their chief. Courage, purpose, endurance,—these are the tests. He did plant a state so deep that all the world has not been able to root it up.

I would call him Napoleon, but Napoleon made his way to empire over broken oaths and through a sea of blood. This man never broke his word. "No RETALIATION" was his great motto and the rule of his life; and the last words uttered to his son in France were these: "My boy, you will one day go back to St. Domingo; forget that France murdered your father." I would call him Cromwell, but Cromwell was only a soldier, and the state he founded went down with him into his grave. I would call him Washington, but the great Virginian held slaves. This man risked his empire rather than permit the slave-trade in the humblest village of his dominions.

You think me a fanatic to-night, for you read history, not with your eyes, but with your prejudices. But fifty years hence, when Truth gets a hearing, the Muse of History will put Phocion for the Greek, and Brutus for the Roman, Hampden for England, Fayette for France, choose Washington as the bright, consummate flower of our earlier civilization, and John Brown the ripe fruit of our noonday [thunders of applause], then, dipping her pen in the sunlight, will write in the clear blue, above them all, the name of the soldier, the statesman, the martyr, TOUSSAINT L'OUVERTURE. [Long-continued applause.]

REV. JOHN R. BEARD [3]

. . . He possessed a rare genius, the efficiency of which was augmented by an unusual power of self-concealment. His life lay in thought and in action rather than in words. Self-contained, he was also self-sufficing. Though he disdained not the advice of others, he was in the main his own council-board. With an intense concentration of vitality in his own soul, he threw into his outer life a power and an energy which armed one man with the power of thousands, and made him great alike in the command of others and in the command of himself. He was created for government by the hand of Nature. That strength of soul and self-reliance which made him fit to rule also gave him subjects for his sway. Hence it was that he could not remain in the herd of his fellow-slaves. Rise he must, and rise he did; first to humble offices, then to the command of a regiment, and then to the command of "the armies of Saint Domingo."

To the qualities which make an illustrious general and statesman, there were added, in Toussaint's soul, the milder virtues that form the strength and the ornament of domestic life. Great as he was in the field and in the cabinet, scarcely less great and more estimable was he as a husband and a father. . . .

But he had learned his duty from the lips of One who taught men to make the love of children and parents subordinate to the love of himself; and assured that he had in some special manner been called and sent to set the captive free, he, in a native benevolence of character which the gospel enriched, strengthened, and directed, concentrated

[3] From Beard, *Toussaint L'Ouverture*, pp. 287–92.

all the fine endowments of his soul on the great work of negro emancipation in the island of his birth.

His mind appeared in his countenance and his manner, yet only as if under a veil. His looks were noble and dignified, rather than refined; . . . his eyes, darting fire, told of the burning elements of his soul. Though little aided by what is called education, he, in the potency of his mind, bent and moulded language to his thoughts, and ruled the minds of others by an eloquence which was no less concise than simple, manly, and full of imagery. As with other men of ardent genius, he fused ideas into proverbs, and put into circulation sayings that are reported to be still current in his native land.

But, after all, he was greater in deed than he was in word. Vast was the influence which he acquired by the mere force of his silent example. His very name became a tower of strength to his friends and a terror to his foes. Hence his presence was so impressive that none approached him without fear, nor left him without emotion.

If the world has reason to thank God for great men, with special gratitude should we acknowledge the divine goodness in raising up Toussaint L'Ouverture. Among the privileged races of the earth, the role of patriots, legislators, and heroes is long and well filled. As yet there is but one Toussaint L'Ouverture. Yet how many of the highest qualities of our nature did that one unite in himself. But his best claim to our respect and admiration consists in the entire devotion of his varied and lofty powers to the redemption of his color from degrading bondage, and its elevation into the full stature of perfect manhood.

I do not intend to paint the Haytian patriot as a perfect man. Moral perfection once appeared on earth. It is not likely to have appeared a second time among the slaves of Hayti. Toussaint has been accused of harshness and cruelty. I am not prepared to affirm that the charges are without foundation. But it is equally true that his enemies have done their utmost to point out stains in his character. Unfortunately, the means for a thorough investigation are wholly wanting. It has also been said that he was an adept at dissimulation. But secrecy in his circumstances was both needful and virtuous; and, if the study of secrecy on his part was undue, let the failing be set down against him at its full value. It has even been intimated that when in power he yielded to the fascinations of the accomplished creole women of the Cape. But the intimation, faint and indirect as it is, rests on no solid grounds. In truth, it was impossible that a man of the origin and aims of Toussaint L'Ouverture should have escaped the shafts of calumny, and, after all due abatements are made, enough of excellence remains to command our admiration and win our esteem. . . .

The history of L'Ouverture, placed by the side of the history of Bonaparte, presents a number of striking parallels. Both born in a humble position, they raised themselves to the height of power by the force of their genius and the intense energy of their character. Both gained renown in legislation and government as well as in war. Both fell the moment they had obtained supreme authority. Both were betrayed by pretended friends, and delivered into the hands of embittered foes. Both were severed from their families. Both finished their lives on a barren rock.

The parallels have their contrasts. Toussaint L'Ouverture fought for liberty; Bonaparte fought for himself. Toussaint L'Ouverture gained fame and power by leading an oppressed and injured race to the successful vindication of their rights; Bonaparte made himself a name and acquired a sceptre by supplanting liberty and destroying nationalities, in order to substitute his own illegitimate despotism. The fall of Toussaint L'Ouverture was a voluntary retirement from power, accompanied by a voluntary renunciation of authority, under circumstances which seemed to guarantee that freedom the attainment of which had been the sole object of his efforts; the fall of Bonaparte was the forced abdication of a throne which was regarded as a European nuisance, and descent from which was a virtual acknowledgment that he had utterly failed in the purposes of his life. In the treachery which they underwent, on one side, Toussaint L'Ouverture was the victim and Bonaparte the seducer; and on the other side the former suffered from those who had been his enemies, the latter from those who in profession were his constant friends. And in the rupture of their domestic ties, Bonaparte was the injurer, Toussaint L'Ouverture the injured.

Nor is it easy to bring one's mind to the conclusion that retribution was wholly absent in the facts to which allusion has just been made. The punishment is too like the crime to be regarded as accidental. Toussaint's domestic bereavement was requited by Bonaparte's domestic sorrows. The drear solitude of the Castle of Joux was experienced over again at Saint Helena by him who inflicted the penalty. Strange to say, it was a friend of the negroes—namely, Admiral Maitland—that conducted the Corsican to his prison. And as if to make the correspondence the more complete, and the retribution the more potent, by an exchange of extreme localities, the man of the temperate regions was transferred to the tropics, to atone for his crime in transferring the man of the tropics to the killing frosts of the temperate regions. Resembling each other in several points of their calamities and pains, the two differed in that which is the dividing line between the happy and the wretched; for, while, with Bonaparte, God was a name, with Toussaint L'Ouverture, God was at once the sole reality and the sovereign good.

VICTOR SCHOELCHER [4]

Toussaint-Louverture belonged to a class of men scarcely out of barbarism. Until the age of fifty he had lived in the state of degradation that is slavery. His story is mixed with that of the first period of the St. Domingue revolution, with the history of a slave population shattering its chains in an environment of dreadful lacerations. How could he escape the serviture of his violent instincts, from which humanity has to some degree delivered itself by the incessant labor of civilization?

One musn't, therefore, expect to find many edifying examples in the life of this Negro who received only exploitation at the hands of human creatures. His life had aspects of a truly extraordinary brilliance that can only excite astonishment, but we must be careful not to write a panegyric. We have endeavored to portray Toussaint-Louverture . . . as he really was: a man who, despite his genius, was unable to rid himself of the effects of a long oppression. Magnificent enough in the struggle to provoke our admiration, he didn't have enough moral force to emancipate himself from his slave past; he declined while in power until he became a tyrant. He reestablished labor in St. Domingue after ten years of war and revolution had overthrown everything, leaving nothing standing; but by what methods? By serfdom. He brought the colony to the highest point of material prosperity, but his memory cannot claim the honor of having founded free labor, without which there is no morality. . . .

Physically, Toussaint was "a small man, with bright, piercing eyes, a repulsive ugliness and poor build," said Norvins, who had seen him often. "His external appearance was repulsive, " said General Ramel, who also knew him. According to Valentin Cullion, another eyewitness, "he was a small man, poorly built, with a disagreeable face, on which, nevertheless, a certain air of goodness could be discerned."

He possessed a robust healthiness, an iron constitution which supported an extreme sobriety. . . . His memory was prodigious. His perpetual activity enabled him to do everything by himself. He was agile, skillful in all exercises of the body. An accomplished horseman, he and his horse were one, so much so that he was nicknamed "the centaur of the savanna. . . ."

Those who accuse him of criminal acts are all too correct; we haven't

[4] From Schoelcher, *Vie de Toussaint-Louverture,* Preface and pp. 384–86, 390–404; trans. George F. Tyson, Jr.

tried to hide or excuse them. But it cannot be forgotten, when judging this violent civilizer, that several years of civil war, in which all parties seemed to vie with one another in barbarity, had taught him to make little of human life. He was deprived of the insights that, alas! do not always serve to give us a horror of blood. However, he is far, very far, from having been the bloodthirsty man that the colonists and negrophobes represented. . . .

Many of his deeds show him to be a generous and compassionate spirit. Laveaux replied to Vaublanc, who had painted a horrible portrait of him in a speech to the *Conseil des anciens:* "Vaublanc has portrayed General Toussaint-Louverture to you as a brigand. Well! This General has never ceased giving proofs of the greatest humanity; he has never ceased having a consideration for the vanquished that would honor the most civilized European. In captured Spanish camps he found some white women; he collected them upon the estates which served as his general quarters; he found a way of keeping them alive while his army died of hunger. I have seen these citizennesses bless him and call him their father. He stormed a fort in which two hundred French *émigrés* were found. . . . They all expected to be put to the sword: 'Take the oath of loyalty to the Republic,' the black general said to them, 'and I grant you life.' Several of these *émigrés* are now in New England; the rest are on their estates, which they have peacefully possessed since then." . . .

Ingratitude doesn't find access to the hearts of blacks, and Toussaint was black to the marrow of his bones. He was always grateful to those to whom he owed something. "Each year," says General Ramel, "he sent the produce of his plantation to M. de Noé, his former master, who was a refugee in the United States." "Fortune," he wrote to him, "has changed my position, but not my heart." . . .

Toussaint shared the touching respect that Negroes hold for the aged. As soon as he spied an old person, he gave him a dramatic salute and yielded the roadway to him. He was extremely fond of children, and the children, knowing it, loved him. "Riding one day from Gonaïves to Ennery, he saw a young girl running after him, crying at the top of her lungs: 'Papa, Papa, take me away with you.' It was a ten year old orphan named Rose. . . . Moved by her childish voice, Toussaint dismounted, put the child on his horse, and continued on his way. On entering his house, he said to Madame Louverture: 'Here is an orphan who has just appointed me her father; I accepted this title, accept also the title of her mother.' " . . .[5]

These traits prove an evident natural goodness. But it is necessary to

[5] Saint-Anthoine, *Notice sur Toussaint-Louverture* (Paris, 1842), p. 24.

look at the other side of the coin, to see that Toussaint was hypocritical, crafty, and deceitful. He had neither confidant or favorite, he gave his trust to no one, not even to some "éminence grise." . . .

Always master of himself, always reserved, he said only what he meant to: all who knew him agreed with Pamphile Lacroix, "that he was impenetrable. His personal secretaries assured General Leclerc that they knew no one in the world who had the least impact upon the iron character of this extraordinary man."

He listened to priests a great deal and served them, but we see nothing in his political career that was due to their counsels: neither priest, nor man, nor woman, nor flatterer has influence upon him. Surrounded by enemies he always had to keep up his guard; he never did the expected. . . .

To his spirit of distrust he allied a sangfroid, a sagacity that always protected him from allowing himself to be flattered. Malenfant knew him to be a veritable sage: "A white colonist desired a post as storekeeper and asked Toussaint for this employment. . . . Toussaint refused. The petitioner's wife tried many times to approach Toussaint but was unsuccessful. Some time later she gave birth to a son and asked the black general to be the godfather. 'Why, Madame, do you wish me to name your son?—your approach to me has no other object than to get me to give a post to your husband, for the feelings of your heart are contrary to the request that you make of me.'

'How can you believe that, General? No, my husband loves you, all the whites are attached to you.'

'Madame, I know the whites. If I had their skin, yes, but I am black and I know their aversion to us. Have you reflected well on the request that you make of me? If I accept, how do you know that when he reaches the age of reason, your son won't reproach you when he sees a Negro as his godfather?'

'But, General. . . .'

'Madame' (Toussaint pointed to the sky), 'He who governs all is alone immortal. I am a general, it is true, but I am black. After my death, who knows if my brothers will not be put back into slavery and will yet perish under the whip of the whites. The work of men is not durable. The French Revolution has enlightened Europeans; we are loved and wept over by them, but the white colonists are enemies of the blacks. . . . You wish a post for your husband. Well, I give him the employment that he asks. Let him be honest, and let him remember that I cannot see everything but that nothing escapes God. I am unable to accept your offer to be the godfather of your child. You may have to bear the reproaches of the colonists and perhaps one day that of your son.' " [6]

This reply indicates a wisdom, a knowledge of the human heart that one is astonished to find in a man who until the age of fifty had been retained in a state of slavery, in which all mental faculties waste away.

Toussaint's conversation with this white petitioner is one of the thinker; with his black brothers he frequently employed apt images, whose worth with them was equal to the best of reasons. . . . "One day, while at Gonaïves, Toussaint learned that the field-negroes of Grand-Rivière had revolted, stating that they would obey neither whites nor men of color. He rushed to Grand-Rivière. Surrounded by furious rioters, he poured some wine and water together in a glass and then showing it to them, said, 'Which of you can now separate one from the other? God wants us to be similarly inseparable, to love one another.' The field-negroes, struck by the justness of the image, renounced their claims and returned to work." [7]

The reader . . . will recall that in his conversations and proclamations Toussaint constantly returned to pious recommendations, to formulas impregnated with holiness. His language was always full of the name of God. It is evident to us that he was sincere, for example, in preserving from childhood the habit of attending confession. But as in the case of so many others, even the educated, his religion accommodated itself to all his needs and tastes. It was unable to restrain . . . the most dominant of human passions. "When Port-au-Prince was taken," says General Pamphile Lacroix, "General Bourdet and I perused the secret documents of Toussaint-Louverture. Our curiosity was intensified after discovering a double bottom in the chest where they were contained. Our astonishment can be imagined when upon forcing this double bottom, we only found there some locks of hair of all colors, some rings, some gold hearts crossed by an arrow, some small keys and an infinity of love letters, all of which left no doubt of old Toussaint's amorous successes. . . ." [8]

All patriotic Frenchmen must honor the memory of this black, for it was due to him that the Republic was able to conserve the colony of St. Domingue for some time. He expended there an unlimited devotion, a perseverance of will that nothing could stop. "I thank you," he wrote to General Laveaux (17 August 1796), "I have taken care of my

[6] Colonel Malenfant, *Des Colonies et particulièrement de celle de Saint-Domingue* (Paris, 1819), pp. 94–95.

[7] "Notes d'Issac Toussaint-Louverture sur l'histoire du Consulat de Thiers," *Journal de Bordeaux,* 18 September 1845.

[8] Pamphile de Lacroix, *Mémoires pour servir,* 2: 104.

health. You tell me to take care; it is true that it will be necessary, but nothing is dearer to me than the reestablishment of order and prosperity in my country, and for that I cannot take care of myself. It is necessary for me to be everywhere."

In effect, at the head of his troops for battle, in the midst of his secretaries for organization, in conference with the diplomats for negotiations, he was always untiring, skillful, and resolute.

When he created his detestable constitution, Toussaint mercilessly put in it the reestablishment of the slave trade because *the prosperity of the colony* required many hands in order to produce more sugar. He acted at that time as a man of order, as the conservative he was by nature. But he came up with some lofty thoughts; he conceived a project whose realization could only make impossible the horrible recruitment of the hands that the old slave in him believed necessary to *the prosperity of the colony*. He proposed to descend upon the African continent with a thousand of his soldiers and a few officers to try to abolish slavery and unfurl the French flag wherever he would have extended his easy conquests. No doubt such a noble crusade would have been successful if he had been able to undertake it; no doubt "coming in friendship" he would have been received with open arms by the African peoples and his well-disciplined black battalions would have dealt easily with the barbarian and Arab chiefs, true land pirates, who for two centuries ravished the country in order to take prisoners to see to the slavers. "He wanted," says M. Saint-Anthoine, the first author to uncover this project, "to resign as Commander-in-Chief of St. Domingue and, at the head of a handful of soldiers, to throw himself upon the African continent in order to abolish the slave trade; without the troubles in St. Domingue during this period and without the Leclerc expedition, he would have put his generous projects into execution: *all the preparations had been made secretly in the United States.* He would have thus anticipated Europe by a half century in the emancipation of the blacks. . . ."

Lamartine said of Toussaint: "This man was a nation." This phrase is as true as it is beautiful. The race that has produced such a man cannot be considered inferior. The history of the St. Domingue revolution remains a striking protest against the still widespread opinion that Negroes occupy a rank below ours in the human family. Anyone who will read it carefully must recognize that blacks, when placed in an environment where they can develop their intellectual qualities, their spiritual resources, show themselves the equals of whites in every respect.

12

Black Americans Look at Toussaint

Despite the many significant contributions made to their history by West Indians such as Edward W. Blyden, Marcus Garvey, and Stokely Carmichael, American blacks have shown relatively little interest in the black peoples inhabiting the islands of the Caribbean Sea. Appreciation of Toussaint has suffered from this neglect. Nevertheless, there have been some Afro-Americans who have perceived the close historical bonds linking the destinies of the two peoples. Perhaps Toussaint's greatest impact was made on black freedom fighters like Gabriel Prosser and Denmark Vesey, who were moved by the example of the Haitian Revolution to open resistance. For less militant blacks, Toussaint served as a model for elevating black pride and purpose—as is obvious from the first selection by Robert C. Benjamin. The second reading is by William Wells Brown, one of the most prominent and reprsentative blacks of his time. A runaway slave, a dedicated antislavery crusader, and an outstanding literary talent, Brown had an enduring interest in the history of Haiti and it figured conspicuously in his voluminous writings. The Caribbean area did take on a certain attraction prior to the Civil War when free blacks in America, despairing of their degraded condition in both the North and South, began to look abroad for a new homeland. Haiti, in particular, as the only independent black nation in the hemisphere, appealed to black separatists. Foremost among the exponents of a mass emigration to Haiti was the Rev. James Theodore Holly. Active from an early age in black colonization movements, Holly believed that blacks could only fully realize their potentials under black rule. Largely as a result of his efforts, the Haitian government in 1858 invited American blacks to settle there. Although the movement was generally a failure, as the Americans became disenchanted with conditions in Haiti and returned to the U.S., Holly stayed on to become Lord Bishop of Haiti. For Holly, as for Benjamin and Brown, Toussaint L'Ouverture was a genuine black hero who stood as living testimony to the Negro's capacity for self-government and as a model to rekindle the black man's pride in himself and his race.

ROBERT C. BENJAMIN [1]

Twice in history there has been witnessed the struggle of the highest individual genius against the resources and institutions of great nations. For years Hannibal strove against Rome, his efforts ended in his defeat at Zama and his death by his own hands. For years Toussaint L'Ouverture struggled against the forces of Spain, England and France, his efforts ended in the establishment of a free and independent government and his incarceration in a dungeon. Hayti owes its liberty to Toussaint L'Ouverture. He was really its father. In that vast tempest which from Europe broke upon Hayti, we see nothing but Toussaint L'Ouverture. He was the moving and directing power. In the tremendous struggle for human freedom he stood forth pre-eminent as a leader, as a statesman, as an unflinching friend and advocate of the oppressed, and to his bravery must be ascribed the success which crowned the independence of Hayti. . . .

In every age men have arisen, and by the force of an original genius and a lofty aspiration, have come to stand as heralds in the forefront of the world's progress, the lives of such men are lessons and inspiration. Of men distinguished by their talents, elevated spheres of action and military prowess. Wellington, Washington, Cromwell, Grant, we have many and excellent biographies, serving as examples for the emulation of the white youth. The Negro youth also needs memoirs of men of their race, distinguished for their patriotism, high literary attainments, naval conflicts upon the seas and grand achievements upon the field of carnage. Such histories cannot fail of stimulating every Negro boy, yea! of helping them to follow the glorious footsteps of the noble descendants of Africa, our fatherland. . . .

As a legislator and chieftain, what age or nation has produced his superior? As a patriot he was independent, honest and uncompromising. What a spotless character he possessed. With what equity, with what moderation he behaved toward his enemies. What intrepidity! What greatness of soul! In short, what a multitude of stirring qualities appear in Toussaint L'Ouverture. He shone as conspicuously in the Cabinet as in the field. His only ambition was the welfare and freedom of his race; his disregard of wealth at a time when he had so many opportunities to enrich himself, is a confirmation of this fact. Endowed by nature with high qualities of mind, he, by his genius, courage, individuality and irrepressible perseverance, conquered difficulties which appeared insurmountable.

[1] From Robert C. Benjamin, *Life of Toussaint L'Ouverture* (1888), pp. vii–viii, 94–95.

Splendid examples of some single qualification no doubt there are. Cæsar was merciful; Hannibal was patient; Scipio was continent; Washington was serene; but it was reserved for Toussaint L'Ouverture to blend them all in one, and, like the lovely masterpiece of the Grecian artist, to exhibit in one glow of associated beauty the pride of every model and the perfection of every master in one transcendant superiority. As a general, he marshalled the slave into a veteran, and supplied by discipline the absence of experience. As a stateman, he originated a comprehensive system of constitutional law, of legislation and diplomacy, of preserving the peace, keeping the honor of, and vindicating the neutral rights of his country and developing its resources He was the first ruler in the world to promote foreign commerce and domestic industry by a system of free trade, and such was the wisdom of his views, that to the soldier and the statesman he added the character of the sage. A conqueror, he was untainted with the crime of blood; a revolutionist, he was free from any stain of treason, for aggression commenced the contest and his country called him to the command. Liberty unsheathed his sword, necessity stained, victory returned it. His body is dead, his deeds are not dead. His name is not dead, his glory is not dead. He is one of the few, the immortal names—"That were not born to die."

WILLIAM WELLS BROWN [2]

Toussaint was of prepossessing appearance, of middle stature, and possessed an iron frame. His dignified, calm, and unaffected features, and broad and well-developed forehead, would cause him to be selected, in any company of men, as one born for a leader. Endowed by nature with high qualities of mind, he owed his elevation to his own energies and his devotion to the welfare and freedom of his race. His habits were thoughtful; and like most men of energetic temperaments, he crowded much into what he said. So profound and original were his opinions, that they have been successively drawn upon by all the chiefs of St. Domingo since his era, and still without loss of adaptation to the circumstances of the country. The policy of his successors has been but a repetition of his plans, and his maxims are still the guidance of the rulers of Hayti. His thoughts were copious and full of vigor, and what he could express well in his native *patois* he found tame and unsatisfactory in the French language, which he was obliged to employ in the deails of his official business. . . . While at the height

[2] From William Wells Brown, *The Black Man* . . . , 2 vols. (Boston, 1863), 2: 103–5.

of his power, and when all around him were furnished with every comfort, and his officers living in splendor, Toussaint himself lived with an austere sobriety which bordered on abstemiousness. He was entirely master of his own passions and appetites. . . . No person knew better than he the art of governing the people under his jurisdiction. The greater part of the population loved him to idolatry. Veneration for Toussaint was not confined to the boundaries of St. Domingo; it ran through Europe; and in France his name was frequently pronounced in the senate with the eulogy of polished eloquence. No one can look back upon his career without feeling that Toussaint was a remarkable man. Without being bred to the science of arms, he became a valiant soldier, and baffled the skill of the most experienced generals that had followed Napoleon. Without military knowledge he fought like one born in the camp. Without means he carried on the war. He beat his enemies in battle, and turned their own weapons against them. He laid the foundation for the emancipation of his race and the independence of the island. From ignorance he became educated by his own exertions. From a slave he rose to be a soldier, a general, and a governor, and might have been king of St. Domingo. He possessed splendid traits of genius, which was developed in the private circle, in the council chamber, and on the field of battle. His very name became a tower of strength to his friends and a terror to his foes. Toussaint's career as a Christian, a statesman, and a general, will lose nothing by a comparison with that of Washington. Each was the leader of an oppressed and outraged people, each had a powerful enemy to contend with, and each succeeded in founding a government in the new world. Toussaint's government made liberty its watchword, incorporated it in its constitution, abolished the slave trade, and made freedom universal amongst the people. Washington's government incorporated slavery and the slave trade, and enacted laws by which chains were fastened upon the limbs of millions of people. Toussaint liberated his countrymen; Washington enslaved a portion of his. When impartial history shall do justice to the St. Domingo revolution, the name of Toussaint L'Ouverture will be placed high upon the roll of fame.

REV. JAMES THEODORE HOLLY [3]

Notwithstanding the remarkable progress of philanthropic ideas and humanitarian feelings, during the last half century, among almost

[3] From Rev. James Theodore Holly, *A Vindication of the Capacity of the Negro Race for Self-Government and Civilized Progress* . . . (New Haven 1857), pp. 1–4, 29–39.

every nation and people throughout the habitable globe; yet the great mass of the Caucasian race still deem the negro as entirely destitute of those qualities, on which they selfishly predicate their own superiority.

And we may add to this overwhelming class that cherish such self-complacent ideas of themselves, to the great prejudice of the negro, a large quota also of that small portion of the white race, who profess to believe the truths, "That God is no respector of persons;" and that "He has made of one blood, all the nations that dwell upon the face of the earth." Yes, I say, we may add a large number of the noisy agitators of the present day, who would persuade themselves and the world, that they are really christian philanthropists, to that overwhelming crowd who openly traduce the negro; because too many of those pseudo-humanitarians have lurking in their heart of hearts, a secret infidelity in regard to the real equality of the black man, which is ever ready to manifest its concealed sting, when the full and unequivocal recognition of the negro, in all respects, is pressed home upon their hearts.

Hence, between this downright prejudice against this long abused race, which is flauntingly maintained by myriads of their oppressors on the one hand; and this woeful distrust of his natural equality, among those who claim to be his friends, on the other; no earnest and fearless efforts are put forth to vindicate their character, by even the few who may really acknowledge this equality of the races. They are overawed by the overpowering influence of the contrary sentiment. This sentiment unnerves their hands and palsies their tongue; and no pen is wielded or voice heard, among that race of men, which fearlessly and boldly places the negro side by side with the white man, as his equal in all respects. But to the contrary, every thing is done by the enemies of the negro race to vilify and debase them. And the result is, that many of the race themselves, are almost persuaded that they are a brood of inferior beings.

It is then, to attempt a fearless but truthful vindication of this race, with which I am identified—however feeble and immature that effort may be—that I now proceed to set forth the following address:

I wish, by the undoubted facts of history, to cast back the vile asper-sions and foul calumnies that have been heaped upon my race for the last four centuries, by our unprincipled oppressors; whose base inter-est, at the expense of our blood and our bones, have made them reiter-ate, from generation to generation, during the long march of ages, every thing that would prop up the impious dogma of our natural and inherent inferiority.

But this is not all. I wish hereby to contribute my influence—how-ever small that influence—to effect a grandeur and dearer object to our race than even this truthful vindication of them before the world. I wish to do all in my power to inflame the latent embers of self-respect, that the cruelty and injustice of our oppressors, have nearly extinguished in our bosoms, during the midnight chill of centuries, that we have clanked the galling chains of slavery. To this end, I wish to remind my oppressed brethren, that dark and dismal as this horrid night has been, and sorrowful as the general reflections are, in regard to our race; yet, notwithstanding these discouraging considerations, there are still some proud historic recollections, linked indissolubly with the most important events of the past and present century, which break the general monotony, and remove some of the gloom that hang[s] over the dark historic period of African slavery, and the accursed traffic in which it was cradled.

These recollections are to be found in the history of the heroic events of the Revolution of Hayti.

This revolution is one of the noblest, grandest, and most justifiable outbursts against tyrannical oppression that is recorded on the pages of the world's history.

A race of almost dehumanized men—made so by an oppressive slavery of three centuries—arose from their slumber of ages, and redressed their own unparalleled wrongs with a terrible hand in the name of God and humanity. . . .

Toussaint, by his acute genius and daring prowess, made himself the most efficient instrument in accomplishing these important results, contemplated by the three French Commissioners, who brought the last decrees of the National Assembly of France, proclaiming liberty throughout the island to all the inhabitants thereof; and thus, like another Washington, proved himself the regenerator and savior of his country.

On this account, therefore, he was solemnly invested with the executive authority of the colony; and their labors having been thus brought to such a satisfactory and auspicious result, two of the Commissioners returned home to France.

No man was more competent to sway the civil destinies of these enfranchised bondmen than he who had preserved such an unbounded control over them as their military chieftain, and led them on to gloriout deeds amid the fortunes of warfare recently waged in that island. And no one else could hold that responsible position of an official mediator between them and the government of France, with so great a surety and pledge of their continued freedom, as Toussaint L'Ouverture. And there was no other man, in fine, that these rightfully jealous freemen would have permitted to carry out such stringent measures in the island, so nearly verging to serfdom, which were so necessary at that time in order to restore industry, but one of their own caste whose unreserved devotion to the cause of their freedom, placed him beyond the suspicion of any treacherous design to re-enslave them.

Hence, by these eminent characteristics possessed by Toussaint in a super excellent degree, he was the very man for the hour; and the only one fitted for the governorship of the colony calculated to preserve the interests of all concerned.

The leading Commissioners of France, then in the island, duly recognized this fact, and did not dispute with him the claim to this responsible position. Thus had the genius of Toussaint developed itself to meet an emergency that no other man in the world was so peculiarly prepared to fulfill; and thereby he has added another inextinguishable proof of the capacity of the negro for self-government.

But if the combination of causes, which thus pointed him out as the only man that could undertake the fulfillment of the gubernatorial duties, are such manifest proofs of negro capacity; then the manner in which we shall see that he afterwards discharged the duties of that official station, goes still further to magnify the self-evident fact of negro capability.

The means that he adapted to heal the internecine dissensions that threatened civil turmoil; and the manner that he successfully counteracted the machinations of the ambitious General Hédouville, a French Commissioner that remained in the colony, who desired to overthrow Toussaint, showed that the negro chieftain was no tyro in the secret of government.

He also established commercial relations between that island and foreign nations; and he is said to be the first statesman of modern times, who promulgated the doctrine of free trade and reduced it to practice. He also desired to secure a constitutional government to St. Domingo, and for this purpose he assembled around him a select council of the most eminent men in the colony, who drew up a form of constitution under his supervision and approval, and which he transmitted, with a commendatory letter to Napoleon Bonaparte, then First Consul of France, in order to obtain the sanction of the imperial government.

But that great bad man did not even acknowledge its receipt to Toussaint; but in his mad ambition he silently meditated when he should safely dislodge the negro chief from his responsible position, as the necessary prelude to the re-enslavement of his sable brethren, whose freedom was secure against his nefarious designs, so long as Toussaint stood at the helm of affairs in the colony.

But decidedly the crowning act of Toussaint L'Ouverture's states-manship, was the enactment of the Rural Code, by the operation of which, he was successful in restoring industrial prosperity to the island, which had been sadly ruined by the late events of sanguinary warfare. He effectually solved the problem of immediate emancipation and un-impaired industry, by having the emancipated slaves produce there-after, as much of the usual staple productions of the country, as was produced under the horrible regime of slavery; nevertheless, the lash was entirely abolished, and a system of wages adopted, instead of the uncompensated toil of the lacerated and delving bondman. . . .

The rural code, by which so much was accomplished, instead of be-ing the horrible nightmare of despotism—worse than slavery, that some of the pro-slavery caluminators of negro freedom and rule would have us believe; was, in fact, nothing more than a prudent government regu-lation of labor—a regulation which made labor the first necessity of a people in a state of freedom,—a regulation which struck a death blow at idleness, the parent of poverty and all the vices—a regulation, in fine, which might be adopted with advantage in every civilized country in the world, and thereby extinguish two-thirds of the pauperism, va-grancy, and crime, that curse these nations of the earth; and thus lessen the need for poor-houses, police officers, and prisons, that are now sus-tained at such an enormous expense, for the relief of the poor and the correction of felons.

This Haytian Code compelled every vagabond or loafer about the towns and cities, who had no visible means of an honest livelihood, to find an employer and work to do in the rural districts. And if no pri-vate employer could be found, then the government employed such on its rural estates, until they had found a private employer. The hours and days of labor were prescribed by this code, and the terms of agree-ment and compensation between employer and employed were also determined by its provisions. Thus, there could be no private imposi-tion on the laborers; and, as a further security against such a spirit, the government maintained rural magistrates and a rural police, whose duty it was to see to the faithful execution of the law on both sides.

By the arrangement of this excellent and celebrated code, everybody in the commonwealth was sure of work and compensation for the same, either from private employers or from the government. Nobody need fear being starved for want of work to support themselves, as is often the case among the laborers of Europe, and is fast coming to pass in the densely populated communities of this country, where labor is left to take care of itself under the private exploitation of mercenary capitalists. Under this code nobody need fear geing exploited by such unprincipled and usurious men, who willingly take advantage of the poor to pay them starvation prices for their labor; because, against such, the law of Toussaint secured to each laborer a living compensation.

By the operation of this code, towns and cities were cleared of all those idle persons who calculate to live by their wits, and who commit nine-tenths of all the crimes that afflict civilized society. All such were compelled to be engaged at active industrial labors, and thus rendered a help to themselves and a blessing to the community at large.

By this industrial regulation, every thing flourished in the island in an unprecedented degree; and the negro genius of Toussaint, by a bold and straight-forward provision for the regulation and protection of his emancipated brethren, effected that high degree of prosperity in Hayti, which all the wisdom of the British nation has not been able to accomplish in her emancipated West India colonies, in consequence of her miserable shuffling in establishing Coolie and Chinese apprenticeship — that semi-system of slavery—in order to gratify the prejudices of her pro-slavery colonial planters; and because of the baneful influence of absentee landlordism, which seems to be an inseparable incident of the British system of property.

Thus did the negro government of St. Domingo, show more paternal solicitude for the well being of her free citizens, than they ever could have enjoyed under the capricious despotism of individual masters who might pretend to care for them; and thus did it more truly subserve the purposes of a government than any or all of the similar organizations of civilization, whose only care and object seem to be the protection of the feudal rights of property in the hands of the wealthy few; leaving the honest labor of the many unprotected, and the poor laborer left to starve, or to become a criminal, to be punished either by incarceration in the jails, prisons and dungeons provided for common felons; or executed on the gallows as the greatest of malefactors.

This genius of Toussaint by towering so far above the common ideas of this age in relation to the true purposes of government; and by carrying out his bold problem with such eminent success, has thereby emblazoned on the historic page of the world's statesmanship a fame more enduring than Pitt, who laid the foundation of a perpetual fund to liquidate the national debt of England.

I say Toussaint has carved for himself a more enduring fame, because his scheme was more useful to mankind. The negro statesman devised a plan that comprehended in its scope the well being of the masses of humanity. But Pitt only laid a scheme whereby the few hereditary paupers pensioned on a whole nation, with the absurd right to govern it, might still continue to plunge their country deeper and deeper into debt, to subserve their own extravagant purposes; and then provide for the payment of the same out of the blood and sweat, and bones of the delving operatives and colliers of Great Britain. Thus, then, Toussaint by the evident superiority of his statesmanship, has left on the pages of the world's statute book, an enduring and irrefutable testimony of the capacity of the negro for self-government, and the loftiest achievements in national statesmanship.

And Toussaint showed that he had not mistaken his position by proving himself equal to that trying emergency when that demigod of the historian Abbott, Napoleon Bonaparte, first Consul of France, conceived the infernal design of reenslaving the heroic blacks of St. Domingo; and who for the execution of this nefarious purpose sent the flower of the French Army, and a naval fleet of fifty-six vessels under command of General Leclerc, the husband of Pauline, the voluptuous and abandoned sister of Napoleon.

When this formidable expedition arrived on the coast of St. Domingo, the Commander found Toussaint and his heroic compeers ready to defend their God given liberty against even the terrors of the godless First Consul of France. Wheresoever these minions of slavery and despotism made their sacrilegious advances, devastation and death reigned under the exasperated genius of Toussaint.

He made that bold resolution and unalterable determination, which, in ancient times, would have entitled him to be deified among the gods; that resolution was to reduce the fair eden-like Isle of Hispaniola to a desolate waste like Sahara; and suffer every black to be immolated in a manly defense of his liberty, rather than the infernal and accursed system of negro slavery should again be established on that soil. He considered it far better, that his sable countrymen should be DEAD FREE MEN than LIVING SLAVES. . . .

Now, with the illustrious traits of character of this brilliant negro before us, who will dare to say that the race who can thus produce such a noble specimen of a hero and statesman, is incapable of self-government? Let such a vile slanderer, if there any longer remains such, hide his diminutive head in the presence of his illustrious negro superior!

I know it may be said that, after all Toussaint was found wanting in the necessary qualities to meet, and triumph in, the last emergency, when he was finally beguiled, and sent to perish in the dungeons of France, a victim of the perfidious machinations of the heartless Napoleon.

On this point I will frankly own that Toussaint was deficient in those qualities by which his antagonist finally succeeded in getting him in his power.

So long as manly skill and shrewdness—so long as bold and open tactics and honorable stratagems were resorted to, the black had proved himself, in every respect, the equal of the white man. But the negro's heart had not yet descended to that infamous depth of subtle depravity, that could justify him in solemnly and publicly taking an oath, with the concealed, jesuitical purpose, of thereby gaining an opportunity to deliberately violate the same. He had no conception, therefore, that the white man from whom he had learned all that he knew of true—religion, I repeat it—he had no conception that the white man, bad as he was, slaveholder as he was—that *even* HE was really so debased, vile, and depraved, as to be capable of such a double-dyed act of villainy, as breaking an oath solemnly sealed by invoking the name of the Eternal God of Ages.

Hence, when the Captain General, Leclerc, said to Toussaint, in presence of the French and Black Generals, uplifting his hand and jewelled sword to heaven: "I swear before the face of the Supreme Being, to respect the liberty of the people of St. Domingo," Toussaint believed in the sincerity of this solemn oath of the white man. He threw down his arms, and went to end the remainder of his days in the bosom of his family. This was, indeed, a sad mistake for him, to place so much confidence in the word of the white man. As the result of this first error, he easily fell into another equally treacherous. He was invited by General Brunet, another minion of Napoleon, in St. Domingo, to partake of the social hospitalities of his home; but, Toussaint, instead of finding the domestic civilities that he expected, was bound in chains, sent on board the Hero, a vessel already held in readiness for the consummation of the vile deed, in which he was carried a prisoner to France.

13

Henry Adams: Toussaint's Foreign Policy

This selection by an eminent American historian contains an excellent summary of Toussaint's foreign relations with the United States and France. In it, Adams makes an interesting comparison between Toussaint and Napoleon, and, while clearly partial to the latter, his account demonstrates how Toussaint's diplomacy shrewdly took advantage of the colonial rivalries of the great powers to play them off against one another while keeping them guessing about his real intentions.[1]

The story of Toussaint Louverture has been told almost as often as that of Napoleon, but not in connection with the history of the United States, although Toussaint exercised on their history an influence as decisive as that of any European ruler. His fate placed him at a point where Bonaparte needed absolute control. St. Domingo was the only centre from which the measures needed for rebuilding the French colonial system could radiate. Before Bonaparte could reach Louisiana he was obliged to crush the power of Toussaint. . . .

The services he rendered to France were great, and were highly rewarded. His character was an enigma. Hated by the mulattoes with such vindictiveness as mutual antipathies and crimes could cause, he was liked by the whites rather because he protected and flattered them at the expense of the mulattoes than because they felt any love for him or his race. In return they flattered and betrayed him. . . .

Gentle and well-meaning in his ordinary relations, vehement in his passions, and splendid in his ambition, Toussaint was a wise, though a severe, ruler so long as he was undisturbed; but where his own safety or power was in question he could be as ferocious as Dessalines and as treacherous as Bonaparte. In more respects than one his character had a curious resemblance to that of Napoleon,—the same abnormal energy of body and mind; the same morbid lust for power, and indifference

[1] From Henry Adams, *History of the United States of America during the First Administration of Thomas Jefferson* (New York, 1962 ed.), 1: 378–94.

to means; the same craft and vehemence of temper; the same fatalism, love of display, reckless personal courage, and, what was much more remarkable, the same occasional acts of moral cowardice. One might suppose that Toussaint had inherited from his Dahomey grandfather the qualities of primitive society; but if this was the case, the conditions of life in Corsica must have borne some strong resemblance to barbarism, because the rule of inheritance which applied to Toussaint should hold good for Bonaparte. The problem was the more interesting because the parallelism roused Napoleon's anger, and precipitated a conflict which had vast influence on human affairs. Both Bonaparte and Louverture were the products of a revolution which gave its highest rewards to qualities of energy and audacity. So nearly identical were the steps in their career, that after the 18th Brumaire Toussaint seemed naturally to ape every action which Bonaparte wished to make heroic in the world's eyes. There was reason to fear that Toussaint would end in making Bonaparte ridiculous; for his conduct was, as it seemed to the First Consul, a sort of negro travesty on the consular *régime*.

When the difficulties between France and America became serious, after Talleyrand's demand for money and sweeping attacks upon American commerce, Congress passed an Act of June 13, 1798, suspending commercial relations with France and her dependencies. At that time Toussaint, although in title only General-in-Chief, was in reality absolute ruler of St. Domingo. He recognized a general allegiance to the French Republic, and allowed the Directory to keep a civil agent— the Citizen Roume—as a check on his power; but in face Roume was helpless in his hands. Toussaint's only rival was Rigaud, a mulatto, who commanded the southern part of the colony, where Jacmel and other ports were situated. Rigaud was a perpetual danger to Louverture, whose safety depended on tolerating no rival. The Act of Congress threatened to create distress among the blacks and endanger the quiet of the colony; while Rigaud and the French authority would be strengthened by whatever weakened Louverture. Spurred both by fear and ambition, Toussaint took the character of an independent ruler. The United States government, counting on such a result, had instructed its consul to invite an advance; and, acting on the consul's suggestion, Toussaint sent to the United States an agent with a letter to the President[2] containing the emphatic assurance that if commercial intercourse were renewed between the United States and St. Domingo it should be protected by every means in his power. The trade was profitable, the political advantages of neutralizing Toussaint were

---

[2] Toussaint to President Adams, 16 Brumaire, An vii (Nov. 6, 1798); MSS. State Department Archives.

great; and accordingly the President obtained from Congress a new Act, approved Feb. 9, 1799, which was intended to meet the case. He also sent a very able man—Edward Stevens—to St. Domingo, with the title of Consul-General, and with diplomatic powers. At the same time the British Ministry despatched General Maitland to the same place, with orders to stop at Philadelphia and arrange a general policy in regard to Toussaint. This was rapidly done. Maitland hurried to the island, which he reached May 15, 1799, within a month after the arrival of Stevens. Negotiations followed, which resulted, June 13, in a secret treaty[3] between Toussaint and Maitland, by which Toussaint abandoned all privateering and shipping, receiving in return free access to those supplies from the United States which were needed to content his people, fill his treasury, and equip his troops.

To this treaty Stevens was not openly a party; but in Toussaint's eyes he was the real negotiator, and his influence had more to do with the result than all the ships and soldiers at Maitland's disposal. Under this informal tripartite agreement, Toussaint threw himself into the arms of the United States, and took an enormous stride toward the goal of his ambition,—a crown.

Louverture had waited only to complete this arrangement before attacking Rigaud. Then the fruits of his foreign policy ripened. Supplies of every kind flowed from the United States into St. Domingo; but supplies were not enough. Toussaint began the siege of Jacmel,—a siege famous in Haytian history. His position was hazardous. A difficult war in a remote province, for which he could not bring the necessary supplies and materials by land; a suspicious or hostile French agent and government; a population easily affected by rumors and intrigues; finally, the seizure by English cruisers of a flotilla which, after his promise to abandon all shipping, was bringing his munitions of war along the coast for the siege,—made Toussaint tremble for the result of his civil war. He wrote once more to the President,[4] requesting him to send some frigates to enforce the treaty by putting an end to all trade with the island except such as the treaty permitted. Stevens again came to his assistance. The United States frigate, "General Greene," was sent to cruise off Jacmel in February and March, 1800, and was followed by other vessels of war. Rigaud's garrison was starved out; Jacmel was abandoned; and Rigaud himself, July 29, 1800, consented to quit the country.

Toussaint's gratitude was great, and his confidence in Stevens unbounded. Even before the fall of Jacmel, Stevens was able to inform

---

[3] Treaty of June 13, 1799; MSS. State Department Archives.
[4] Toussaint to President Adams, Aug. 14, 1799; MSS. State Department Archives.

Secretary Pickering that Toussaint was taking his measures slowly but certainly to break connection with France.[5] "If he is not disturbed, he will preserve appearances a little longer; but as soon as France interferes with this colony, he will throw off the mask and declare it independent." Hardly was Rigaud crushed, when the first overt act of independence followed. Toussaint imprisoned Roume, and on an invitation from the municipalities assumed the civil as well as military authority, under the title of governor. In announcing to his Government that this step was to be taken, Stevens added:[6] "From that moment the colony may be considered as forever separated from France. Policy perhaps may induce him to make no open declaration of independence before he is compelled." A few days afterward Toussaint took the Napoleonic measure of seizing by force the Spanish part of the island, which had been ceded to France by the treaty of Bâle five years before, but had not yet been actually transferred. In thus making war on the ally of France, Toussaint had no other motive, as Stevens explained,[7] than to prevent the French government from getting a footing there. Bonaparte had given a new Constitution to France after the 18th Brumaire. Toussaint, after the deposition of Roume, which was his *coup d'état* and 18th Brumaire, gave a new Constitution to St. Domingo in the month of May, 1801, by which he not only assumed all political power for life, but also ascribed to himself the right of naming his own successor. Bonaparte had not yet dared to go so far, although he waited only another year, and meanwhile chafed under the idea of being imitated by one whom he called a "gilded African."

Perhaps audacity was Louverture's best policy; yet no wise man would intentionally aggravate his own dangers by unnecessary rashness, such as he showed in Bonaparte's face. He was like a rat defying a ferret; his safety lay not in his own strength, but in the nature of his hole. Power turned his head, and his regular army of twenty thousand disciplined and well-equipped men was his ruin. All his acts, and much of his open conversation, during the years 1800 and 1801, showed defiance to the First Consul. He prided himself upon being "First of the Blacks" and "Bonaparte of the Antilles." Warning and remonstrance from the Minister of Marine in France excited only his violent anger.[8] He insisted upon dealing directly with sovereigns, and not with their ministers, and was deeply irritated with Bonaparte for answering his letters through the Minister of Marine. Throwing one of these des-

[5] Stevens to Pickering, Feb. 13, 1800; MSS. State Department Archives.
[6] Stevens to Pickering, April 19, 1800; MSS. State Department Archives.
[7] Ibid.
[8] Stevens to Pickering, May 24, 1800; MSS. State Department Archives.

patches aside unopened, he was heard to mutter before all his company the words, *"Ministre!* . . . *valet!* . . ." [9] He was right in the in-
stinct of self-assertion, for his single hope lay in Bonaparte's consent
to his independent power; but the attack on Spanish St. Domingo, and
the proclamation of his new Constitution, were unnecessary acts of
defiance.

When Jefferson became President of the United States and the Senate confirmed the treaty of Morfontaine, had Louverture not lost his
balance he would have seen that Bonaparte and Talleyrand had out-
manœuvred him, and that even if Jefferson were not as French in policy as his predecessor had been hostile to France, yet henceforth the
United States must disregard sympathies, treat St. Domingo as a French
colony, and leave the negro chief to his fate. England alone, after the
month of February, 1801, stood between Toussaint and Bonaparte.
Edward Stevens, who felt the storm that was in the air, pleaded ill-
health and resigned his post of consul-general. Jefferson sent Tobias
Lear to Cap Français in Stevens's place, and Lear's first interview
showed that Toussaint was beginning to feel Talleyrand's restraints.
The freedom he had enjoyed was disappearing, and he chafed at the
unaccustomed limitations. He complained bitterly that Lear had
brought him no personal letter from the President; and Lear in vain
explained the custom of the Government, which warranted no such
practice in the case of consuls. "It is because of my color!" cried Toussaint.[10] Justice to President Jefferson and a keener sense of the diplomatic situation would have shown him that such a letter could not be
written by the President consistently with his new relations of friendship toward France; and in fact almost the first act of Pichon, on taking
charge of the French Legation in Washington after the treaty, was to
remonstrate against any recognition of Toussaint, and to cause Lear's
want of diplomatic character which offended Louverture.[11]

Rarely has diplomacy been used with more skill and energy than by
Bonaparte, who knew where force and craft should converge. That in
this skill mendacity played a chief part, need hardly be repeated. Toussaint was flattered, cajoled, and held in a mist of ignorance, while one
by one the necessary preparations were made to prevent his escape; and
then, with scarcely a word of warning, at the First Consul's order the
mist rolled away, and the unhappy negro found himself face to face
with destruction. The same ships that brought news of the preliminary
treaty signed at London brought also the rumor of a great expedition

[9] Pamphile de Lacroix, *Mémoires*, 2: 52.
[10] Lear to Madison, July, 1801; MSS. State Department Archives.
[11] Pichon to Decrès, 18 Fructidor, An ix (Sept. 5, 1801); Archives de la Marine, MSS.

fitting at Brest and the gossip of creole society in Paris, which made no longer a secret that Bonaparte meant to crush Toussaint and restore slavery at St. Domingo. Nowhere in the world had Toussaint a friend or a hope except in himself. Two continents looked on with folded arms, more and more interested in the result, as Bonaparte's ripening schemes began to show their character. As yet President Jefferson had no inkling of their meaning. The British government was somewhat better informed . . . but none of them grasped the whole truth, or felt their own dependence on Toussaint's courage. If he and his blacks should succumb easily to their fate, the wave of French empire would roll on to Louisiana and sweep far up the Mississippi; if St. Domingo should resist, and succeed in resistance, the recoil would spend its force on Europe, while America would be left to pursue her democratic destiny in peace.

Bonaparte hurried his preparations. The month of October, 1801, saw vast activity in French and Spanish ports, for a Spanish squadron accompanied the French fleet. Not a chance was to be left for Toussaint's resistance or escape. To quiet English uneasiness, Bonaparte dictated to Talleyrand a despatch explaining to the British government the nature of the expedition.[12] "In the course which I have taken of annihilating the black government at St. Domingo," he said, "I have been less guided by considerations of commerce and finance than by the necessity of stifling in every part of the world every kind of germ of disquiet and trouble; but it could not escape me that St. Domingo, even after being reconquered by the whites, would be for many years a weak point which would need the support of peace and of the mother country; . . . that one of the principal benefits of peace, at the actual moment, for England was its conclusion at a time when the French government had not yet recognized the organization of St. Domingo, and in consequence the power of the blacks; and if it had done so, the sceptre of the new world would sooner or later have fallen into the hands of the blacks. . . ."

. . . Toussaint's resistance broke the force of Bonaparte's attack. Although it lasted less than three months, it swept away one French army, and ruined the industry of the colony to an extent that required years of repair. Had Toussaint not been betrayed by his own generals, and had he been less attached than he was to civilization and despotic theories of military rule, he would have achieved a personal triumph greater than was won by any other man of his time. His own choice was to accept the war of races, to avoid open battle where his troops

[12] *Correspondance*, 7: 319; Bonaparte to Talleyrand, 22 Brumaire, An x (Nov. 13, 1801).

were unequal to their opponents, and to harass instead of fighting in line. He would have made a war of guerillas, stirred up the terror and fanaticism of the negro laborers, put arms into their hands, and relied on their courage rather than on that of his army. He let himself be overruled. "Old Toussaint," said Christophe afterward, "never ceased saying this, but no one would believe him. We had arms; pride in using them destroyed us." [13]

[13] Pamphile de Lacroix, *Mémoires,* 2: 228.

14

Aimé Césaire

Aimé Césaire is one of the most brilliant and influential black writers of the century. Born and raised in Martinique, he is one of the founders, along with Leopold Senghor, of the ideology of Négritude—a doctrine that urges the black man to cease perceiving himself in terms of racial stereotypes imposed on him by his white oppressors and to appreciate his cultural uniqueness and the significant contributions of his race to the history of mankind. A long-time communist (although he resigned from the Communist Party in 1956 in protest against the Soviet invasion of Hungary), Césaire has played an active role in the political life of his native Martinique, where he has served as a Deputy to the French National Assembly and as Mayor of Fort de France. Not only did he help to shape the ideology of colonial independence movements throughout the world, but he also rallied world opinion on their behalf. His study of Toussaint reflects these concerns. He views Toussaint as the catalyst that turned a slave rebellion into a genuine social revolution and a movement of national liberation. Even if Toussaint could never bring himself to initiate the final struggle against France, Césaire concludes that he still must be considered as the real founder of Haitian independence.[1]

After the *"moment"* Boukman the *"moment"* Toussaint Louverture began.

Two moments of the same movement, but different.

The *moment* Boukman is the moment when the black insurrection, swept along by a single élan, could easily have been vanquished by a single blow; the moment of fiery inspiration and prophecy.

The moment of Toussaint [is] . . . the moment of the fallout, the moment of cold reflection that corrects errors and resets methods.

In short, as soon as the upheaval by its persistence had won a chance of transforming itself into insurrection, Toussaint joined it.

[1] From Aimé Césaire, *Toussaint Louverture: La Révolution française et le problème coloniale* (Paris, 1960), pp. 180–81, 275–77, 299–300; trans. George F. Tyson, Jr. Reproduced in English translation by permission of Club Français du Livre.

But once Toussaint had engaged himself in it, he didn't stop until he had widened it into a revolution.

And that meant essentially to discipline the revolt and to elevate it. To elevate its military level certainly, but more still, its political level. And, at first, to make it conscious of one thing: that beyond men it was a system that must be destroyed. The goal, the single, valid goal, could only be liberty, general liberty. . . .

There was a magic word that Toussaint always refused to pronounce: *independence.*

You can say that he lacked the "word of command." The idea of word of command makes sense only in relation to the notion of structure. The word of command deserving of the name is the one that reveals to the masses the *structure* of a troublesome situation and at the same time structures the struggle that guides the masses out of this situation. When in 1794 Toussaint said "general liberty," the word was excellent, perfectly demystifying and sufficiently dynamic. But in 1801, what sense was there in repeating the same word? None, except negative: "no reestablishment of slavery." But a negative word of command is hardly a word of command. What was necessary, and what Toussaint failed to do, was to indicate the means of escaping the impasse. The only word that constituted the dialectical overcoming of the notion of *individual liberty* contained in the word of command of 1794 was the one he failed to pronounce: the word *independence.*

Did he believe it premature?

In that case, it was he who was behind the masses. . . .

Briefly, the prisoner of outworn habits and of a style that for the first time showed signs of becoming rigid, he negotiated with Leclerc as he had with Hédouville, without realizing that the situation was fundamentally different.

The consequences were grave.

Affirming his attachment to France, his fidelity to the Republic— in a word, denying his claim to independence—was undoubtedly a tactic but, in reality, an incorrect one.

Whom was he able to deceive? The enemy? Leclerc? Bonaparte?

They were precisely the ones who were not deceived. . . . It was his own people who were the victims of the snare so vainly set for the enemy.

Is it possible to conquer independence without the people's knowledge and almost without their perceiving it? Can an action which can only be achieved through open force put up with such an ambiguity? That was Toussaint's weakness. . . .

Toussaint's activity was obvious, his doctrine devious. He was incapable of knowing how to propose a great, simple, and clear goal to his people. The result was that the French realized a certain success in their maneuver of separating the people from Toussaint. If the French can be believed, there was only one obstacle to immediate peace and general happiness: Toussaint. . . .

With Toussaint dead, France would believe St. Domingue decapitated, at her mercy.

But it is then that the true dimensions of the man are perceived: the importance of his work, which infinitely surpassed its author.

At the very moment of believing their way clear, they will encounter this work . . . and against it Bonaparte's enterprise will be definitely smashed.

More than Môle Saint-Nicolas, more than Crête-a-Pierrot, more than the fortifications that had been erected throughout the old buccaneer island, it was the spirit of Toussaint Louverture, the spirit he forged, that resisted the power of the French, their cannon fire and the charges of their soldiers.

Today it is fashionable in Haiti to diminish Toussaint in order to aggrandize Dessalines.

It cannot be a question of denying Dessalines's merits or of Toussaint's shortcomings.

But the debate can be closed in a word: At the beginning is Toussaint Louverture, and without Toussaint there would have been no Dessalines to continue his work.

Certainly Toussaint's historic situation was difficult, like that of all men of transition.

But it is great, irreplaceable: This man, as no other, constitutes a historical articulation.

In any case, there is one good way to appreciate his role and value. It is to apply the criteria of Péguy: to measure from what low level he raised his country and the conscience of his people.

He had inherited the rebel bands; he made them into an army. He had inherited a *jacquerie;* he transformed it into a Revolution. He made a population into a people. A colony he made a state, or rather, a nation.

Whether it wants to or not, everything in this country converges toward Toussaint and is radiated from him anew.

Toussaint is really a center.

The center of Haitian history, the center, undoubtedly, of West Indian history.

When he burst upon the historical scene for the first time, many movements were already underway, started by others, but stopped in

mid-course, languid, powerless to consummate themselves: the movement of the whites toward autonomy and free trade; the movement of
the mulattoes toward social equality; the movement of the blacks toward freedom.

Toussaint united all these movements, continued them, deepened
them.

When he departed, the triple movement was achieved or in process
of becoming.

In truth, St. Domingue went with him. But Haiti was born. The
first of all black nations.

15
François Duvalier and Lorimer Denis

This selection by the late President of Haiti, François Duvalier, and the noted ethnologist, Lorimer Denis, is taken from their important essay Problème des classes à travers l'histoire d'Haiti, *which is both a provocative interpretation of Haiti's historical development and a manifesto for the future. Both men were leading members of a group of Haitian intellectuals known as* Les Griots, *which was founded in 1938 to investigate and popularize the African roots of Haitian culture and resuscitate the folklore traditions of the Haitian peasantry. Politically the group opposed the American occupation and espoused the cause of the black masses against the selfish exclusivism of the western-oriented mulatto elite. In* Problème *Duvalier and Denis argue that the class problem in their country is intrinsically linked to race. They denounce the mulatto ruling class for its long history of ignoring the needs of the black masses and predict the emergence of a popular leader from the midst of the blacks, who, in the tradition of Toussaint, will reunite the population in a mighty effort of national regeneration. They describe Toussaint as the first Haitian patriot, who prepared his people for independence and national unity. His efforts were frustrated by the greed of the whites and the prejudice of the mulattoes. Nevertheless, his vision of a unified nation under the leadership of an elite dedicated to the real interests of the people must continue to serve as an inspiration to all Haitian leaders. When the essay was first published in 1948, the new leader Duvalier and Denis had in mind for this task was the President of Haiti, Dumarsais Estimé, a dark-skinned man from the country, who indeed actively promoted a national cultural revival oriented toward African and Haitian folklore traditions. Later, however, there can be no doubt that "Papa Doc" envisaged himself as this inspired savior, and the essay is highly suggestive of the popular nationalistic ideology that cloaked his brutal dictatorship over the Haitian people.[1]*

[1] From Lorimer Denis et François Duvalier, *Problème des classes à travers l'histoire d'Haiti* (Port-au-Prince, 1948), pp. vii–viii, 4, 11, 16–32, 35, 40–42, 55–65, 66–67; trans. Josetta Paquin.

We have written this book for the education of the generations.
No sectarian sentiment has guided our course. After having stud-
ied . . . our History as much in the colony of St. Domingo as during
the Haitian period of our public life, we have understood that the
backwardness of our Country with regard to certain South American
communities was partly due to the heavy colonial heritage, a serious
handicap to the great understanding between the two classes—an understanding which must condition the evolution and the very life of
the Haitian Nation. And to obviate it, the irritating question of color,
contrary to the old custom, has to be brought into the open, so it can
be solved rationally by education and social policies. It is the only
way to fight against this enervating cancer which threatens to destroy
us as a social body. . . .

In Haiti, as soon as one considers the aspects of the class problem,
one finds himself as a fisherman in troubled water. It is to disturb or
grapple with unwholesome questions that are likely to involve serious
consequences. It is like reviving the old quarrel between the blacks
and browns. Why? Because in our country color prejudice is grafted
onto the class probem, which is of a universal and scientific order. If
we look back into our colonial past, we will see that the colonists instituted this obvious sophism in order to justify the slavery of the
black. From this resulted the dogma of inferiority invented in order
to erase the black race from the human species. In essence, it comes
down to a question of class: The colonist in St. Domingo wanted to
divide the two social categories which were bound to unite—a union
which must inevitably be fatal for him. . . .

To understand the complexity of this jungle which contemporary
Haitian Society represents . . . it is necessary to return to our colonial
past in order to study from the statistical and dynamical point of view
the substratum of St. Domingo's society: its classes. . . .

The French colony of St. Domingo was composed of three classes:
that of the large plantation owners, that of the *affranchis,* and finally
that of the slaves, comprising a majority of blacks and a minority of
mulattoes. This slave society was characterized by the exploitation of
the human material represented by the vast majority of the blacks imported from Africa. All the same, the status conferred on the intermediate class—the mulattoes—at the social and economic levels was
an insult to the dignity of human nature. But when the first hour of
vindication struck in St. Domingo it was right to expect that from
both a biological and a political point of view the leaders of this intermediate class would join their interests and their future with that of
the great mass of blacks. Unfortunately, History reports that Ogé,

scorning all sentiments of solidarity, put forward claims only on behalf of his own kind. Therefore, the struggle against the oppressors in St. Domingo was inaugurated by the absence of unity between two classes that had common claims to put forward. It was necessary that leaders rise from the depth of the slave caste: They were Boukman, Jean-François, Biassou, etc. But one of them, Toussaint Louverture, not only claimed the heavy task of defending the interests and rights of the poor blacks but became their living conscience by incarnating their aspirations, their desires to the point of dreaming of Independence for this flock of pariahs.

The mulatto class, as previously stated, did not enjoy any civil and political rights: neither did it share social equality with the whites. What then, could be its supreme aspiration? It would be to obtain these primordial rights. In spite of the Declaration of the Rights of Man, the whites persisted in denying them satisfaction. Two men claimed the honor of being the defenders of the rights of the *affranchis:* Vincent Ogé and Julien Raymond, who could be considered as the spokesman or doctrinaire of his class. Tired of fighting in St. Domingo, they transferred their struggle and activities to the stage of the [mother country]. . . . Symbolizing the conscience of his class, Vincent Ogé repudiated all solidarity with the slaves. Here, two variables conditioned his conduct: COLOR PREJUDICE and INTEREST. Remember that the *affranchis* possessed a third of the land and a quarter of the slaves.

Beauvais and Pinchinat,[2] imbued with the experience of the past, first associated with a free negro: Lambert, and then with a great number of slaves, the 300 "Swiss." This was a political maneuver to the detriment of the "Swiss," since the *affranchis,* once the Concordat of Damien[3] was concluded, reconciled themselves with the whites, their fathers, thereby putting into application the machiavellian dogma of Julien Raymond that stipulated that the colony must be defended by the men of color against the slaves.

Now, what can be learned from these historical facts? It is evident that a sincere and ardent leader of the black masses could not emerge from the *affranchis* or mulatto class. Why? Because there had never been community of interest, purpose, and thought between these two social entities. Those personalities, who as living crystallization of the

[2] [Leaders of the mulatto revolt in the West immediately following the slave revolt of August 1791—Ed.]

[3] [Signed on 19 October 1791 after the whites agreed to grant full equality to the *affranchis.* Following the agreement the "Swiss" were turned over to the whites, who first deported them, and when they were returned to St. Domingo by the English, murdered all but twenty of them.—Ed.]

sufferings of the slaves will incarnate their thirst for vengeance and justice, had to spring from the Great Pain of the Workers. Thus appeared on the political scene of St. Domingo a Mackandal and a Toussaint Louverture, whom Destiny had chosen to be the Martyrs of the Regeneration of their Class. If, when we look ahead to consider the relations of classes in Haitian Society today, we come to the evidence that they conserve unchanged their old colonial structure, is it astonishing that after one hundred and forty-four years of independence, the descendants of the new freemen are still being maintained in their outcast condition? Moreover, is it astonishing to discover that, as formerly in the old colony of St. Domingo, the pains and sufferings of the proletariat in our cities and countryside only finds a sympathetic echo in the conscience of men of the majority class who have equally suffered and grieved. Isn't it that we are actually living in another epoch of our History when collective aspirations are crystallized in some self-conscious leaders of the class so as to become the highest exponent of the process of emblemization and symbolization of the aspirations and traditions of an entire class of men? . . .

We have tried to extricate the personalities of Mackandal and Toussaint Louverture upon the scene of St. Domingo while trying to shed the light of their teaching on the happenings of contemporary history. Why have we done this? Because . . . the individual has a notable influence upon the formation of the revolutionary conscience, and one cannot neglect to acknowledge this fact in a psycho-demographic explanation of revolutions. These representative individuals collect in themselves the influences of generations, the echo of the voice of the people of the towns and countryside, the pains and hopes of multitudes. . . . This is why they can utter words that others don't know how to say and make themselves executors of the unexpressed collective will. Primarily instruments of history, they are also partly creators of it. Instrument and creator of history, Toussaint was the organizer of the slave revolt of August 1791. Symbol of the profound aspirations and tendencies of the black masses of St. Domingo, he will draw from these same collective aspirations and tendencies the variable determining the great actions he will accomplish before History. . . .

Although dominated by the idea of reintegrating his brothers to the eminent dignity of human beings, he will prove himself hardly an exclusivist. Immediately after he had conquered Marmelade, he will be conferring ranks as much to whites as to blacks and mulattoes. This explains why Vernet (mulatto and his unsuccessful adversary) was elevated to the rank of general. And another important thing to note is that while serving under the Spanish flag he was obsessed by the idea of granting liberty to the slaves. . . . When, in the name of France, Sonthonax proclaimed the freedom of the slaves in the North, Toussaint was meditating on how to make it general and absolute. He wanted to proclaim it with his arms and maintain it by labor. When he will realize that Spain, contrary to its declarations, had tendencies to remain in favor of slavery, he will think of disengaging himself from Her Majesty's service. Here, we intend to point out, contrary to certain historians, that this decision of Toussaint was not a simple submission, but the result of a lofty political conception. He waited for the psychological moment, when Laveaux was reduced to the point where he could only claim Port-de-Paix and Fort Dauphin as still belonging to France, to employ his black legions to restore the situation as much to the benefit of France as to that of the great mass of slaves. To show that he had the future in mind, the Genius of our Race first thought of offering his submission to his natural ally, the mulatto Villate. What kind of reception did he receive? Bound by the prejudice of caste, Villate answered him, . . . that he did not want to negotiate with a worthless slave devoted to the cause of servitude. This answer . . . made Toussaint all the more indignant because it had come from a man of color who had quickly forgotten his primitive condition. From that moment he considered surrendering to Laveaux, but making sure to proclaim General Liberty wherever he hoisted the French flag. Henceforth, one could say that St. Domingo was under the aegis of the Hero who had promised himself to make St. Domingo the birthplace of liberty for his Race in the New World. This he accomplished: simultaneously he laid the foundations of a Black Civilization in the Western Hemisphere. Already, speaking for ourselves, we can add that love for liberty had reached those deepest stratums of this superman's conscience where burning desires are sublimated in order to blend with our tendencies and inclinations towards the Absolute. Will we be astonished that this man, interpreter of the great human dramas played out on the blood soaked soil of St. Domingo, could reveal himself to be a true Mystic Center? . . .

When, in a collectivity and in a given era great things must be accomplished in order to realize greater justice and enlightenment among men, there springs up from the Womb of the Race one of those leaders who in their personal equation synthesizes the conscience of this collectivity. In ancient times these were Tiberius and Caïus Graccus, grandchildren of Scipio the African, and also Vespasian, considered the second founder of Rome; in revolutionary France it was Graccus Babeuf; finally and closer to our time, the Ghazi Mustapha Kemal Attaturk, founder of modern Turkey.

If the collectivities are subject to the laws of historical determinism, if our community is truly confronting, at this crossroads of its existence, a genuine internal disequilibrium, a mixture of apparently chaotic events, there will spring up, as formerly in St. Domingo, one of these representative individuals, . . . who in his personal synthesis polarizes the anguish, the hopes and also the will of a class of men, generator of such men as Toussaint Louverture, Dessalines, Christophe, founders of empire and Nation. . . .

During the Galbaud revolt[4]—20 June 1793—and pressured by circumstances, the Civil Commissioners had to call the slaves to their rescue—the only force capable of saving the Government; one of the consequences of this act was to fortify the indigenous in the awareness of their power. Each rebel band was integrated to form an indivisable Whole. When Toussaint Louverture returned to the tricolor, this act of solidarity among the rebel bands will reach its highest degree of polarization, because the secular tendencies and aspirations will find their greatest exponent in the personality of that Leader. At that moment a group of men became aware of their class. This new factor will modify the equation of forces in St. Domingo. . . .

Thereafter, the struggle was unleashed between the new freemen and the representatives of the [Mother Country] on the one side and the former freemen and the big planters on the other. . . .

But this class antagonism will evolve towards a struggle for preponderance. A struggle that will explode between the prototypes of the two classes: Toussaint Louverture and Villatte. Who was Villatte? A knowledgeable man, says Schoelcher, a soldier of great courage and great capacity, who won all his ranks with the sword. Being very disinterested, also because of a weak character, he let the monopolists grow rich during his government, but never took anything for himself. Who were these monopolists? According to Schoelcher, many mulattoes had come to live in Le Cap in order to be under the administration of one of their congeners. Villatte had favored them beyond measure. They occupied almost all the municipal and civil offices. The National Guard was composed almost entirely of mulattoes. However, the city's prisons were filled up with blacks.

The exclusivism of the *affranchis* had attained its peak.

But Toussaint was watching. . . .

For a long time he had been struggling with Villate's partisans. . . .

The explosion came on 22 March, when . . . Laveaux came to Le Cap to put in order the finances being shared out by the mulattoes.

---

[4] [Galbaud, Governor of St. Domingo, led the revolt of the royalists and *petits blancs* against the Commissioners in June, 1793. —Ed.]

Villate allied himself with the colonial aristocracy in order to make the coup, but he underestimated the Black factor devoted to Toussaint Louverture. . . .

Toussaint arrived in Le Cap from Gonaives, liberated Laveaux . . . incarcerated by Villate, and remained the only Master of the situation. The Negroes, by supporting the "Representatives of France were also supporting Toussaint Louverture, who the conspirators detested as much as the Governor." This affair, says St.-Remy, took on the proportions of a war of caste. The attempted coup, as ill-conceived as it was criminal, resulted in the establishment of black preponderance in the North. . . .

In this antagonism of factions in St. Domingo, it was, we would say, providential that Toussaint Louverture thought of CLASS, and that he succeeded after so many struggles in realizing the domination of the Northern Province destined to play such a great role in the wars for National Independence. And, it is almost certain that if he had failed in this great struggle of classes, the future of the Blacks would have definitely been precarious, because with Villate acquiring supremacy in the North and Rigaud already preponderant in the South, Independence would have been conquered to the sole benefit of the men of color in league with the colonial aristocracy. . . .

Considering its importance, the Villate Affair must be considered as a landmark in the development of the social process of events in St. Domingo. Toussaint Louverture, by dominating the crisis provoked by Villatte's ambition, reestablished the equilibrium to the benefit of the Blacks. . . .

For accomplishing all this, Toussaint was elevated to the rank of General of Division. He used this promotion to organize his army in the North and the Center. . . .

What was the behavior of the Blacks and the reaction of the mulattoes to the promotion and adulations of which Toussaint Louverture had been the object from the [Mother Country]?

Naturally, all these marks of favor, . . . had the effect of increasing Toussaint Louverture's prestige among the blacks, while arousing the jealousies of the mulattoes. In particular, Rigaud, who was only General of Brigade, had been deeply irritated by the nomination of his rival to the rank of General of Division; he couldn't restrain his anger over the thought that he would be obliged to obey a former slave. Another event soon brought Rigaud's exasperation to its peak; it was when he learned that the Commissioners had conferred the title of "General-in-Chief of the Army of St. Domingo" on Toussaint Louverture. . . . Rigaud, who was more or less living in complete independence in the South since Sonthonax's departure, was fearful of the preponderance of the black element in the North and the Artibonite.

Absolute master in the South, he could not stand the Blacks. His administration was totally military and essentially aristocratic: the Commandants of the fortified towns were performing the municipal functions; the District Commanders, Justices of the Peace and Agricultural Inspectors were officers. Rigaud, one will recall, had an Army of eight thousand men; all of his superior officers were mulattoes. The Blacks couldn't go beyond the rank of Captain; all public offices were the monopoly of the men of color; and under the pretense of suppressing vagrancy, Rigaud had sent all the Blacks to the plantations and had subjected them to a kind of servitude that resembled slavery in certain ways.

Meanwhile, how was Toussaint Louverture shaping his politics in the North? Aiming at hegemony, at National Independence, he rid himself, one after the other, of Laveaux and Sonthonax by sending them to represent St. Domingo in the [Mother Country]. . . .

The Genius of our Race, the Great Toussaint Louverture, was obsessed by the idea of the Union of the two classes, indispensable factor to the realization of National Independence. Visionary that he was, he will forget his pride and try to make Rigaud, who was sick of France, understand that the salvation of the two classes rested upon their unification. Unfortunately, blinded by the colonial ideology and his hereditary tendencies, Rigaud was unable to raise himself to the level of these magnanimous conceptions of Toussaint, to combine in the same ideal of common rehabilitation the destiny of two human groups which nevertheless belong to only one race: the black race. . . .

What did Rigaud do about these counsels imprinted with wisdom and grandeur? . . .

Here is how General Rigaud enflamed the minds of the people of St. Domingo:

> Brothers of the South, know it well, there exists in the country two classes of men, the disgusting and incapable class, and the sympathetic and intelligent class. Let us be of the latter, and let us chase the former to the mountains where its home is destined to be, far from our life, among inferior beings incapable of society. . . .

Confronted with this attitude that was profitable to neither class, one understands Toussaint's indignation in his speech in the Church of Port Republican, where he pointed out the real causes of the antagonism between the two classes:

People of color, who since the beginning of the revolution have betrayed the blacks, what do you want today? No one is ignorant of it; you want to command the colony as masters; you want the extermination of the whites and the enslavement of the blacks! . . . But consider it, you perverse men forever dishonored by the deportation and then the slaughter of the black troops known under the denomination of "Swiss." Have you hesitated to sacrifice to the hatred of the *petits blancs* those unfortunates who had shed their blood for your cause? Why have you sacrificed them? It is because they were black. Why does General Rigaud refuse to obey me? It is because I am black. It is because he has sworn me an implacable hatred because of my color. Why else would he refuse to obey a French General like himself, who has contributed more than anyone else to the expulsion of the English. Men of color, because of your foolish pride, because of your perfidy, you have already lost your share of political power. As for General Rigaud, he is lost. I see him at the bottom of an abyss; rebel and traitor to the Country, he will be devoured by the troops of liberty. Mulattoes, will he continue? I see in the depth of your souls that you were ready to rise against me; but although all the troops are incessantly leaving the Western province, I leave there my eye and my arms: my eye to watch you, and my arms that will know how to strike you. . . .

16
C. L. R. James: The Black Jacobin [1]

Perhaps the most perceptive study of Toussaint and the Haitian Revolution in any language came from the pen of this Trinidadian marxist, who recognized not only the importance of the revolution within the larger framework of the "Atlantic Revolution," but also its relevance to the social and colonial upheavals that have shaken the entire world in the twentieth century. By identifying Toussaint as a leader of a genuine national liberation movement, confronted with problems intrinsic to all social and political revolts, James adds a dimension to his character that could only be appreciated in the light of the world revolutionary movement initiated by the Russian Revolution. Accordingly, it is Lenin, and not Napoleon or Cromwell, with whom he compares Toussaint. For James, Toussaint was an inspirational leader, a true military and political genius, who ultimately failed to reconstruct a viable postrevolutionary society because he lacked an ideology and because he lost contact with the masses.

He set his face sternly against racial discrimination. He guarded his power and the rights of the labourers by an army overwhelmingly black. But within that wall he encouraged all to come back, Mulattoes and whites. The policy was both wise and workable, and if his relations with France had been regularised he would have done all he hoped to do. But San Domingo did not know where it stood in relation to France. There were still fears for liberty, and the black labourers did not approve of Toussaint's policy. They felt that he showed too much favour to their old enemies.[2]

These anti-white feelings of the blacks were no infringement of liberty and equality, but were in reality the soundest revolutionary policy.

[1] From C. L. R. James, *The Black Jacobins: Toussaint L'Ouverture and the San Domingo Revolution*, 2nd rev. ed. (New York: Vintage Books, Random House, Inc., 1963), pp. 261–65, 282–92. Reprinted by permission of the author.

[2] Proclamation of Christophe I, 1814. Printed in Beard, *Life of Toussaint L'Ouverture*, p. 326.

It was fear of the counter-revolution. They had loved Sonthonax, called down blessings on his head, and made their children pray for him at night. Fifty years afterwards their old eyes would glow as they told travellers of this wonderful white man who had given them liberty and equality, not only in words but in deeds. But men like Sonthonax, Vincent, Laveaux, and Roume were few and with the decline of the revolution in France had come a man like Hédouville. The black labourers had their eyes fixed on the local whites and resented Toussaint's policy. It was not the whites at home whom Toussaint feared. It was the counter-revolution in France. But the blacks could see in the eyes of their former owners the regret for the old days and the hatred. Shortly after Toussaint issued one of his stern proclamations confining the blacks to the plantations, some of these whites issued a proclamation of their own to the labourers. "You say that you are free. Yet you are going to be forced to come back to my house and there I shall treat you as before and shall show you you are not free."[3] This was the spirit which so constantly provoked massacres of the whites. Toussaint fined the culprits heavily, ordered that all who could not pay should be imprisoned, even women, and reduced such officers as were concerned to the ranks. But he still continued to favour the whites. Every white woman was entitled to come to all "circles." Only the wives of the highest black officials could come. A white woman was called madame, the black woman was citizen. Losing sight of his mass support, taking it for granted, he sought only to conciliate the whites at home and abroad. . . .

Toussaint prepared for the inevitable war. That was one of the reasons which drove him to demand that his generals be mercilessly strict with the labourers.

He bought 30,000 guns from America. He armed the labourers. At reviews he would snatch a gun, wave it, and shout, "Here is your liberty!" He was not afraid to arm the masses. He trusted them for he had no interests apart from theirs. He hid stocks of ammunition and supplies in secret places in the interior. He called up the able-bodied for military training, and drilled the regular army. Bold in innovation, he introduced a system of commands by whistles. In every conceivable way (except one) he prepared. The blacks would have to fight. This war would devastate San Domingo as no war had ever devastated it before, ruin his work and let loose barbarism and savagery again, this time on an unprecedented scale. But any large expedition could have no other aim than the restoration of slavery. In that cruel dilemma he worked feverishly, hoping against hope, writing to Bonaparte, begging

[3] Ardouin, *Études sur l'histoire* . . . , Vol. IV, p. 256.

for skilled workmen, teachers, administrators, to help him govern the colony.

Bonaparte would not answer, and Toussaint could guess why. If Bonaparte wrote a personal letter he would have either to accept or condemn. If he accepted, then Toussaint's position would receive the final sanction. If he condemned, then Toussaint would openly declare independence and perhaps clinch a bargain with the British if one were not made already.

Toussaint, however, immediately after the victory in the South, had decided to regularise his own position and put an end to internal troubles for the future by giving San Domingo a Constitution. For this purpose he summoned an assembly of six men, one from each province, consisting of rich whites and Mulattoes: there was not one black. As always now, he was thinking of the effect in France, and not of the effect on his own masses, feeling too sure of them. The members of his assembly were merely figureheads. The Constitution is Toussaint L'Ouverture from the first line to the last, and in it he enshrined his principles of government.[4] Slavery was forever abolished. Every man, whatever his colour, was admissible to all employments, and there was to exist no other distinction than that of virtues and talents, and no other superiority than that which the law gives in the exercise of a public function. He incorporated in the Constitution an article which preserved their rights to all proprietors absent from the colony "for whatever reason" except if they were on the list of émigrés proscribed in France. For the rest, Toussaint concentrated all power in his own hands.

Every municipal administration was composed of a mayor and four administrators. They were nominated by the Governor for two years from a list of 16 submitted to him.

The Church was strictly subordinate to the State. The Governor apportioned to each minister of religion the extent of his administration, and the clergy were not allowed under any pretext whatever to form an association in the colony. Laws were to be preceded by this formula: "The Central Assembly of San Domingo, on the proposal of the Governor. . . ." They were to be promulgated with the formula: "The Governor commands. . . ." Every department of administration, finance, police, army, was confided to him, and he corresponded directly with France on everything relating to the colony. He had the censorship of all printed matter.

[4] The Constitution is printed in full in Nemours, *Histoire Militaire,* Vol. I, pp. 95–112.

The Central Assembly could accept or reject laws, but the Assembly was in the hands of the Governor, being elected by the principal administrators, whom he nominated. The Constitution appointed Toussaint Governor for life, with power to name his successor.

Constitutions are what they turn out to be. France in 1802 could have no quarrel with Toussaint over this Constitution on the score of despotism. What would strike any Frenchman, however, was that the Constitution, though swearing allegiance to French, left no room for any French official. Toussaint wanted them to come out and help govern, but under the local government. It was virtual independence, with France as elder brother, guide and mentor. He had no precedents to guide him, but he knew what he wanted. When remonstrated with as to where was the place of France in such a government, he replied, "The French Government will send Commissioners to speak with me." Absolute local independence on the one hand, but on the other French capital and French administrators, helping to develop and educate the country, and a high official from France as a link between both Governments. The local power was too well safeguarded for us to call the scheme a protectorate in the political content of that dishonest word. All the evidence shows that Toussaint, working alone, had reached forward to that form of political allegiance which we know to-day as Dominion Status. . . .

Criticism is not enough. What should Toussaint have done? A hundred and fifty years of history and the scientific study of revolution begun by Marx and Engels, and amplified by Lenin and Trotsky, justify us in pointing to an alternative course.

Lenin and the Bolsheviks after the October Revolution faced much the same problem as Toussaint. Russian bourgeois culture was a relatively poor thing, but Lenin admitted frankly that it was superior to that of the proletariat and would have to be used until the proletariat had developed itself. He rigidly excluded the bourgeoisie from political power, but he proposed that they should be given important posts and good salaries, higher than those of Communist Party members. Even some Communists who had suffered and fought under Tsarism were after a time dismissed and replaced by competent bourgeois. We can measure Toussaint's gigantic intellect by the fact that, untrained as he was, he attempted to do the same, his black army and generals filling the political rôle of the Bolshevik Party. If he kept whites in his army, it was for the same reason that the Bolsheviks also kept Tsarist officers. Neither revolution had enough trained and educated officers of its own, and the black Jacobins, relatively speaking, were far worse off culturally than the Russian Bolsheviks.

The whole theory of the Bolshevik policy was that the victories of
the new régime would gradually win over those who had been con-
strained to accept it by force. Toussaint hoped for the same. If he
failed, it is for the same reason that the Russian socialist revolution
failed, even after all its achievements—the defeat of the revolution in
Europe. Had the Jacobins been able to consolidate the democratic republic in 1794, Haiti would have remained a French colony, but an attempt to restore slavery would have been most unlikely.

It was in method, and not in principle, that Toussaint failed. The
race question is subsidiary to the class question in politics, and to think
of imperialism in terms of race is disastrous. But to neglect the racial
factor as merely incidental is an error only less grave than to make it
fundamental. There were Jacobin workmen in Paris who would have
fought for the blacks against Bonaparte's troops. But the international
movement was not then what it is to-day, and there were none in San
Domingo. The black labourers saw only the old slave-owning whites.
These would accept the new régime, but never to the extent of fighting
for it against a French army, and the masses knew this. Toussaint of
course knew this also. He never trusted Agé, his Chief of Staff who was
a Frenchman, and asked Agé's junior, Lamartinière, to keep an eye on
him. But whereas Lenin kept the party and the masses thoroughly
aware of every step, and explained carefully the exact position of the
bourgeois servants of the Workers' State, Toussaint explained nothing,
and allowed the masses to think that their old enemies were being favoured at their expense. In allowing himself to be looked upon as
taking the side of the whites against the blacks, Toussaint committed
the unpardonable crime in the eyes of a community where the whites
stood for so much evil. That they should get back their property was
bad enough. That they should be privileged was intolerable. And to
shoot Moïse, the black, for the sake of the whites was more than an error, it was a crime. It was almost as if Lenin had had Trotsky shot for
taking the side of the proletariat against the bourgeoisie.

Toussaint's position was extraordinarily difficult. San Domingo was,
after all, a French colony. Granted that, before the expedition was a
certainty, plain speech was impossible; once he understood that it was
coming, there should have been no hesitation. He should have declared
that a powerful expedition could have no other aim than the restoration of slavery, summoned the population to resist, declared independence, confiscated the property of all who refused to accept and dis-
tributed it among his supporters. Agé and the other white officers
should have been given a plain choice: accept or leave. If they had accepted, intending to be traitors, the black officers would have been on

guard against them, the men would have known where they stood and would have shot them at the slightest vacillation before the enemy. The whites should have been offered the same choice: accept the black régime which has guaranteed and will guarantee your property, or leave; traitors in war-time would be dealt with as all traitors in war. Many of the planters favoured independence. They would have stayed and contributed their knowledge, such as it was, to the new State. Not only former slaves had followed Toussaint. Lamartinière was a Mulatto so white that only those who knew his origins could tell that he had Negro ancestry, but he was absolutely and completely devoted to the cause of Toussaint. So was Maurepas, an old free black. With Dessalines, Belair, Moïse and the hundreds of other officers, ex-slave and formerly free, it would have been easy for Toussaint to get the mass of the population behind him. Having the army, some of the better educated blacks and Mulattoes and the labourers who had supported him so staunchly in everything, he would have been invincible. With the issue unobscure and his power clear, many who might otherwise have hesitated would have come down on the side that was taking decisive action. With a decisive victory won it was not impossible to re-open negotiations with a chastened French government to establish the hoped-for relations.

It was the ex-slave labourers and the ex-slave army which would decide the issue, and Toussaint's policy crippled both.

He left the army with a divided allegiance. There were Frenchmen in it whose duty would be to fight for France. They, the Mulattoes and the old free blacks had no fears about their liberty.

Instead of bringing the black labourers nearer he drove them away from him. Even after the revolt it was not too late. Lenin crushed the Kronstadt revolt with a relentless hand, but, in a manner so abrupt as to call forth protests from sticklers for party discipline, he proposed the New Economic Policy immediately afterwards. It was this quick recognition of danger that saved the Russian Revolution. Toussaint crushed the revolt as he was bound to do. But instead of recognising the origin of the revolt as springing from the fear of the same enemy that he was arming against, he was sterner with the revolutionaries than he had ever been before. It happened that the day on which Moïse was executed, November 21st, was the very day fixed by Bonaparte for the departure of the expedition.

Instead of reprisals Toussaint should have covered the country, and in the homely way that he understood so well, mobilised the masses, talked to the people, explained the situation to them and told them what he wanted them to do. As it was, the policy he persisted in reduced the masses to a state of stupor.[5] It has been said that he was thinking of the effect in France. His severity and his proclamation reassuring the whites aimed at showing Bonaparte that all classes were safe in San Domingo, and that he could be trusted to govern the colony with justice. It is probably true, and is his greatest condemnation.

Bonaparte was not going to be convinced by Toussaint's justice and fairness and capacity to govern. Where imperialists do not find disorder they create it deliberately, as Hédouville did. They want an excuse for going in. But they can find that easily and will go in even without any. It is force that counts, and chiefly the organised force of the masses. Always, but particularly at the moment of struggle, a leader must think of his own masses. It is what they think that matters, not what the imperialists think. And if to make matters clear to them Toussaint had to condone a massacre of the whites, so much the worse for the whites. He had done everything possible for them, and if the race question occupied the place that it did in San Domingo, it was not the fault of the blacks. But Toussaint, like Robespierre, destroyed his own Left-wing, and with it sealed his own doom. The tragedy was that there was no need for it. Robespierre struck at the masses because he was bourgeois and they were communist. That clash was inevitable, and regrets over it are vain. But between Toussaint and his people there was no fundamental difference of outlook or of aim. Knowing the race question for the political and social question that it was, he tried to deal with it in a purely political and social way. It was a grave error. Lenin in his thesis to the Second Congress of the Communist International warned the white revolutionaries—a warning they badly need—that such has been the effect of the policy of imperialism on the relationship between advanced and backward peoples that European Communists will have to make wide concessions to natives of colonial countries in order to overcome the justified prejudice which these feel toward all classes in the oppressing countries. Toussaint, as his power grew, forgot that. He ignored the black labourers, bewildered them at the very moment that he needed them most, and to bewilder the masses is to strike the deadliest of all blows at the revolution.

His personal weakness, the obverse side of his strength, played its part also. He left even his generals in the dark. A naturally silent and reserved man, he had been formed by military discipline. He gave orders and expected them to be obeyed. Nobody ever knew what he was doing. He said suddenly that Sonthonax must go and invited his generals to sign the letter or not, as they pleased. When Vincent spoke to

[5] Idlinger, Treasurer to the Colony. Report to the French Government, *Les Archives du Ministère des Affaires Etrangères. Fonds divers, Section Amérique*, No. 14.

Christophe and Moïse about the Constitution, they knew nothing about it. Moïse's bitter complaint about Toussaint and the whites came obviously from a man to whom Toussaint had never explained the motives of his policy. They would not have needed much persuasion to follow a bold lead. Moïse was feeling his way towards it, and we can point out Toussaint's weakness all the more clearly because Dessalines had actually found the correct method. His speech to the army was famous, and another version—he probably made it more than once—ran this way: "If France wishes to try any nonsense here, everybody must rise together, men and women." Loud acclamations greeted this bold pronouncement, worth a thousand of Toussaint's equivocal proclamations reassuring the whites. Dessalines had not the slightest desire to reassure whites.

The whites were whites of the old régime. Dessalines did not care what they said or thought. The black labourers had to do the fighting —and it was they who needed reassurance. It was not that Toussaint had any illusions about the whites. He had none whatever. When the war had actually begun, he sent a curt message to his commanders: "Leave nothing white behind you." [6] But the mischief had been done.

Yet Toussaint's error sprang from the very qualities that made him what he was. It is easy to see to-day, as his generals saw after he was dead, where he had erred. It does not mean that they or any of us would have done better in his place. If Dessalines could see so clearly and simply, it was because the ties that bound this uneducated soldier to French civilisation were of the slenderest. He saw what was under his nose so well because he saw no further. Toussaint's failure was the failure of enlightenment, not of darkness. . . .

The defeat of Toussaint in the War of Independence and his imprisonment and death in Europe are universally looked upon as a tragedy. They contain authentic elements of the tragic in that even at the height of the war Toussaint strove to maintain the French connection as necessary to Haiti in its long and difficult climb to civilisation. Convinced that slavery could never be restored in San Domingo, he was equally convinced that a population of slaves recently landed from Africa could not attain to civilisation by "going it alone." His tergiversations, his inability to take the firm and realistic decisions which so distinguished his career and had become the complete expression of his personality, as we watch his blunders and the inevitable catastrophe, we have always to remember that here is no conflict of the

[6] Mauviel, Bishop of San Domingo. Memorandum to Napoleon, *Les Archives Nationales*, AF. IV. 1187.

insoluble dilemmas of the human condition, no division of a personality which can find itself only in its striving for the unattainable.
Toussaint was a whole man. The man into which the French Revolution had made him demanded that the relation with the France of liberty, equality, fraternity and the abolition of slavery without a debate,
should be maintained. What revolutionary France signified was per-
petually on his lips, in public statements, in his correspondence, in the
spontaneous intimacy of private conversation. It was the highest stage
of social existence that he could imagine. It was not only the framework
of his mind. No one else was so conscious of its practical necessity in the
social backwardness and primitive conditions of life around him. Being
the man he was, by nature, and by a range and intensity of new experi-
ences such as is given to few, that is the way he saw the world in which he
lived. His unrealistic attitude to the former masters, at home and abroad,
sprang not from any abstract humanitarianism or loyalty, but from a
recognition that they alone had what San Domingo society needed. He
believed that he could handle them. It is not improbable that he could
have done it. He was in a situation strictly comparable to that of the
greatest of all American statesmen, Abraham Lincoln, in 1865: if the
thing could be done at all, he alone could do it. Lincoln was not allowed to try. Toussaint fought desperately for the right to try.

If he was convinced that San Domingo would decay without the
benefits of the French connection, he was equally certain that slavery
could never be restored. Between these two certainties, he, in whom
penetrating vision and prompt decision had become second nature,
became the embodiment of vacillation. His allegiance to the French
Revolution and all it opened out for mankind in general and the people of San Domingo in particular, this had made him what he was. But
this in the end ruined him.

Perhaps for him to have expected more than the bare freedom was
too much for the time. With that alone Dessalines was satisfied, and
perhaps the proof that freedom alone was possible lies in the fact that
to ensure it Dessalines, that faithful adjutant, had to see that Toussaint
was removed from the scene. Toussaint was attempting the impossible
—the impossible that was for him the only reality that mattered. The
realities to which the historian is condemned will at times simplify the
tragic alternatives with which he was faced. But these factual statements and the judgments they demand must not be allowed to obscure
or minimise the truly tragic character of his dilemma, one of the most
remarkable of which there is an authentic historical record.

But in a deeper sense the life and death are not truly tragic. Prome-
theus, Hamlet, Lear, Phèdre, Ahab, assert what may be the permanent

impulses of the human condition against the claims of organised society. They do this in the face of imminent or even certain destruction, and their defiance propels them to heights which make of their defeat a sacrifice which adds to our conceptions of human grandeur.

Toussaint is in a lesser category. His splendid powers do not rise but decline. Where formerly he was distinguished above all for his prompt and fearless estimate of whatever faced him, we shall see him, we have already seen him, misjudging events and people, vacillating in principle, and losing both the fear of his enemies and the confidence of his own supporters.

The hamartia, the tragic flaw, which we have constructed from Aristotle, was in Toussaint not a moral weakness. It was a specific error, a total miscalculation of the constituent events. Yet what is lost by the imaginative freedom and creative logic of great dramatists is to some degree atoned for by the historical actuality of his dilemma. It would therefore be a mistake to see him merely as a political figure in a remote West Indian island. If his story does not approach the greater dramatic creations, in its social significance and human appeal it far exceeds the last days at St Helena and that apotheosis of accumulation and degradation, the suicide in the Wilhelmstrasse. The Greek tragedians could always go to their gods for a dramatic embodiment of fate, the *dike* which rules over a world neither they nor we ever made. But not Shakespeare himself could have found such a dramatic embodiment of fate as Toussaint struggled against, Bonaparte himself; nor could the furthest imagination have envisaged the entry of the chorus, of the ex-slaves themselves, as the arbiters of their own fate. Toussaint's certainty of this as the ultimate and irresistible resolution of the problem to which he refused to limit himself, that explains his mistakes and atones for them.

Bibliographical Note

Toussaint's own writings are largely confined to his official letters, proclamations, and speeches. Almost all of them, along with the most important documents on the Haitian Revolution can be found only in the French archives. The National Archives contain a vast amount of material, including most of the official reports and letters. Some of Toussaint's military correspondence, along with Leclerc's, is located in the Archives of the Ministry of War. Also, a rich collection of material can be found in the Archives of the Ministry of Colonies. Three volumes of Toussaint's important correspondence with Laveaux and much of Sonthonax's correspondence are deposited in *La Bibliothèque Nationale,* along with many other miscellaneous memoirs and tracts. Gerard M. Laurent, ed., *Toussaint Louverture à travers sa correspondance 1794–1798* (Madrid, 1953), which draws chiefly from the Toussaint-Laveaux correspondence, is the only book in any language devoted to Toussaint's writings. Various proclamations, speeches, and letters of Toussaint are scattered throughout many of his biographies. His *Memoir* is reproduced in its entirety in Rev. John R. Beard, *Toussaint L'Ouverture: A Biography and Autobiography* (Boston, 1863). Victor Schoelcher, *Vie de Toussaint-Louverture* (Paris, 1889), also reprints at length a number of important documents. Many documents, as well as a fine discussion of Toussaint's foreign policy, can be found in Louis M. Lecorps, ed., *La Politique exterieure de Toussaint-Louverture* (Port-au-Prince, 1935). Toussaint's dealings with the Adams Administration can be followed in "Letters of Toussaint Louverture and Edward Stevens, 1798–1800," *American Historical Review,* Vol. 26 (October 1910). Letters of Toussaint to British officials and miscellaneous proclamations can be found in the Public Record Office (London, C.O. [Colonial Office] 137/88–112). Surprisingly little material on or by Toussaint is located in Haitian archives. However, some interesting documents have been published in Haitian periodicals such as *Revue Le Document* and *Revue de la Société d'histoire et de géographie d'Haiti.*

Although a multitude of biographies of Toussaint have been published, few are worthy of consideration by the serious student of history. The most comprehensive is H. Paulèus-Sannon, *Histoire de Toussaint-Louverture,* 3 vols. (Port-au-Prince, 1920–1933). The best 19th-century study is Schoelcher's biography, cited above. Critical portraits include Joseph Saint-Rémy, *Vie de Toussaint Louverture* (Paris, 1850), which offers the standard mulatto interpretation, and Louis Dubroca, *The Life of Toussaint Louverture* (London, 1802), which gives the Napoleonic view. Insightful recent biographies, generally favorable, are Timoléon C. Brutus, *Rançon du génie, ou La Leçon de Toussaint Louverture* (Port-au-Prince, 1945); Aimé Césaire, *Toussaint Louverture: La Révolution française et le problème coloniale* (Paris, 1960); Roger Dorsinville,

Toussaint Louverture, ou La Vocation de la liberté (Paris, 1965); Gerard M. Laurent, *Coup d'oeil sur la politique de Toussaint-Louverture* (Port-au-Prince, 1949). Unabashed panegyrics, which nevertheless contain some useful information, are Thomas P. Gragnon-Lacoste, *Toussaint-Louverture . . .* (Paris, 1877) and Alfred Nemours, *Toussaint Louverture fonde à Saint-Domingue la liberté et l'egalité* (Port-au-Prince, 1945). The view of Toussaint as an example of inspired Christianity can be found in Rev. John R. Beard, *Toussaint L'Ouverture: A Biography and Autobiography* (Boston, 1863) and Rev. Charles Mossell, *Toussaint Louverture, the Hero of Saint Domingo* (Lockport, 1896). Bibliographical essays by Afro-Americans who have recognized Toussaint's outstanding contributions to the history of their race include: Robert C. Benjamin, *Life of Toussaint L'Ouverture* (1888); William Wells Brown, *The Black Man . . . ,* 2 vols. (Boston, 1863); B. O. Flower, "The Greatest Black Man Known to History," in *The Arena,* 24 (July–December 1900); Elizabeth R. Haynes, *Unsung Heroes* (New York, 1921); and David A. Straker, *Reflections on the Life and Times of Toussaint L'Ouverture* (ca. 1886). Two provocative, interpretative essays by outstanding Haitian scholars are Jean Price-Mars, "Toussaint-Louverture," in *Revue de la Société d'histoire et de géographie d'Haiti* (April 1945) and Duraciné Vaval, "Le Génie politique de Toussaint," in *Revue de la Société d'histoire et de géographie d'Haiti* (July and October 1948). A fine study of Toussaint's struggle with Hédouville, but also an excellent examination of the entire period, is Antoine Michel, *La Mission du Général Hédouville à Saint-Domingue* (Port-au-Prince, 1929). Toussaint's last months in France are discussed by Alfred Nemours, *Histoire de la captivité et de la mort de Toussaint Louverture* (Paris, 1929) and Governor Caffarelli, "Toussaint-Louverture au Fort de Joux," in *Nouvelle revue rétrospective,* 18 (10 April 1902). Other biographies of Toussaint include: Stephen Alexis, *Black Liberator* (New York, 1945); Mary A. Healy, "The Contributions of Toussaint Louverture to the Independence of the American Republics," in *The Americas,* 9 (April 1953); Ralph Korngold, *Citizen Toussaint* (Boston, 1944); Emil H. Maurer, *Der Schwarze Revolutionar, Toussaint Louverture* (Meiseheim, 1950); Karl Otten, *Der Schwarze Napoleon: Toussaint Louverture und der Negeraufstand auf St. Domingo* (Berlin, 1930); Faine Scharon, *Toussaint Louverture et la révolution de Saint-Domingue,* 2 vols. (Port-au-Prince, 1957); Raphael Tardon, *Toussaint Louverture, le Napoléon noir* (Paris, 1951); and Michel Vaucaire, *Toussaint-Louverture* (Paris, 1930). Two popular biographies, closer to fiction than fact, are: Anatoli Vinogradov, *The Black Consul* (London, 1935) and Percy Waxman, *The Black Napoleon* (New York, 1931).

For an understanding of Toussaint's foreign policy and the response of the great powers, the reader can consult several fine surveys. The most authoritative exposition of Toussaint's policy is found in Alfred Nemours, *Histoire des relations internationales de Toussaint-Louverture* (Port-au-Prince, 1945). Rayford W. Logan, *The Diplomatic Relations of the United States with Haiti, 1776–1891* (Chapel Hill, 1941) is an outstanding introduction to American policy toward Toussaint. But the reader should also consult relevant sections in Henry Adams, *History of the United States of America during the First Ad-*

ministration of Thomas Jefferson, Vol. 1 (New York, 1891–1896), Alexander DeConde, *The Quasi War* (New York, 1966); Ludwell L. Montague, *Haiti and the United States 1714–1938* (Durham, 1940); and Charles C. Tansill, *The United States and Santo Domingo 1789–1873* (Baltimore, 1938). The definitive study of Napoleon's policy is G. Roloff, *Die Kolonialpolitik Napoleons I* (Munich, 1899). Napoleon's secret instructions to Leclerc are reprinted and discussed in Carl L. Lokke, "The Leclerc Instructions," in *Journal of Negro History,* 10 (January 1925). A good short essay is Henry Adams, "Napoleon I and San Domingo," in *Historical Essays* (New York, 1891). A detailed study of British policy remains to be written. Besides the suggestive general interpretation of Eric Williams in his *Capitalism and Slavery* (1944) there is only the short and superficial essay by H. B. L. Hughes, "British Policy Towards Haiti 1801–1805," in *Canadian Historical Review,* 25 (1944). The interested student should consult The Public Records Office (London, C.O. 137/88–112 and C.O. 245/1–10). The latter volumes, which are devoted exclusively to St. Domingue, are particularly rich. There is also a substantial collection of material in the War Office Records.

Essential reading for anyone interested in the historical background to the Haitian Revolution is Pierre de Vassière, *Saint-Domingue, la société et la vie créoles sous l'ancien régime* (Paris, 1909). This book contains an incisive description of the colony's social structure on the eve of the revolution. Moreau de Saint-Méry, *Description topographique, physique et politique de Saint-Dominque,* 2 vols. (Philadelphia, 1797) is also a mine of information on all sections of society. The last years of the ancien régime are vividly depicted in François A. S. Wimpffen, *A Voyage to Saint Domingo, in the Years 1788, 1789 and 1790* (London, 1797). The reader should also consult the voluminous writings of the dean of French West Indian historians, Gabriel Debien. Some of his most important essays dealing with St. Domingue can be found in *Études antillaises* (Paris, 1956) and *Plantations et esclaves à Saint-Domingue* (Dakar, 1962). The standard study on the free people of color, Auguste Lebeau, *De la condition des gens de couleur libres sous l'ancien régime* (Poitiers, 1903), remains indispensable, but the reader also should see the recent work by Yvan Debbasch, *Couleur et liberté: L'Affranchi dans les possessions françaises de la Caraibe* (Paris, 1967). The best account of slavery in the French colonies is still Lucien Peytraud, *L'Esclavage aux Antilles Françaises avant 1789* (Paris, 1897). Two more recent studies—Gaston-Martin, *Histoire de l'esclavage dans les Colonies Françaises* (Paris, 1948) and Antoine Gisler, *L'Esclavage aux Antilles Françaises . . .* (Fribourg, 1965)—serve as adequate introductions but are disappointing in light of recent scholarship on comparative slavery.

Many good surveys of the Haitian Revolution exist. If possible, the reader should consult two works by J. P. Garran-Coulon, *Débats entre les accusés et les accusateurs dans l'affaire des colonies,* 6 vols. (Paris, 1798) and *Rapport sur les troubles de Saint-Domingue,* 6 vols. (Paris, 1799). The single outstanding analysis of the entire revolutionary period is C. L. R. James, *The Black Jacobins* (New York, 1963). Other informative surveys are: Jonathan Brown, *The History and Present Condition of St. Domingo,* 2 vols. (Philadelphia, 1837);

James Franklin, *The Present State of Hayti* (London, 1828); Theophilus G. Steward, *The Haitian Revolution 1791–1804* (New York, 1914); and T. Lothrop Stoddard, *The French Revolution in San Domingo* (Boston, 1914). A good short essay is Adelaide Hill, "Revolution in Haiti, 1791–1820," in *Présence Africaine* (June–July 1958). Two highly influential English studies are Bryan Edwards, *A Historical Survey of the French Colony of San Domingo . . .* (London, 1797) and Charles Mackenzie, *Notes on Haiti . . .*, 2 vols. (London, 1830). The former presents the argument that it was the agitations of the *Amis des Noirs* that provoked the slave revolt of 1791, while the latter was used by British abolitionists to support their contention that blacks could be productive and disciplined without slavery. Venault de Charmilly, *Answer to Bryan Edwards* (London, 1797) is a refutation of Edwards by the most influential French lobbyist for British intervention in St. Domingue. An adequate survey of the period, concentrating on the role of Henri Christophe, is Hubert Cole, *Christophe, King of Haiti* (New York, 1967). For the importance of the discussions of slavery and the free people of color in the French Assemblies see the fine account by C. O. Hardy, *The Negro Question in the French Revolution* (Menasha, 1919), and consult the excellent series of documents recently reprinted in *La Révolution française et l'abolition de l'esclavage*, 14 vols. (Paris, n.d.). The activities of the planters and people of color in Paris and St. Domingue in the early years of the revolution are ably discussed in H. E. Mills, *The Early Years of the French Revolution in San Domingo* (New York, 1892); Philip D. Curtin, "The Declaration of the Rights of Man in Saint-Domingo 1788–1791," in *Hispanic American Historical Review* (May 1950); and P. Boissonade, *Saint-Dominique à la veille de la révolution et la question de la représentation aux etats-généraux* (Paris, 1906). A fine appreciation of the role of voodoo in the formation of the slave revolt of 1791 is L. Riguad, "Le rôle du Vaudou dans l'indépendence d'Haiti," in *Présence Africaine* (February–May 1958). Auguste Nemours, *Histoire militaire de la guerre d'indépendence de Saint-Domigue*, 2 vols. (Paris, 1925) presents an excellent survey of the military campaigns up to 1802, emphasizing Toussaint's military genius. The official French version of these campaigns is Col. A. de Poyen, *Histoire militaire de la révolution de Saint-Domingue* (Paris, 1899). Sir John Fortesque, *History of the British Army*, vol. 9 (London, 1906) treats the role of the British Army in St. Domingue with much sympathy but is highly critical of Pitt's policy, which sent so many Englishmen to almost certain death in the tropics. Highly informative accounts of the final war of independence can be found in Pamphile de Lacroix, *Mémoires pour servir à l'histoire de la révolution de Saint-Domingue*, 2 vols. (Paris, 1819) and Antoine M. T. Métral, *Histoire de l'expedition des Français à Saint-Domingue sous le Consulat de Napoléon Bonaparte* (Paris, 1825). Other useful surveys of the revolution include: William Welles Brown, *St. Domingo: Its Revolutions and Its Patriots* (Boston, 1855); Henry-Louis Castonnet des Fosses, *La perte d'une colonie—la révolution de Saint-Domingue* (Paris, 1893); M. Dalmas, *Histoire de la révolution de Saint-Dominque*, 2 vols. (Paris, 1814); Rev. Jas. Theo. Holly, *A Vindication of the Capacity of the Negro Race for Self-Government and Civilized Prog-*

ress . . . (Boston, 1854); Saint-Victor Jean-Baptiste, *Haiti, sa lutte pour l'emancipation* (Paris, 1957); P. J. Laborie, *The Coffee Planter of Saint-Domingo* (London, 1798); Placide-Justin, *Histoire de l'Ile d'Haiti* (Paris, 1826); Marcus Rainsford, *St. Domingo, or An Historical, Political and Military Sketch of the Black Republic* . . . (London, 1802); and Baron Pompée de Vastey, *An Essay on the Causes of the Revolutions and Civil Wars of Hayti* (Exeter, 1823).

General surveys of Haitian history that contain informative interpretations of the revolutionary period are: H. P. Davis, *Black Democracy: The Story of Haiti* (New York, 1928); Beaubrun Ardouin, *Études sur l'histoire d'Haiti*, 6 vols. (Paris, 1853); Thomas Madiou, *Histoire d'Haiti, 1492–1846,* 4 vols. (Port-au-Prince, 1847–1904); Lorimer Denis et François Duvalier, *Problème des classes à travers l'histoire d'Haiti* (Port-au-Prince, 1948). Anyone interested in Haitian history must read James G. Leybrun, *The Haitian People* (New Haven, 1941), which not only has an excellent summary of the revolutionary period but also is by far the best interpretation in any language of the development of Haitian society.

Index

FARGVER THE BUCKET LIBRARY

GARDNER WEBB COLLEGE LIBRARY